W0007465

*Into  Tibet*

*Great Travellers*
General Editor: GEORGE WOODCOCK

**Alexander Mackenzie and the North West**
Roy Daniells

**Australia's Last Explorer: Ernest Giles**
Geoffrey Dutton

**Bokhara Burnes**
James Lunt

**Henry Walter Bates, Naturalist of the Amazons**
George Woodcock

**Papal Envoys to the Great Khans**
I. de Rachewiltz

**Thomas Gage in Spanish America**
Norman Newton

*other books by George Woodcock*

CANADA AND THE CANADIANS
KERALA: A PORTRAIT OF THE MALABAR COAST
ASIA, GODS AND CITIES: ADEN TO TOKYO
INCAS AND OTHER MEN: TRAVELS IN THE ANDES
THE GREEKS IN INDIA
FACES OF INDIA: A TRAVEL NARRATIVE
THE DOUKHOBORS
(with Ivan Avakumovic)

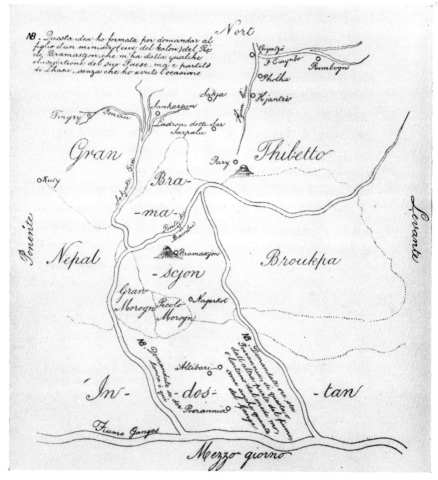

1. Sketch map of Tibet and the neighbouring countries, made by Samuel Van de Putte in the early eighteenth century and preserved in the Museum at Middleburg in Holland

# INTO TIBET

## The Early British Explorers

*by*

George Woodcock

FABER AND FABER
3 Queen Square
London

*First published in 1971*
*by Faber and Faber Limited*
*Printed in Great Britain by*
*Butler & Tanner Ltd Frome and London*
*All rights reserved*

*ISBN 0 571 08394 3*

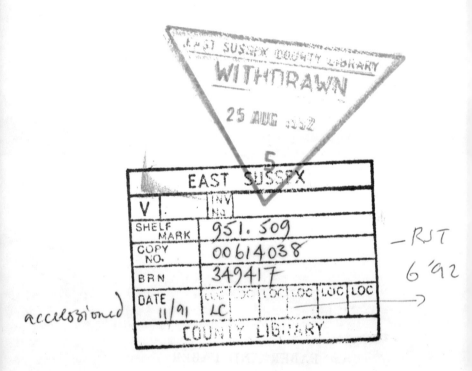

EAST SUSSEX COUNTY LIBRARY

WITHDRAWN

25 AUG 1992

EAST SUSSEX

| V | INV No | |
|---|---|---|
| SHELF MARK | 951.509 | |
| COPY NO. | 00614038 | |
| BRN | 349417 | |
| DATE 11/91 | LOC LC | LOC LOC LOC LOC LOC |

COUNTY LIBRARY

accessioned

— RST
6 '92

© *George Woodcock, 1971*

## *Prefatory* ᴊᴠᴜᴜ

I am indebted to many people for help in the preparation
of this book, and especially to the following: my colleague,
Dr. Ivan Avakumovic, of the University of British Columbia,
who on my behalf searched for material relating to Bogle's
journey in the Public Record Office, the British Museum and
the India Office Library; to Mr. C. W. Black of the Mitchell
Library in Glasgow, who provided me with information on
the Bogle family papers; to Dr. Ram Rahul of the Indian
School of International Studies, who informed me on material
in India relating to Bogle; to Dr. Hugh Richardson who
replied courteously and copiously to my questions; to Mrs.
Catherine Easto, who typed the final version. To all of them
I give my thanks.

The English transliterations of Tibetan and Bhutanese
names have varied considerably over the years, and in most
cases I have kept to those used by the travellers themselves,
with an occasional hint (as when I mention that Tassisudon
is the modern Thimbu) to help the reader in finding his
geographical bearings. However there are a number of
modern versions which are so familiar that in the text I have
used them, retaining the earlier version in quotations. Thus,
Bogle's Pari-jong becomes *Phari*, his Giansu becomes
*Gyantse*, his Teshu Lumbo becomes *Tashilunpo*. In the case of
the Teshu Lama, as Bogle calls him (Teshoo Lama in
Turner), I substitute the title for this hierarch more often
used by Tibetans and modern Europeans, *Panchen Lama*. For
the spiritual ruler of Bhutan I use the more correct form of

7

*Dharma Raja* instead of the Lama Rimpoche used by Bogle, and in the case of the Gesub Rimpoche of Bogle—the Ti-mu-fu of Manning—I have substituted the title of *Regent* and otherwise used the personal names of the various Regents to distinguish them. A few other names of Tibetans have been slightly changed to accord with modern transliterations, but these do not differ sufficiently from the spelling used in quoted passages to raise any doubt.

# Contents

I Introduction         *page* 13

PART I: MISSIONS TO THE PANCHEN LAMA

| | | |
|---|---|---|
| II | John Company and the Panchen Lama | 31 |
| III | The Choice of an Envoy | 43 |
| IV | In Bhutan | 57 |
| V | Into Tibet | 84 |
| VI | With the Panchen Lama | 106 |
| VII | The Mirage of Lhasa | 148 |
| VIII | Return to Bengal | 158 |
| IX | Pressing on the Door | 171 |
| X | Turner's Mission | 183 |

PART II: LHASA ATTAINED

| | | |
|---|---|---|
| XI | The Unlikely Hero | 197 |
| XII | The Way to Lhasa | 206 |
| XIII | Manning in Lhasa | 238 |
| XIV | Epilogue | 263 |
| | Bibliographical Notes | 271 |
| | Index | 273 |

9

# *Illustrations*

## PLATES

1. Sketch map of Tibet and the neighbouring countries, made by Samuel Van de Putte in the early eighteenth century and preserved in the Museum at Middleburg in Holland. *frontispiece*

2. George Bogle, reproduced from *India and Tibet* by Sir Francis Younghusband, John Murray 1910. *facing page* 96

3. The map of Tibet by D'Anville, published originally in 1735, which was used by Hastings in planning Bogle's expedition and which accompanied Bogle on his journey. 97

4. Buxa Duar. 112

5. Plan, Section and Elevation of the Bridge of Chains at Chuka. 113

6. Chuka. 113

7. Tibetan Yak. 192

8. The Mausoleum of the Panchen Lama who entertained Bogle. 193

9. Thomas Manning (artist unknown), reproduced by kind permission of the Royal Asiatic Society. 208

10. The Potala at Lhasa. This illustration, from Kircher's *China Illustrated* (1667), is based on Father Grueber's account of Lhasa. By the time of Manning's arrival the building was larger. 209

11

*Illustrations 4, 5, 6, 8, 9 are copies of prints from the second edition (1806) of Samuel Turner's 'An Account of an Embassy to the Court of the Teshoo Lama'*

## MAPS

|                                                    | *page* |
|----------------------------------------------------|--------|
| General map of Tibet.                              | 16–17  |
| Map showing routes taken by Bogle and Manning.     | 58     |

# I

## *Introduction*

### (i)

'Farewell, ye honest and simple people. May ye long enjoy
that happiness which is denied to more polished nations;
and while they are engaged in the endless pursuits of avarice
and ambition, defended by your barren mountains, may ye
continue to live in peace and contentment, and know no
wants but those of nature.'

So, in 1775, George Bogle, child of the eighteenth century,
bade his farewell to Tibet and the Tibetans. The first native
of Britain to cross the frontiers of that remote Himalayan
country, he had succumbed to a charm that in later years
was to conquer so many of his countrymen among the
Buddhist peoples of the mountains that seal the northern
frontiers of India. During a winter as the guest of the
Panchen Lama, second in status among the great hierarchs
of Tibet, he had lived in what seemed to him, when he
wrote of it immediately after his departure, a 'fairy dream'.
'The novelty of the scenes, and the people I have met with,
and the novelty of the life I have led, seem a perfect illusion.'

Bogle was hardly a romantic. His record with the East
India Company was one of relatively rapid success, and the
qualities of commercial realism and administrative toughness which had brought him in his early thirties to important
positions in the government of Bengal were reflected in the

sangfroid with which he had accepted the hardships of Himalayan travel two centuries ago, and the patience with which he had followed the inconclusive tortuosities of Central Asian diplomatic encounters. Yet—though he started on his long journey through Bhutan to the Panchen Lama's monastic citadel of Tashilunpo with little expectation of pleasure —there is no doubt that the archaic and mediaeval life he encountered attracted him as much as the geniality of the people, whose apparent forthrightness he appreciated after the fawning manner and naïve deviousness that had exasperated him among the Bengalis.

Until it became evident in the present century that the 'barren mountains' were not in fact impregnable against a determined enemy, the idea of Tibet as the last stronghold of a pristine kind of life, lost elsewhere but here uncontaminated by the evils of the modern world, persisted among those Europeans who were aware of the country's existence.

Yet there was a profound difference between the degree and even the kind of interest in Tibet that existed among Europeans in Bogle's day, and that which has developed in our own century. The difference is suggested by the fate of the narratives left by the three travellers—George Bogle, Samuel Turner and Thomas Manning—who form the subject of this book.

Bogle entered the country in 1774, and Samuel Turner— another officer of the East India Company—followed him nine years later to Tashilunpo on a second official mission. In 1811 Thomas Manning exceeded the achievements of both Bogle and Turner by making his way to Lhasa, the goal they had vainly sought. Manning was the first Englishman to reach what his nineteenth-century countrymen described accurately as a 'forbidden city'; not until the early twentieth century, more than ninety years later, did another

Englishman set foot there, and indeed, apart from Manning, only two other Europeans reached Lhasa during the whole of the nineteenth century—the French Lazarist priests Huc and Gabet who were allowed to stay in the city for a few weeks in 1846. Manning succeeded, almost certainly, because rather than in spite of his lack of any clear official status; he went on his own initiative with a minimum of help from the Company's officers in Calcutta, he travelled in a ludicrously penetrable disguise, and the circumstances of his journey were never less than difficult and sometimes positively dangerous.

Yet, though Bogle, Turner and Manning broke new territory so far as Europeans were concerned (for much of the routes they followed into Tibet had only been used beforehand by Asian travellers), and though all of them kept fairly copious journals of their travels, the general interest in the subject of Tibet was so scanty at this period of endemic European wars that only Turner's narrative was made into a book, and even that was published almost two decades after the journey it described (*An Account of an Embassy to the Court of the Teshoo Lama*, 1800). Turner's *Account* went into a second edition in 1806, and then was forgotten until interest in Tibet revived towards the end of the century. Bogle died in 1781, too early to put his papers into publishable shape, and, for reasons on which we shall later speculate, Thomas Manning never chose to transmit to his contemporaries the vast knowledge of Central and Eastern Asia which he accumulated in the eleven years from 1806 to 1817 which he spent in China, Tibet and Indo-China. Yet their journals remained, waiting for the curious scholar, and it is significant that only a hundred and one years after Bogle's regretful farewell to Tashilunpo and sixty-four years after Manning came back from Lhasa with tangled beard and ragged

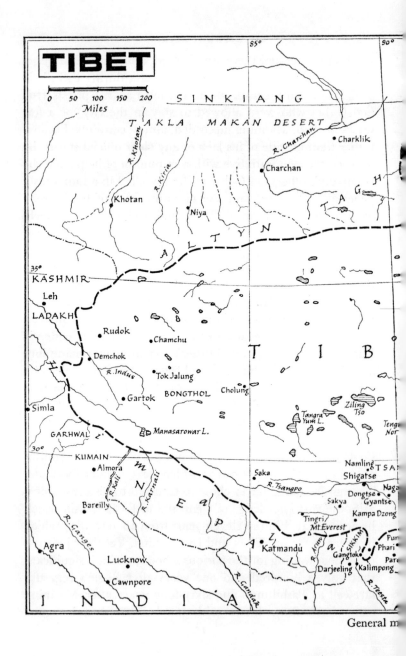

General m

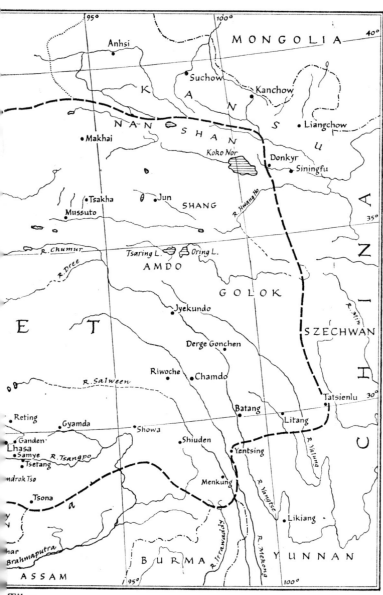

Tibet

B

Chinese robes, did that scholar appear and put their rough notes and narratives into print. He was Clements Markham, who in 1876 published, with introduction and notes, the *Narratives of the Mission of George Bogle to Tibet and of the Journey of Thomas Manning to Lhasa.*

Markham was not merely a distinguished geographer. He was also employed by the India Office, and this fact too is significant, for it gives one of the reasons why in the later nineteenth century a close interest in Tibet had developed of a kind that did not exist when Bogle, Manning and Turner made their journeys.

The political situation, indeed, had changed entirely. India was no longer the exclusive and jealously guarded province of a trading company regarded in England with suspicion and often hatred. The horrors of the Mutiny had drawn the British public into Indian affairs in a highly emotional way, and the new Raj that emerged after 1857, with a Queen Empress eventually replacing the last of the discredited and deposed Moghuls, was much more a matter of constant British public interest than John Company's India. Even before the Mutiny, the need to consolidate the northern frontiers had become urgent, and once India came under direct rule this took place, partly by conquest and partly by negotiation, but in any case by the acquisition of lands (such as the Darjeeling region and the Duars to the east) which belonged to hill states that were neighbours of Tibet, in the case of Nepal and Bhutan, or even tributary to Lhasa, in the case of Sikkim. As a result of these territorial changes, British India and Tibet made contact in the west, and also in the Chumbi valley on the east, where Kalimpong remained until the Communist conquest of Tibet in the 1950's a centre of trade through the mountains to Lhasa. The establishment of common frontiers led to a curiosity about the land beyond them which was partly strategic in origin but also motivated by the spirit of scientific inquiry that inspired the military men and civil servants who undertook the great nineteenth-century surveys of India. At this period the frontiers of Tibet were so jealously guarded by Chinese and native distrust of the white man that it was impossible for Europeans to undertake exploratory trips before the Younghusband Expedition forced its way to Lhasa in 1903; when the Chinese in 1885 actually agreed to a mission being sent to Lhasa under Colman Macaulay, it could not proceed because of Tibetan hostility which led to an armed clash on the borders of Sikkim. But the frontiers of Tibet were not closed against Asians; Indians and members of the hill tribes regularly crossed them as pilgrims or petty traders, and this enabled the British to compile a great deal of information about Tibet long before the Young-husband Expedition set off. They did so by sending in the celebrated 'pundits', Indian mock-pilgrims who carried concealed in their voluminous garments such simple geographer's equipment as pocket compasses and chronometers, boiling-point thermometers and folding sextants.

The first of the pundits, known to history merely as A, set off in 1865, eleven years before the revival of interest in Tibet induced a London publisher to print Markham's version of Bogle's and Manning's journals. Many other native explorers followed, to be immortalized by Kipling in the character of Hurree Babu; *Kim*, indeed, contributed greatly to the complex romantic image of Tibet that emerged among the British at the end of the nineteenth century. Lord Curzon's anxieties over Russian ambitions had made the country a focus of the 'Great Game', the half-imaginary contest of secret agents which gave Lhasa at the turn of the century the same kind of repute as a centre of political intrigue which Katmandu, certainly more justifiably, enjoys today. The Younghusband Expedition in 1903-4, the Chinese invasion of Tibet in 1910 and the consequent flight of the Thirteenth Dalai Lama to British protection in Darjeeling, the expulsion of the Chinese in 1912 and the return of the Tibetan hierarch to rule over a country that had gained *de facto* independence and remained isolated and unchanging behind its mountain frontiers until the later Chinese invasion of 1951: all these events contributed to the image of Tibet as a strange mediaeval polity preserving its integrity in the heart of Asia through the delicate balances of world power which—as effectively as the Himalayas— sustained its precarious freedom. Those rare travellers— mostly British officials—who were allowed to enter Tibetan territory and to proceed to Lhasa, gradually filled in with their accounts (notably those of Sir Charles Bell who became an intimate friend and adviser of the Thirteenth Dalai Lama) the picture of a traditional theocratic society, a society which, as conquest overcame archaic kingdoms in other parts of the world, acquired a political uniqueness enhanced by the fact that its vast mountains had remained one of the few parts of the world still incompletely explored.

But in the world of Bogle and Manning and Turner, Tibet appeared neither as a potential battleground where spies contested, nor as a place of unique archaism and inaccessibility. The world was still full of ancient kingdoms awaiting conquerors and of empty maps awaiting explorers. And, during the first half of the nineteenth century, the process of conquest and exploration went on at such a pace that it is not to be wondered at if the accounts of these Englishmen wandering in the Himalayas lay unattended until the rivalry of western powers in Central Asia brought Tibet into the eye of world attention.

Nor, in that age when the rational illumination of the Enlightenment still delineated men's thoughts, was there that other interest in Tibet, as a land of spiritual mysteries, which, in our day, has survived the Communist conquest by means of a diaspora of Himalayan gurus into the western world. Bogle, it appears, acquired a certain sympathy for the Mahayanist doctrines enunciated by his friend the Panchen Lama; Turner was certainly fascinated by meeting that Lama's successor and reincarnation in the form of a precocious and charming child; Manning—himself an object of amusement to an equally youthful Dalai Lama—appears to have been very little interested in the deeper religious complexities of a country which he regarded mainly as a stage on a never-completed journey to his personal Mecca of Peking.

Certainly one catches in none of them the flavour of magical fantasy that emerges from Alexandra David-Neel's accounts, published more than a century later, of the necromantic mysteries of Tantric Buddhism. And, indeed, Madame David-Neel went to Tibet out of a completely different mental climate from that which had produced such matter-of-fact merchant administrators as Bogle and Turner or even such a traditional English eccentric as Manning. It was a climate affected by the upsurge of academic interest in eastern religions associated particularly with the work of German scholars like Max Müller; affected also by the more dubious excursions into oriental mysticism which led to the Theosophical movement and allied manifestations of western occultism at the turn of the century. Anyone who reads the records of Bogle, Manning and Turner in search of the thaumaturgical lamas celebrated by Madame David-Neel or the occult masters evoked by Madame Blavatsky, will certainly be disappointed. What he will encounter are mountain roads, a land, a people, described for the first time by men of his language. There will be wonder, as there always is in the unfamiliar; there will be adventure, as there always is when men go to new places or travel in disguise on forbidden roads; there will be the personalities of the travellers, differentiating themselves in their reactions to what they see and those they meet. But the journey will not lead to a land of wizards or—despite the lyrical outburst from Bogle with which this chapter begins —to the kind of haven free from earthly troubles that James Hilton projected when, in *Lost Horizon*, he gave voice to another modern conception of Tibet as far from reality as that projected by the occultists. Perhaps I should end this comparison between the modern romantic view of Tibet and the soberer view of earlier travellers with the comment that, during a decade which has brought me into the company not only of many lay Tibetans but also a great variety of religious leaders beginning with the Dalai Lama and the Sakya Lama, I find the pictures evoked by Bogle and Turner and Manning nearer to the real Tibetans, even as they are today, than the fantasies of those who have tried to abstract from the symbolism of Tantric cults a world of chimerical marvels.

(ii)

If Bogle and Turner and Manning are divided by changing historical circumstance and philosophic viewpoint from many who have written of Tibet in modern times, they stand in equal isolation from the earlier travellers to that country. These, with a single exception, were Catholic missionaries, of the Jesuit and Capuchin orders, intent primarily upon conversion. The exception, and the only European layman to enter Tibet before Bogle, was certainly one of the world's great travellers, yet only the bare outline of his travels is known, and is unlikely ever to be fleshed out with the detail of impression and experience. He was Samuel Van de Putte. His father was a Dutch Admiral, and he himself became a Doctor of Law at Leyden University, and gave promise, when, in 1715, he became Alderman of Flushing, of settling into a respectable stay-at-home career. Three years later, at the age of twenty-eight and inspired by a consuming curiosity about unknown lands, Van de Putte set off on what he announced as a three years' journey into Asia. It was to end after twenty-seven years when he died in Batavia at the age of fifty-five, at last on his way home. Van de Putte's vast journey had led him by caravan from Aleppo to Isfahan, and thence, after several years of wandering in Iran, to the Persian Gulf, whence he took ship to Cochin, and, disguising himself as an Indian, found his way to Delhi. Eventually he crossed the mountains to Tibet, probably by way of the valley of Katmandu which, under the Newari Kings, still formed the main route by which trade passed between India and Lhasa. In Lhasa he lived for several years, learnt Tibetan and appears to have gained the respect of the Lamas to such a degree, by his ascetic life, that he was allowed to accompany a party of them on a journey by the great lake of Kokonor and the Wall of China to Peking. He came back through Lhasa to India and arrived in time to witness the sacking of Delhi by Nadir Shah in 1737. Later he continued by way of Malaya to Java, and when he died there he specified in his will that all his papers should be destroyed. The will was unfortunately followed, and Van de Putte's map of Tibet and a few scattered notes are all that have remained, so that we are mainly indebted to Catholic missionaries who were in China and Tibet at the time for what we know of this extraordinary traveller's experiences and exploits.

If travellers' tales of their own adventures are to be universally believed, the earliest Catholic priest and the first European to reach Tibet was the amazing Friar Odoric of Pordenone, who went to the Mongol court in 1320, travelling via the Middle East, India and Canton to Peking, returning overland through central Asia. He claimed to have gone back through Tibet. It is certain that he met Tibetan monks in northern China, and learnt from them some details of Tibetan life; he may even have passed through Tibetan-speaking regions on the western marches of China, but modern historians are inclined to doubt that the unnamed Tibetan city he mentions as the capital of Tibet was in fact Lhasa.

The first Europeans who undoubtedly reached Tibet were Jesuits, and the pioneers among them were the Portuguese Fathers Andrada and Marques, who in 1624 climbed the high passes of the Himalayas to Lake Mansarowar in Tibet and established a short-lived mission at Tsaparang. Three years later two other Jesuits, Fathers Cacella and Cabral, reached Shigatse, near the Panchen Lama's abbey of Tashi-lunpo, and preached there until Cacella's death in 1630. Not until 1661 did the Jesuit Fathers Grueber and D'Orville, on their way to India via Nepal, reach Lhasa, where they spent two months and wrote a brief account of the Dalai Lama and of the religious system of Tibet.

Like Van de Putte, these early missionaries appear to have experienced no difficulties in entering Tibet other than those imposed by the physical nature of the land; indeed, those who went to Tsaparang and Shigatse were welcomed hospitably by the local kings and encountered everywhere that spirit of tolerance which is traditionally associated with the Buddhist creed.

The change in the Tibetan attitude towards foreigners

dates from the eighteenth century, and in particular from the imposition about 1720 of a more direct control of Tibetan affairs by the Manchu Emperors of China. Under the pretence of keeping the peace and protecting the Tibetans from Mongol interference, Chinese magistrates or Ambans were established at Lhasa, with a small army to defend them, and as time went on they began to interfere vigorously in Tibetan internal politics, to the extent, in 1750, of murdering the last secular King of Lhasa, Gyurmé Namgyal, and thus assuring the dominance of the Dalai Lama and of his supporters in the great monasteries that existed in the mountains around the capital. Chinese suspicion of foreigners—demonstrated at this period in the restrictions placed on trading along the China coast—was one reason why foreigners became unwelcome in Tibet. But it also seems likely that, as in other similar situations, the Europeans did much to make themselves unpopular.

In particular, the quarrel between the Jesuits and the Capuchins as to who should control Catholic missions in Tibet helped greatly to discredit Europeans in the eyes of Tibetans. After Fathers Grueber and D'Orville left in 1661 to travel through Nepal into India, the hard roads and the high passes of Tibet saw no Europeans until, in 1707, the Capuchin Fathers d'Ascoli and de Tours arrived in Lhasa to set up a mission with Papal blessing. They were kindly received, as their predecessors had been, and started their mission, which continued for almost forty years. Their desire to maintain the field to themselves helped to defeat them.

Less than a decade after the Capuchins had established themselves, in 1716, another Jesuit found his way into Tibet coming over the passes from Kashmir and Ladakh. This was the Italian priest Ippolito Desideri, the first of the great

European Tibetologists. The Capuchins rendered brotherly hospitality to Desideri, but made it clear that they considered themselves to have exclusive rights of conversion. They even wrote to the Pope so as to make sure that Jesuit intrusion was banned from Rome. But messages took long to travel over the vast and perilous spaces of Central Asia and the Middle East, and it was not until five years had passed that Desideri knew the Papal verdict had gone against him and that he must depart from a people he had come to respect, a people who in turn had learnt to appreciate his own exceptional qualities. For, debarred from ordinary mission work, Desideri devoted himself to learning the Tibetan language and observing Tibetan religion and customs with a zeal not to be equalled until Sir Charles Bell began to publish his series of great books on Tibet and its people two centuries after Desideri's departure from Lhasa. Desideri saw the establishment of the power of the Manchu Emperors in Tibet in 1720, and his comments on the political situation at that crucial period gave a topical character to his *Account of Tibet*, which is deepened by the care with which he wrote on Tibetan beliefs. His own views were not shaken by his exposure to Lamaist Buddhism, which he did not fully understand, but even the attempt to master Buddhist concepts led to the development of a great mutual esteem between him and the learned Lamas of Lhasa. He actually wrote in Tibetan a discourse attempting to refute the teachings of the Buddha, and the Tibetan sages, who have always been greatly addicted to religious debates, hailed it as a noble effort but remained unconverted; Desideri in turn confessed that there were times when the religious devotion he saw among the Tibetans made him feel ashamed of his own Christian faith, so lukewarm in comparison.

The Capuchin fathers were less adaptable than Desideri,

and the Tibetans found them less congenial. Among other errors, they denounced rather too boldly the 'magical' or Tantric practices of certain Tibetan monks. By this kind of interference they made themselves offensive in the eyes of pious Tibetans, while their dispute with Desideri had not gone unnoticed, and helped to lower the prestige of Christian teachers. When, in 1745, they were expelled from Lhasa and forced to find refuge in the Nepali kingdom of Patan, it was as much from pressure on the part of the Buddhist monks as from the growing influence of Chinese xenophobia. After the Capuchins departed from Lhasa—leaving a chapel bell twentieth-century visitors were still to find hanging in the great temple of Lhasa—no Europeans reached that city until Manning arrived two generations later.

How far the first English travellers to Tibet were able to profit by the experiences of their predecessors it is hard to estimate. Desideri's full *Account* was not published until long after their journeys, and only brief narratives of the other missionary journeys had found their way into print, originally in French or Italian, and by the middle of the eighteenth century in English as well through such compilations as *Astley's Collection of Voyages and Travels*, 1745–7, and the great *Description . . . de l'Empire de la Chine et de la Tartarie Chinoise* (Paris, 1735) which Father Du Halde based on the accounts of his fellow Jesuits and which in 1742 appeared in an English translation. Warren Hastings, briefing Bogle before his journey to Tashilunpo in 1772, had certainly studied the accounts presented by both Astley and Du Halde, and, since Bogle took with him to Tibet the maps which Jean Baptiste d'Anville drew to accompany Du Halde's book, it is likely that he also was familiar with whatever had been printed in English of earlier travels to Tibet. The same would apply to Samuel Turner, also to be briefed by Warren Hastings. As for Thomas Manning, there is little chance that his almost obsessive interest in anything relating to China would have left him ignorant of any of the existing sources of information in either England or France, where, as we shall see, he began his serious Chinese studies.

Yet, given this degree of continuity between the English travellers to Tibet and their missionary predecessors, the actual quantity of information transmitted was relatively slight, owing to the fact that the only account which was not brief or fragmentary, that of Desideri, remained so long unpublished, while even D'Anville's map was of little practical value on the road. Bogle and Turner and Manning were, to all practical intents and purposes, seeing a land of which, in detail, contemporary Europeans knew very little, and this is why their experiences contributed so significantly to the special English view of Tibet which developed during the latter decades of the nineteenth century.

# Part I

# MISSIONS TO THE PANCHEN LAMA

# II

## *John Company and the Panchen Lama*

### (i)

From the beginning of English connections with India, the
traders who went to reconnoitre the empire of the Great
Moghul were familiar with the shadowy fame of Tibet.
Ralph Fitch, who left London in 1583 on his long journey to
India and the countries of South-East Asia, heard tales of the
land high in the Himalayas, though he made no attempt to
get there. Nor did the traders who followed him to set up the
first factories of the East India Company on the shores of
India. Their interests were localized, confined to making the
best trading terms they could with coastal rulers. But by the
eighteenth century a change occurred in the very nature of
the Company's activities. While continuing to control all the
trade with London, it began in India to leave local commercial transactions to Indian or English 'country traders',
and to become involved in functions of a political rather
than a commercial nature. The need for self-defence against
hostile native powers and against its French rivals had led
the Company by a process at first hardly perceptible but
fatally cumulative to establish itself as a military force. And
as a military force it had been drawn into the power vacuum
created by the disintegration of the Moghul Empire.
Directly, or indirectly under the guise of farming taxes for

rulers who quickly became puppets, the Company rapidly developed from a military into a territorial force.

In Bengal it was Clive's success at the battle of Plassey in 1757 that confirmed this transformation of the Company into a political power, still interested in trade, but increasingly directed towards preserving the integrity of the territory from which it gained a profitable return in the form of taxes, now gathered through the Company's own officials (whose accurately descriptive title of 'Collector' still survives to describe the highest rank of local official in independent India). Bengal became virtually a province of the East India Company, and it was inevitable that within a decade of Plassey its officers were vitally interested in the Himalayan states whose frontiers marched with its northern borders. Aggressive rulers in these states might form a threat to territory; friendly ones might offer the promise of profitable trade. Moreover, in varying degrees all these states were tributaries of China, and when the Company's officers looked north to Nepal, Sikkim or Bhutan, which were actual neighbours, or to Tibet whose territories at this period did not yet adjoin Bengal, it was with a thought that here might be a channel for the Chinese tea trade less difficult than Canton, where the local Chinese authorities placed onerous restrictions on the Company's traders.

Bhutan was recognized as a threat from the beginning, for its people, despite their Buddhist religion, were a race of warlike hillmen who had kept up a tradition of raiding through the low Southern passes or Duars of their country into the rich lowlands of Assam and Cooch Behar. Nepal was in a state of dangerous transition. The old Newari kingdoms of the valley of Nepal—Katmandu, Patan and Bhatgoan—though they were constantly fighting among themselves, rarely allowed their differences to interfere with the flow of trade from India through their territories into Tibet, for this was the life-blood of their treasuries, and, being city-states with small domains, they presented no territorial threat at all. By the early 1760's, however, the dissensions among the Newaris had allowed the hill kings of Gurkha, members of a Hindu warrior caste, to create a warrior state in the mountains of Nepal, from which they looked down with predatory eyes on the cities of the valley. They were encouraged by the dissensions among the Newari rulers, particularly when the king of Bhatgoan called on the Gurkha chieftain, Prithvi Narayan, for help against the kings of Katmandu and Patan, and thus enabled the Gurkhas to get a foothold in the valley. It was evident that the ambitions of the Gurkhas went beyond Nepal, and in fact they were shortly afterwards to invade Sikkim and even Tibet.

The Company's officers felt a natural anxiety over the situation in Nepal which made them willing in 1767, when the valley kings were at last united against Prithvi Narayan, to respond to the pleas of the king of Patan and send to the support of the Newaris a small military expedition led by Captain Kinloch. It was the first British intervention in the Himalayan region, and an unsuccessful one, for Kinloch's men suffered severely in the fever-ridden scrub of the Terai, the foothill region of Nepal which has to be crossed before one climbs the passes into the valley of Katmandu. Captain Kinloch never reached the endangered Newari kingdoms, and though his appearance on the borders of Nepal may have created a minor diversion of Gurkha attention, it is very doubtful if it delayed in any way the fate of the valley of Katmandu, which by 1769 had been swallowed up in the expanding Gurkha state.

Kinloch's failure had shown the sheer physical difficulties

that any military approach to the Himalayan kingdoms would encounter, but this did nothing to lessen the Company's interest in the region, and in the interval between Kinloch's abortive expedition and the final downfall of the valley kingdoms the Court of Directors wrote to Henry Verelst, Governor at Fort William: 'We desire you will obtain the best intelligence you can whether trade can be opened with Nepaul, and whether cloth and other European commodities may not find their way thence to Thibet, Lhassa and the western parts of China.' What the Directors hoped to obtain from these regions in return for the Company's broadcloth and other English manufactures was a supply of gold to offset the drain of specie incurred by the tea trade at Canton where—until the Company eventually found high-grade opium an acceptable commodity—the Chinese merchants preferred to be paid in silver rather than in trade goods. Early in 1769 Surgeon James Logan was chosen to conduct a mission to the valley of Katmandu in the hope of reviving the trade which was already being disrupted by Gurkha aggressions. Logan prepared a memorandum justifying his mission which showed a sound knowledge of the situation in Nepal and stressed the need to support the Newari kings, so that a trade might be established 'with Tibett and the Western Provinces by way of Neypall'; in view of later events perhaps the most interesting point Logan made was that support for the Newaris would be pleasing to the Tashi Lama of Tibet, who had long been on close terms with these Buddhist rulers.

If the Newari kingdoms had not finally collapsed shortly after Logan wrote his report, he might well have been the first Englishman to enter Tibet. As it was, any possibility of approaching that country through Nepal was destroyed by the triumph of the Gurkhas who, with the memory of

Kinloch's expedition in their minds, were neither interested in fostering trade between India and Tibet nor inclined to establish friendly relations with the East India Company.

The Company, in its turn, accepted the situation realistically; the trade to Tibet still seemed a desirable prize, but in 1771 the Directors in London shifted their gaze to the eastern edges of their maps and suggested to the officers in Calcutta that they should now explore the possibilities of trade through Assam or Bhutan. Accordingly, the Collector at Rangpur, the district of Bengal nearest the northern frontier, was instructed to begin by finding out the prospects of selling British goods in Bhutan.

At this point, in April 1772, Warren Hastings began his career as Governor of Bengal. Almost everything that Hastings did was touched with the dramatic quality created by his energetic personality, and while the idea of Tibet as a source of trade and as a possible avenue to China had already claimed the attention of his predecessors, it was he who gave precise and practical form to their vaguely formulated intentions. He did so, as great men often do, by taking advantage of the initiatives of others.

(ii)

It was the Bhutanese who started the process by behaving in a way that at first appeared to make nonsense of the Court's decision to explore the possibilities of trade with their country. Bhutan in the eighteenth century was ruled by a dual system of authority not unlike that which nominally operated in Europe during the Middle Ages, when the Pope was spiritual ruler and the Emperor was supposed to rule as his agent in temporal affairs. In Bhutan it was the Dharma Raja or Lama Rimpoche who held spiritual power; he was a monk, the successor and according to Lamaist doctrine

35

the incarnation of a seventeenth-century Tantric guru named Sheptoon La-Pha who had established a position for himself like that of the Dalai Lama in Tibet. A later Dharma Raja had devoted himself entirely to spiritual exercises, and this had allowed his chief minister, the Deb Raja, to gather power into his own hands. In general this arrangement continued into the first half of the present century, but there were occasions when the monks and the lay chieftains of the country rebelled against the exactions of some particular Deb Raja; at such times the Dharma Raja would regain for a time some of the temporal power which Sheptoon La-Pha had originally wielded.

In 1772 Bhutan was under the control of a ruler, Deb Judhur, who in five years had consolidated his rule into a virtual despotism. Having established his power at home, Deb Judhur determined to better his fortunes by invading the plains of India which the rough mountain clansmen of Bhutan had always regarded as a legitimate field of plunder. In 1772 his levies, armed with primitive matchlocks and with the bows which they used with much greater accuracy, poured down through the Duars of Daling and Buxa into the little buffer state of Cooch Behar to the north of Bengal. The Raja of Cooch Behar, whose miniature army was helpless against these thousands of highland warriors, appealed to Warren Hastings for help and protection. The Company would have had to intervene in any case to prevent the Bhutanese from overflowing out of Cooch Behar and endangering Rangpur, but, since the Raja appealed, Hastings exacted his price: that the principality accept the Company's suzerainty, which meant its extinction as a separate political entity. This concession did not save the Raja himself from being captured and imprisoned by the Bhutanese and taken into their territory, but it provided the excuse for the Company's forces to go into action, and a battalion of sepoys, commanded by Captain John Jones, marched into Cooch Behar.

Jones stormed and captured the fortress of Behar. He drove the Bhutanese back through the Duars and seized three of their frontier fortresses. In every engagement the badly armed and undisciplined Bhutanese proved inferior to the well-armed sepoys led by British officers (a lesson not wasted on the watchful Gurkha king in Nepal, who reorganized his army on European lines). But, like Captain Kinloch a few years before, Jones found the land a more tenacious enemy than its inhabitants, and he himself was one of the many members of his expedition who fell victim to malaria.

Yet the campaign had been a success. Cooch Behar itself became a vassal state in the Company's empire. And the remnants of the Company's forces stood poised on the borders of Bhutan. Hastings was wise enough not to risk these forces on the perilous task of trying to conquer a poor and thinly populated mountain country, but the British victory alarmed the rulers of the other native countries of the region and the results favoured the Company's interests. Before his defeat Deb Judhur had suggested to the rulers of Nepal and Assam an alliance against the Company and they had promised him assistance, which would undoubtedly have been forthcoming if the Bhutanese had in any way been successful. Witnessing the rout of Deb Judhur's levies, the Nepali ruler Prithvi Narayan viewed apprehensively the prospect of the Company's army marching into Bhutan itself, which he had already marked out as part of the future Gurkha empire. Disinclined to risk his army, he chose diplomacy instead, and was wise enough to realize that any direct approach to Hastings on his part, as the conqueror of the Newari kingdoms, would certainly be rebuffed.

Instead he sent his messengers into Tibet, to the Panchen Lama at his great monastery of Tashilunpo near the southern Tibetan city of Shigatse. Lobsang Palden Yeshe, the Third Panchen Lama, was at this time a man in the vigour of late middle age, who like many Tibetan hierarchs combined a reputation for piety with an able shrewdness in worldly affairs. The Dalai Lama, Jampel Gyatso, nominal ruler of Tibet, was at this time a minor, and the monk who ruled as Regent in Lhasa, Demo Rimpoche, was unpopular among the Tibetans, so that the Panchen Lama—although in temporal affairs he was inferior in rank to the Dalai Lama—had acquired a great influence not only in southern Tibet, but also in the Himalayan states which bordered the country to the south and which owed a rather nebulous fealty to its rulers. Prithvi Narayan represented to the Panchen Lama that the Deb Raja of Bhutan, vassal of Tibet, was in perilous straits, and that an appeal from him—the Panchen Lama—might mitigate the wrath of the British and preserve the Himalayan states from intervention.

The Panchen Lama responded, perhaps in part because he accepted Prithvi Narayan's argument, but even more—as he later insisted—because it was his function as a Buddhist priest to seek for peace and happiness among human beings. Early in 1774 his envoys set out from Tashilunpo on the long ride by horseback over the high Tibetan passes into Bhutan, and through the western valleys of that country towards the borders of Cooch Behar. At Tassisudon (the modern Thimbu), which then as now was the capital of Bhutan, Deb Judhur joined the party and accompanied the envoys to the border fortress at the Buxa Duar.

Then occurred an event which throws a shadow of ambiguity over the Panchen Lama's intentions. A messenger following Deb Judhur down to Buxa carried news that a palace revolution had taken place in Tassisudon. The Dharma Raja had stepped outside his spiritual function and with his followers had deposed Deb Judhur and appointed a new Deb Raja in his place. Orders had been issued for the arrest of the deposed minister, and, realizing his peril, he immediately fled, accompanied by his favourites, in the direction of Lhasa, where he hoped to arouse support. Those of his officers who fell into the hands of the Dharma Raja's party were, with unBuddhist ferocity, put to death.

The excitements at Buxa did not prevent the Panchen Lama's envoys from proceeding to Calcutta; they reached Fort William at the end of March, 1774. One of them was a Tibetan named Padma, a lay official in the Panchen Lama's court. The other was a more curious figure, a young Hindu sadhu who went by the name of Purangir Gosain; he will appear often in the pages of this narrative. The Gosains were a class of Bengali holy men who at this period wandered freely in the mountains between India and Tibet, visiting the holy places that were revered by both Hindus and Buddhists. Many of them took advantage of their immunity from interference to become traders, specializing in light and valuable items, and often accumulating considerable fortunes under the guise of devotion to religion. Their freedom of travel gave them opportunities to act as spies and envoys, and many of them became double or even multiple agents, making their services available to several rulers.

The letter which Padma and the orange-robed Gosain handed to Warren Hastings was the first communication from a Tibetan hierarch to a European ruler. It was written, not in Tibetan or English, but in the Persian tongue that in Asia west of China was the habitual language of diplomacy and government, and whose turns of phrase and

39

flourishes of courtesy gave its opening phrases a fulsomeness of tone hardly in keeping with the Tibetan character.

> In every respect [it begins] the affairs of this quarter flourish. I am night and day employed in prayers for the increase of your happiness and prosperity. Having been informed by travellers from your country of your exalted fame and reputation, my heart, like the blossom of spring, abounds with gaiety, gladness and joy; praise God that the star of your fortune is in its ascendancy; praise God that happiness and ease are the surrounding attendants of myself and my family.

The voice of the Tibetan monk breaks in among the Persian rhetoric as the Panchen Lama remarks that his aim is 'neither to molest nor persecute', and that members of his sect deprive themselves of sleep if injury is done to a single being. This leads him to the point of intercession for the offending Deb Judhur. That the Deb is of 'a rude and ignorant race' the Panchen Lama admits with no concealment of the superiority with which Tibetans habitually regard the lesser Himalayan peoples. That the Deb's 'avarice' has led him into 'misconduct' on frequent occasions the Lama also admits, and he grants it likely that 'the ravages and plunder which he may have committed on the skirts of the provinces of Bengal and Behar have given you provocation to send your avenging army against him'. But the Deb is now brought low; his army has been defeated, many of his people have been killed, three of his forts have been occupied and it is time for a generous man to consider that the 'deserved punishment' has been meted out. That Hastings possesses such generosity the writer implies when he notes that 'if you had been desirous of it, you might, in the space of two days, have entirely extirpated him, for he had no power to resist your efforts'.

The Panchen Lama offers himself as mediator. Deb Judhur, he remarks, is a dependant of the Dalai Lama, and in the Dalai Lama's minority 'the charge for the government and administration for the present is committed to me' (a pretension that would not have gone uncontradicted in Lhasa). He has admonished the Deb to be 'submissive to you in all matters'.

> As for me, I am but a monk, and it is the custom of my sect, with rosary in hand, to pray for the welfare of all mankind . . . and I do now, with my head uncovered, entreat that you may cease all hostilities against the Deb in future.

The eloquences of this letter were reinforced by the gifts ('a few things' the Panchen Lama happened 'to have in hand') that accompanied it: little ingots of gold and silver and bags of gold dust panned from Tibetan streams; musk and woollen cloth; brocaded silk from China and stamped and gilded leather that had come from Russia by caravan through Sinkiang. In kind as well as in word, the tokens of a new and strange land lay before Hastings as the presents were unpacked from their skilfully made boxes, and beside him stood the men from that land who could answer the questions which the books he read had aroused in his mind. But however much his educated curiosity may have been provoked by the Panchen Lama's letters and gifts and messengers, it was his instinct as the first great political architect of British India that aroused him to immediate action.

The door to Tibet, at whose blank surface the Company's officials had been looking for years, was suddenly ajar, and, surprisingly, it had unlatched from inside. To push it wider, so that trade and envoys could pass, was his immediate intent, and at once he took the action he believed would deepen the Panchen Lama's benevolence. By Padma and

Purangir Gosain he sent back gifts and a courteous reply, proposing a general treaty of amity between the states of Bengal and Tibet. And, within a month of receiving the Panchen Lama's letter, he had signed a treaty with the new Deb Raja of Bhutan, by which the latter undertook to allow no more incursions on Company territory, to pay an annual tribute of five Tangun ponies (which was a way of acknowledging the Company's suzerainty), and to give up the captured Raja of Cooch Behar. In return the Company withdrew its forces from Bhutanese territory, evacuated the frontier fortresses and abolished the customs duties for Bhutanese merchants travelling to the annual fair at Rangpur in Bengal. In making such an agreement, Hastings was granting nothing that he would not in any case have given, for he had no intention of invading Bhutan, and the maintenance of garrisons within its border was vexatious and expensive, while, as a result of the former Deb Raja's incursions, he achieved one of the Company's main aims, which was the establishment of trade between Bengal and Bhutan.

But the door to Tibet still stood tantalizingly ajar. Courtesy alone would justify an attempt to reciprocate the advances made by the Panchen Lama, and interest made courtesy seem urgent. By the beginning of May, 1772, Hastings had decided to send the first British mission to Tibet, and had chosen George Bogle as his envoy.

# III

## *The Choice of an Envoy*

Apart from an insipid and characterless miniature made in his youth, no portrait of George Bogle exists. Yet it is not difficult, when we read his narrative, when we accompany him on the hard journey over the passes from one smoke-grimed but hospitable hovel to the next, when we join him as he puts on his warm and easy Tibetan garb to engage the Panchen Lama in one of those long informal talks in Hindustani and later in Tibetan which both of them liked, to form a visual image of him. Young, of course; he died before he was thirty-five, and was only twenty-seven when he set out on his journey; yet already touched by the heats and humidities and fevers of Bengal, where his four years in India had been spent, so that the freshness of his Lanarkshire complexion would have been sallowed, and his face etched by the lines of exhaustion that come even now when a European spends more than three years without leave in such a climate. Touched also by the lines of care, for already his intelligence had picked him out in the eyes of Warren Hastings as a young man to be given responsibility, so that after less than two years in India he had been chosen from the ruck of young clerks to be named Assistant Secretary of the Board of Revenue.

There was a physical toughness in Bogle, and there must also have been a sangfroid that enabled him to come off with reasonable honours in Asian bargaining, yet, strong personality though he obviously was, this did not mean that he lacked sensibility or sentiment. He confessed to hating farewells, and he obviously felt with a deep personal warmth the relationships which he established with his Tibetan friends, just as he remembered his family and his Scottish friends, and retained a special feeling for his sister Anne, to whom, before he set out on his journey to Tibet, he wrote a letter that one reads now with the slight sense of embarrassment induced by listening to private family talk.

> Your letters, my dear Chuffles, [he writes as the palm trees of Fort William grow misty in his mind's eye and the green fields of Lanarkshire fill their place] are the very nutmeg of delight, so long, so particular about everything my friends are doing. I have read them over again and again, and find new beauties in them every day. They are just as if you were chattering, with this advantage, that they cannot give me a headache, and I can stop them if I choose, which, you know, is not always an easy matter with your ladyship. They want, however, the snap of the fingers and the hearty laugh. The good news of all my friends gives me the most sincere delight. God grant I may long continue to receive such comfortable news! My heart overflows with gratitude to heaven, but it is not unmixed with regret.

Bogle was obviously a man whose affections were strong and easily aroused; at the same time he projected an air of great openness of nature, and this endeared him to the Tibetans. But there were other sides to Bogle. His frankness of manner masked an inner shrewdness which Hastings had sensed when he decided to appoint him to a sensitive and important mission in which he would need all the tact as well as all the mental adaptability he could muster. We shall encounter also a sharpness of calculation and a willingness to condone actions that would seem to us harsh. He was, in other words, a very typical eighteenth-century Scot, with a great capacity to like and to make himself liked, but with a core of the hardness that was needed to survive in the eighteenth century, that age of wedded contrasts when men could be moved to the depths of their souls by the sublimities of Handel and accept as justice the hanging of a poor woman for stealing a shilling.

The self-portrait that emerges from almost everything that Bogle left in writing retains the immaculate surface which the mannered prose he used was intended to create; the more personal idiosyncrasies are usually concealed as capably as the features of a No-player behind his mask, and it is rarely that a break in the self-dignifying but self-effacing manner reveals Bogle off his guard. The difference between him and Thomas Manning is in this respect astonishing, for Manning, at least in his journal, is never on his guard. All the idiosyncrasies are there, and are given their head. It is more than the difference between two kinds of personality; it is the difference, also, between the world of the Enlightenment and the world of the Romantics. Bogle is—and Turner will be—eminently the rational traveller, deferring at times to sentiment but keeping his emotions always in control and usually in hiding. Manning is eminently the emotional traveller, and, as we shall see, in some ways strikingly modern in his actions, combining comedy and self-pity in a way which travel writers in our day have fairly consistently imitated. Bogle was not comic, though he was genial. Nor did he ever pity himself, at least on paper.

That vein of stoicism had been bred into him from the beginning. He came of solid upper-middle-class Lowlands stock. His father, also George Bogle, educated at Leyden, had been a Glasgow merchant; his mother was the daughter of Sir John Sinclair, and his maternal grandmother the daughter of Sir John Lockhart, who had been one of the Lords of Justiciary under Charles II. Young George was the last of nine children; the toughness of the Bogle stock is shown by the fact that in that age of infant mortality no less than seven survived to adulthood. Bogle's childhood was passed in the atmosphere of scholarly rusticity that fostered so many of the great Scots of his age. In the letters he wrote his sister from Bengal, he remembers the theatrical pageants which the children would create out of a few simple props, a knowledge of the lives of classical heroes like Julius Caesar, and liberal imaginations. There is one passage in which a memory of spartan Scottish beds is curiously combined with the opening of one of those windows to the personality which Bogle so habitually kept curtained.

> Need I ask you if you remember one night that the beds were to be filled with fresh chaff and afterwards lay upon the floor, what diversion we had in tumbling one another from the top of the drawers? Do you remember how we broke open the window, at the bottom of one of the beds, to get at some shells? Never shall I wish for anything so much as I did to get at those shells, which we could always see and never get at.

Remembering so vividly, as he lay back in the great rattan chair on his Calcutta verandah, the child longing to lay his hands on those exotic and unattainable objects, doubtless brought into Glasgow by a seaman from some distant tropical beach, Bogle touched on the key pattern of his life —the desire to reach and to grasp what seemed unattainable, the desire always to excel one's present. Such a desire to go beyond the immediate was encouraged by the quality of his boyhood. He was sent first to a school in Haddington, east of Edinburgh, and perhaps sixty miles from Daldowie's

Clydeside. That mere fraction of the great distances Bogle was later to travel then seemed a veritable journey to Siberia. And it was only once a year, during 'this Latin and Greek period' as he called it, that he came home to Daldowie and still found Anne there, 'the brown maiden in her scarlet girdle'. There was a time at a school in Glasgow, when he could spend his Saturday nights at Daldowie, and six months studying logic at Edinburgh University, before his greater wanderings began when he followed his elder brother Robert into England and spent three further years studying at the private academy run in Enfield by a compatriot named Kinross. Bogle left the Enfield school in the autumn of 1764, at the age of eighteen, and accompanied to Europe a consumptive friend travelling towards the sun in a last hope of survival. The friend died at Toulouse before the first month was out, and Bogle spent the rest of the winter and all of the spring travelling in France.

His Little Tour ended, it was time to start a career, and the family tradition was mercantile. His brother Robert had set up an import business in London with a partner named Scott, and George began to learn the business as clerk in the counting house. Four years afterwards, in 1769, the business broke up. Robert went to Grenada to run a sugar plantation, and George was appointed through influence to the staff of the East India Company. He returned briefly to Daldowie, saw his family and home for the last time, and on the 25th January, 1770, he boarded the East Indiaman *Vansittart* for the long and tedious journey to Fort William. It was a month before the ship got clear of the Channel, and the weeks dragged away as it sailed down the sultry African coast, with Bogle filling the expanses of time by the study of Persian. The ship put in at the Cape of Good Hope, at the Comoro Islands off Madagascar, and at Madras; at last on the 19th August, in the swelter of the rainy season, it dropped anchor in the Hoogly and Bogle went ashore to take up his duties as Writer, the lowest rank among the Company's officers in India.

What he saw on his first arrival in Bengal bit deeply into his mind, and it may well have influenced the whole of his career in that country. For this was the year of the great famine, brought on by the crop failures of 1769, and aggravated, as Indian famines always have been, by the activities of native speculators who cold-bloodedly hoarded grain to force up the prices. Talking of the Calcutta that first met his shocked eyes, Bogle reported to his father:

There were sometimes 150 dead bodies picked up in a day, and thrown into the river. In the country the distress was greater, as it was farther removed from the sea and not so easily supplied from distant countries. Whole families perished of hunger, or fed upon leaves of trees, or, contrary to their religion, ate animal food; some even subsisted on the dead carcasses. Their distress is unparalleled, and it shocks one to think of it.

The London of 1770 which Bogle had left was stained by appalling areas of want, and no European going to India under normal circumstances at that time would feel the same kind of shock as a modern westerner experiences on first seeing the wretchedness of human existence in Calcutta, which for the poor has changed little over two centuries. But 1770 was a year like no other in memory, and Bogle was horrified enough by what he saw to keep adverting to the famine in his letters to his family, and reporting, in accents of relief, the improvements in the condition of the people. But the famine, before it ended, had taught him a lasting lesson in Asian psychology, for, if he looked with horror on the disaster itself, he looked with astonishment on the way in which men reacted to it.

> There is one thing that must amaze everyone that has been used to a free country. There is an indolence and indifference about them that is astonishing, and despair rather increases it. They have died without a single effort to obtain grain either by force or even by toil or labour. What mobs and commotions there would be with us were grain to increase to three times its price, and in many places it was a hundred times what it usually is.

One feels that Bogle would have been happier if there had been riots and commotions, and that the contempt he later showed for the Bengalis, which led him to compare them unfavourably with the more independent Himalayan peoples, may have sprung from his observation of their passivity in the face of starvation and death. What a young man brought up on the good farm food of Lanarkshire could not understand was the apathy that malnutrition prolonged from generation to generation had bred into the Indian poor.

Bogle began in the office of the Select Committee at Fort William, which transacted the political affairs of the Company in Bengal and conducted its foreign relations; as this was the time when affairs in Nepal had reached their disturbing extremity with the extinction of the Newari kingdoms, and the Court of Directors had ordered a shift of attention to Bhutan and Assam as possible sources of trade, there is no doubt that from the beginning of his time in India Bogle's attention was drawn towards the northern frontiers and the Himalayan states beyond them. We can be sure that, while spending much of his spare time perfecting himself in Persian, in which he became fluent within the first year, he did not neglect to learn what he could of Tibet and its neighbouring mountain lands.

Yet it was not until the arrival of Warren Hastings at Calcutta in February, 1772, that Bogle's career began to move forward. With the innovatory resourcefulness which earned him so many enemies among the Company's older officers in India, Hastings sought out younger officers who could be trusted to carry out the great reforms in policy and administration which he was planning. Bogle was one of the juniors whose character attracted his interest, and another was Bogle's close friend, Alexander Elliott, younger brother of Gilbert Elliott who, as Lord Minto, became one of the great early Governors General of India.

Hastings became President of the Council in April, 1772, and within six months Bogle's career moved into the ascendant. In October he was appointed Assistant Secretary to the Board of Revenue, and in the same month set out with Hastings and a number of other high officers on a winter tour of the back areas of Bengal which lasted for four months and was devoted to regularizing the system of land holdings and rationalizing the process of collecting revenue. This brought him into daily contact with Hastings, for whom he acquired an admiration that stopped just short of hero worship. Hastings, he told his family in a letter written home at this time, had reformed many abuses, made government departments more efficient, and begun to frame a legal system that paid due deference to the ancient Indian codes of law. Bogle praised the steadiness and moderation he saw in his chief, his quickness in business, his understanding of native customs and languages, his ready accessibility to petitioners. Yet, he had to add, Hastings was 'not affable'; one is left to wonder whether in his usage the phrase did not mean merely that Hastings was not over-familiar in his behaviour. Certainly Bogle displayed a loyalty which did not swerve when in 1775 Hastings was in difficulties with the hostile majority of his Council at Fort William. Hastings for his part appreciated Bogle's industry, his receptive intelligence, and his calm common sense. In fact, Bogle so well earned Hastings's approval on the inspection tour of 1772–3 that almost immediately after the commission's return to Calcutta he was appointed Registrar of the Sadr Diwani Adalat, a court of appeal for Bengalis, and, shortly afterwards, promoted to the prestigious post of Secretary to the Select Committee, which meant that he was in close touch with the progress of the Bhutanese war in 1773, and was almost certainly called into consultation by Hastings when the Panchen Lama's letter arrived during the following March. Given his position and his character, he was the obvious choice when a young but responsible officer was required to head the mission that would carry the Company's greetings to the Panchen Lama and would endeavour to open more widely the door of access to Tibet.

Hastings's decision was first recorded in a Minute prepared for the Company's local Board, in which he told of his plan to send a mission to the Panchen Lama with a view to proposing a 'general treaty of amity and commerce' between Bengal and Tibet, and of his decision to place in charge of the negotiation 'a European, and servant of the Company . . . in preference to any native . . .'. Hastings did not regard Purangir Gosain, who up to now had handled communications between Calcutta and Tashilunpo, as an entirely reliable representative; after all, he had first appeared as the Panchen Lama's messenger. He chose Bogle as his envoy 'for the coolness and moderation of temper he seems to possess to an eminent degree'. And as Bogle's companion he picked a young assistant surgeon named Alexander Hamilton. They were to take with them not only presents for the Panchen Lama and his high officials, but also samples of the trade goods which the Company hoped would find a market in Tibet.

The appointment was confirmed on the 13th May in a letter of instructions which on that day Hastings handed to Bogle. It reveals preconceptions of the actual situation in Tibet which Bogle was soon to discover were mistaken, for Hastings instructs his envoy to 'the Teshu Lama' to proceed to 'Lhasa, his capital', and not to Tashilunpo. Clearly Padma and the Gosain had talked loudly and misleadingly about the extent of the power wielded by the Panchen Lama, and Bogle appears to have started out on his journey with no real knowledge of the division of authority which existed between the Panchen Lama in Tashilunpo, and the Regent who in Lhasa administered the government of Tibet in the name of the juvenile Dalai Lama.

Hastings's more particular instructions were divided between those stated officially in the letter of commission, and those embodied in a list of 'private commissions' handed to Bogle three days later. 'The design of your mission', state the official instructions, 'is to open a mutual and equal communication of trade between the inhabitants of Bhutan and Bengal, and you will be guided by your own judgment in using such means of negotiation as may be most likely to effect this purpose.' Bogle is to enquire what commodities the Company may profitably try to sell in Tibet, and also what merchandise imported from other lands may be available in that country, 'especially such as are of great value and easy transportation, such as gold, silver, precious stones, musk, rhubarb, munjit, &c.'.

Bogle is further instructed to enquire into the roads and means of communication in the Himalayan countries, and to transmit the results of his observations, 'whether of useful knowledge or curiosity', when he reports on the progress of his negotiations. Finally, he is to give advice as to whether 'a residence may be usefully established at Lhasa without putting the Company to any expense, but such as may be repaid by the advantages which may be hereafter derived from it'.

It is clear from the letter of commission that Hastings trusted implicitly in Bogle's responsibility and discretion, for he is told to judge what length of time he needs to gain a sufficient knowledge of the country, and Hastings places no limitation on his expenditure, 'knowing that I need not recommend to you to observe a strict frugality and economy where the good of the service to which you are commissioned shall not require a deviation from these rules'.

The private commissions are somewhat more interesting because they reveal the fusion of scientific curiosity and mercantile foresight which characterized the viewpoint of an imaginative administrator like Hastings—a viewpoint Bogle appears to have shared to the full. Indeed, they reveal so clearly the mental temper in which Bogle's expedition was conceived that they deserve quotation *in extenso*.

Private Commission to Mr Bogle

*Fort William, 16th May, 1774.*

1. To send one or more pair of the animals called tūs, which produce the shawl wool. If by a dooley, chairs, or any other contrivance they can be secured from the fatigues and hazards of the way, the expense is to be no objection.
2. To send one or more pair of the cattle which bear what are called cowtails.
3. To send me carefully packed some fresh ripe walnuts for seed, or an entire plant, if it can be transported; and any other curious or valuable seeds or plants, the rhubarb and ginseng especially.

53

4. Any curiosities, whether natural productions, manu-factures, paintings, or what else may be acceptable to persons of taste in England. Animals only that may be useful, unless any that may be remarkably curious.

5. In your inquiries concerning the people, the form of their government, and the mode of collecting their revenue, are points principally meriting your attention.

6. To keep a diary, inserting whatever passes before your observation which shall be characteristic of the people, the country, the climate, or the road, their manners, customs, buildings, cookery, &c., or interesting to the trade of this country, carrying with you a pencil and a pocket-book for the purpose of minuting short notes of every fact or remark as it occurs, and putting them in order at your leisure while they are fresh in your memory.

7. To inquire what countries lie between Lhasa and Siberia, and what communication there is between them. The same with regard to China and Kashmir.

8. To ascertain their trade with Bengal by their gold and silver coins, and to send me samples of both.

9. Every nation excels others in some particular art or science. To find out this excellence of the Bhutanese.

WARREN HASTINGS.

10. To inform yourself of the course and navigation of the Brahmaputra, and of the state of the countries through which it runs.

W. H.

When he talked of 'Bhutanese' in this context, Hastings meant, not the people of present-day Bhutan, but the people of Tibet. The word Bhutan was then often applied to Tibet, and indeed is closer than the usual Western term to the Tibetans' own name for their country, which is Bhod. By the cattle 'which bear what are called cowtails', Hastings was of course referring to the yak, while the *tūs*, an archaic transliteration of the Tibetan word for sheep, was in fact a kind of long-haired goat related to if not identical with the Kashmir goat whose fine wool provides the celebrated shawl of that region.

These were instructions to an explorer as much as a plenipotentiary, and such indeed, as events dictated, was the role in which Bogle was most successful. Hastings accompanied the 'private commissions' with a long memorandum condensing the information he had been able to gather from a study of the available texts on Tibet; some of it was garbled history, some of it accurate information regarding customs, including such *exotica* as the prevalence of polyandry, the method of choosing the holy child into whom the spirit of the Dalai Lama has transmigrated, and the magical qualities of the Dalai Lama's excrement.

It was clear that Hastings was deeply concerned over the possibilities of the expedition not only as a means of opening to the Company a new and profitable area of trade in Tibet and perhaps even in western China, but also as a source of new knowledge that would be of use to scientists and geographers, and that he went to great deal of trouble to give Bogle an adequate briefing on what he might expect to encounter. It was the paucity of detailed information on Tibet then available in English rather than any omission on Hastings's part that led to the rather momentous inaccuracies in his instructions. Yet nothing was more characteristic of Hastings and his earnest utilitarian desire to benefit humanity than his verbal order that Bogle carry with him a supply of potatoes, not to eat, but to plant here and there on his way through Bhutan and Tibet in the hope that in this way a new and hardy crop might be introduced into these agriculturally rather desolate uplands. The choice of the potato—that native of the Peruvian sierra—doubtless arose out of the idea, which Hastings also expounded to

Bogle, that there might be a resemblance in climate and other respects between the situation of Lhasa and the valley of Quito in the Andes, whose characteristics had recently been so interestingly described by the explorer de la Condamine. He may well have hoped that Bogle's discoveries would be as momentous as those of the great South American explorer.

# IV

## *In Bhutan*

It was not until the middle of May that Bogle and Hamilton
set out from Calcutta. 'It was then the hottest season of the
year; the thermometer was often above the degree of blood
heat, and the sun being almost vertical, it was necessary to
travel chiefly during the nighttime.' They went northward
through Bengal to Murshidabad, and thence north-eastward
to Dinajpur and Rangpur, both of them now in East
Pakistan. Bogle does not tell how they travelled, but in that
land of many waters it is likely that they went by boat to
Murshidabad, and by an alternation of boat and palanquin
from Murshidabad to Rangpur; the road system of northern
Bengal (rudimentary as it is even today) was not yet existent.
In Rangpur Bogle encountered a Kashmiri merchant named
Mirza Settar who had travelled through Tibet as far as
Lhasa and who knew the Tibetan language. He questioned
him, but after some thought did not immediately engage
him, since Purangir Gosain, still in Calcutta, would be join-
ing the party, and Bogle did not know how the Kashmiri
Moslem and the Hindu Gosain, each of whom claimed to
be something of an authority on Tibet, would agree together.

Bogle left Rangpur almost immediately. He was hurrying
to get out of the plains before the rains began, and by the
end of May he and Hamilton had crossed the frontier of
Bengal into Cooch Behar. At Behar, the fortress-capital of

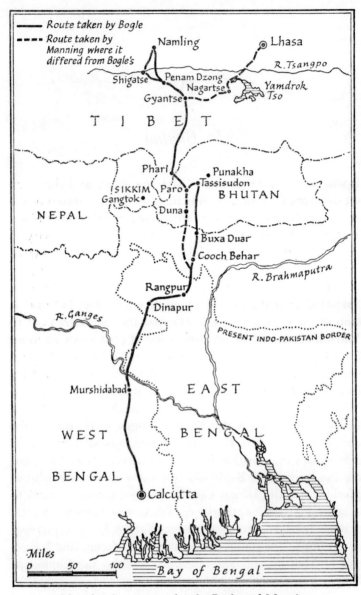

Map showing routes taken by Bogle and Manning

the little state, they stayed a few days to equip their party, which included the large contingent of Bengali servants necessitated by the need to preserve the prestige of the Company's mission as much as by the peculiarities of Hindu caste taboos which created a minute division of menial labour even in a travelling household.

Behar lies in the steamy flats of the Brahmaputra basin, and Bogle and his party trailed a few miles through the rice paddies of the inhabited countryside around the town before they reached the dense scrub that is characteristic of the lowlands which adjoin the foothills of the eastern Himalayas; ' . . . we entered a thicket formed of reeds, brushwood and long grass closely interwoven; frogs, watery insects, and dank air: one can hardly breathe'. After ten miles the thicket gradually changed to a forest of tall trees, through which they came to the river that separated Cooch Behar from Bhutan.

On the way Bogle met a number of Hindu holy men coming down on their way out of Tibet, but their descriptions of the road were so vague as to be almost useless, and the information Hastings had provided contained nothing regarding the actual route through Bhutan to Tibet. D'Anville's map, which Bogle carried, was equally unhelpful. Standing on the bank of the river, and looking over to the opposite shore where there were no guides to see him on his way, he became very conscious that 'none of the Company's servants, and I might say almost no European, had ever visited the country which I was about to enter', and that he was 'equally in the dark as to the road, the climate, or the people'. Doubtless, at this moment, he regretted that in Rangpur he had neglected to engage Mirza Settar. But he could see the long line of hills that defined the Bhutanese frontier, through which the Duars cut down into deep jungle-clogged valleys, and there was a ferry made of dugout canoes tied together by which he and his party could cross. They did so, following a trail that led them past the great earth banks, dominated by ruined wooden stockades, which marked the site of Bhutanese fortresses, destroyed by Captain Jones's men during last year's war and not yet occupied by the forces of the new Deb Raja. At last they came to a little village of new houses, rebuilt after the devastation of the war. The people, though subjects of Bhutan, were still Hindus, belonging to one of the local farmer castes, and Bogle noted that in their colouring, features and physique they much more resembled the Bengalis than the real Mongoloid hill peoples.

The villagers were carousing on rum when Bogle arrived, and the headman was enjoying himself in tipsily Rabelaisian manner with a female pedlar who 'sojourned with him'. Bogle looked with some appreciation at her by no means hidden charms: 'good features and shape, fine teeth, and Rubens' wife's eyes; whole dress one blanket wrapped round her, and fastened over the shoulders with a silver skewer'. There was a hospitable welcome for the strangers, and one of the houses was turned over to Bogle and Hamilton. It was of a type still used in these southern jungle margins of the Himalayas, thatched with grass, 'the floor of lath of bamboo, and raised four feet from the ground; the walls of reeds, tied together with slips of bamboo; and the stair a stump of a tree, with notches cut in it. It had much the look of a birdcage, and the space below being turned into a hogstye contributed little to its pleasantness. There was not a bit of iron or rope about it.' In the other houses that night, Bogle noted, 'men, women and children' slept 'higgledy-piggledy together'.

Next morning, when Bogle and Hamilton set out in the

first light of dawn, the mountains, although eighteen miles away, seemed already to tower over their heads, so loftily and abruptly did they rise out of the valley. There are eighteen Duars cutting down from Bhutan into the plains of Bengal and Assam; Bogle had chosen the Buxa Duar, since this led into the valley of the Chinchu river which in turn led to the Bhutanese capital of Tassisudon. The face of the country began to change. The trees grew taller. The slow murky streams of Bengal were replaced by 'rivulets clear, and running on sand, pebbles, and stones'. The rains still held off, which was fortunate, since as soon as they begin the streams of the Duars turn into dangerous torrents, the air becomes dense and humid, and malaria spreads, even today. As it was, they were able to enjoy the increasing coolness as they came at about two in the afternoon to the foot of the hills and the road began to rise unevenly, climbing gently through woods, and then becoming a narrow path that serpentined steeply up the hillsides. 'What a road for troops!' Bogle reflected as he remembered the hardships suffered by Jones's little army. They threaded their way slowly round magnificent natural amphitheatres, filled with tall trees and musical with the noise of waterfalls; they stopped to drink the fresh, safe water of the mountainside springs, and towards evening they came to the fortress of Buxa, 'situated on a hill, with much higher ones above it, glens under it, and a 3-feet wall of loose stones about it; a fine old banian tree; that's all'.

Modest as Buxa appeared, and dilapidated as it was from the demolitionary efforts of Captain Jones, it was the first outpost of Bhutanese authority, with its garrison of rough kilted soldiers and an absentee commandant whose steward came to pay the necessary compliments to Bogle, laying across his hands the white scarf that honours the guest in the Buddhist realms of the Himalayas, and offering him gifts

61

of butter, of milk, and of the coarse tea which the Bhutanese like the Tibetans mix into a soup-like brew by adding salt and soda and churning in a liberal proportion of yak butter. The steward also provided Bogle with the necessary passports from the Deb Raja to secure his passage through Bhutanese territory, and found him another birdcage house of reed and bamboo.

This was the 7th June. Now Bogle had to change his mode of travel in the densely wooded mountains to the north and up on to the high bare ranges beyond. The rivers were too rapid for boats, the roads too narrow for wheeled vehicles (which in any case were unknown in Bhutan) and even for palanquins. Horses were the only means of passenger transport, and Bogle and Hamilton were provided with 'two Tangun ponies of mean appearance'. The Tangun pony is the tough mountain horse, with hooves so hard that they did not need shoeing, that was commonly used in Tibet and Bhutan. Bogle confessed to being prejudiced at first against these unprepossessing mounts. 'On better acquaintance they turned out patient, sure-footed, and could climb the Monument. Many a time afterwards, when, on the edge of a precipice, I was mounted on a skittish young horse, with a man holding him by the head and another steering him by the tail, have I thought of them.'

But there were not enough ponies to carry the mission's baggage, and Bogle had to rely on the porterage system which until only recently operated throughout the Himalayas by means of a kind of *corvée*.

The carriers [Bogle explained] are pressed from among the inhabitants, receive an allowance for victuals at the pleasure of the person on whose service they are employed, and are relieved by others procured in the same manner at the next village by order of the head man, without which not a coolie is to be had. This is a service so well established that the people submit to it without murmuring. Neither sex, nor youth, nor age exempt them from it. The burden is fastened under the arms upon their backs, with a short stick to support it while they rest themselves. Naturally strong, and accustomed to this kind of labour, it is astonishing what loads they will carry. A girl of eighteen travelled one day 15 or 18 miles, with a burden of 70 or 75 pounds weight. We could hardly do it without any weight at all.

It took two days to round up enough coolies, and it was not until the 9th June that the party began to move up the steep paths that would take them over the tall mountain of Pichakonum which seemed to overhang the fortress of Buxa. It was a narrow path, circling around the steep side of the mountain, 'the upper part paved with stones of bastard marble, put together like ill-formed steps'. By midday, almost at the top of the mountain, when the road turned northward, the wind had become bitterly cold, blowing down out of Tibet. The mountainsides fell away in deep precipices, but Bogle did not find them 'frightful' because they were covered with trees and he enjoyed the illusion that a fall might easily be broken. Light-heartedly, he amused himself tumbling stones into the clattering ravines below; and then, at the highest point of the road, where tall poles flying great white flags bearing Buddhist mantras had been raised, he stopped to look at the double prospect, down over the plains, up into the mountains. He was the first European to have seen either view; Captain Jones had not gone beyond Buxa.

It is impossible to conceive any change of country more abrupt, or any contrast more striking. To the southward the atmosphere was clear. The eye stretched over a vast tract of land, and the view was bounded only by the circular horizon. This part of the view, however, is striking only because it is extensive. There are no hills, spires or other objects to distinguish it. The country—one continuous flat—is marked only by its being cleared or woody, by the course of the rivers, or by some smoking villages. Whether it be that I am partial to hills or not, I beheld the opposite part of the prospect with much greater pleasure. The rapid descent, the deep glens, the hills covered with trees the most lofty and luxuriant, the town of Buxa-Duar immediately below at a great distance, and behind nothing but mountains with their tops hid in the cloud. It was lucky for them, as I fancied them much higher than they really are.

From the summit they descended over the forested mountainsides. 'We went down against the grain, for we must climb it up again,' Bogle wryly remarked. Far below them small villages were scattered, and laboriously built terraces threaded along the hillsides with glistening threads of water carefully diverted into them; they grew small patches of wheat, barley and maize. Everywhere there were the signs of a way of life which demanded more labour than in the flat damp countryside of Bengal, and Bogle saw a wisdom of nature in the fact that—unlike the Bengalis—the Bhutanese were robust enough to carry all they needed on their own backs over this terrain where no road ran level.

At Jaigugu the travellers came within sight of the Chinchu (now more commonly called the Wang Chu) running down its long valley from Tassisudon; 'it runs so fast and dashes over so many stones, that it is half a cascade'. The valley was deep enough and the climate warm enough for more birdcage houses of bamboo and reeds, though there were, to be sure, only three of them, 'and two Nepal dogs'. The people were rough-mannered and at times rather surly; they were as dirty as Bogle was later to find the Tibetans, but by no means as affable. The men 'dressed in short trousers, like the

Highland philabeg; woollen hose, soled with leather and gartered under the knee; a jacket or tunic, and over all two or three striped blankets'. The women wore the long, folded-over Tibetan gown or chupa. They vacated one of the bird-cage houses for the travellers to sleep, and in the morning, before he left, Bogle planted his first ten potatoes in one of the gardens among the turnips and giant white radishes.

Instead of continuing along the Chinchu to Tassisudon, as Bogle had hoped, the road continued to clamber over the mountainsides, avoiding the precipitous river banks, and only occasionally, at some high point, did the white waters become visible in the far distance. All the way to Muri-jong, a twenty-mile stage with the porters in good tramping form, the road went steeply up and down, with distant villages nestling among their terraces on the hillsides. During the night there had been rain, and the road was often soggy and slippery. But scenically it was magnificent and Bogle's love of the picturesque was stirred by the many waterfalls; ' . . . one fell perpendicular about 40 feet from the top of a rock; another a stream foaming and tumbling over large stones; another embosomed in a fine grove, with arches formed by the trees and rocks. There were wooden bridges over all the rivulets that ran from them.' The symbols of a deeply held religion were scattered thickly in this wild land-scape. By the roadside stood the mani walls, the holy formula 'Om mani padmi hum' graven repeatedly into their stones 'and small basso-relievo figures, with gilt faces cut in black marble, and placed in the middle and at each end'. Around these the people tramped in a clockwise direction, whirling their little copper prayer wheels and sending the mantras inscribed within them to float on the spirited air to con-tribute to the diffused power of good. Occasionally, where a stream crossed the road, Bogle and his companions found it turning a small water wheel to which was attached a barrel-like contraption, also inscribed *Om mani padmi hum* in the Tibetan script and stuffed with holy sayings set in motion by the waters as the prayer flags were set in motion by the wind.

At last the travellers came in sight of Muri-jong. The evening gong was beating beside the village chörten, the solid square structure, without doors or windows, that contained sacred relics and was the centre of local religious life. Many prayer flags stirred in the evening winds over the roofs of the twenty houses. The climate was becoming more rigorous, and now only the poorest homes were 'birdcages'; most were built of stone and timber in the solid Tibetan manner, two and three stories high with tiled roofs weighted with stones to prevent their being blown away in the high winds. Bogle liked Muri-jong, for in some ways it reminded him of the temperate European world to which he belonged. There were oak trees around the chörten, and the houses stood in orchards of peaches, apples and pears, of apricots and mulberries. Meadows of lush grass spread out on every side of the village; there were many cattle. In each house the butter lamps burnt before domestic altars, and at evening conch shells and flowers were laid before the images of Buddha and the Mahayanist deities, dressed in their tiny garments of brocade, while the village hummed with the drone of chanted prayers. The people made tea for the travellers, sipping from the cup in the curious Bhutanese manner before they offered it. Bogle honoured Muri-jong by planting fifteen potatoes.

The next day's stage was a long and difficult one, over high mountains where they had often to go on foot and were drenched by rain which, Bogle remarks, 'does not fall from the clouds, but comes upwards'. The road became trapped in the ravine of the Chinchu, and they had to climb a rock

66

that literally hung over the river 'by steps, almost perpendicular', but even here the Tangun ponies that Bogle and Hamilton were riding showed their mettle by climbing as nimbly as the men. Near the top of the rock a narrow tunnel had been cut and through this they came out in sight of another curious monument of Bhutanese engineering, the iron bridge that led over the broad and tumultuous river into Chuka, a somewhat larger village which served as a district centre; in Bhutan, then as now, there were no real towns, but only villages and fortresses or dzongs which served as governmental strongpoints and centres of administration. The iron bridge fascinated Bogle, and he measured and described it carefully.

> Five chains are stretched from one side to the other, and covered with laths and mats of bamboo, which form the floor. Two other chains are extended across the river at about seven feet perpendicular above the outermost of those on each side, and joined to them with twisted rattans. It is 147 feet long, and 6 feet broad. As soon as one steps upon it, it moves from one end to the other.

The river was a kind of topographical frontier from which the country and its prospects steadily opened out.

> The mountains are still very high [Bogle noted] but being more sloped have more arable land, and being at a greater distance from one another, leave room for villages in the hollows between them. On the former part of the journey there were nothing but glens, now there are valleys. But the sides of the mountains are more bare; there are few large trees, mostly fir; the road is more level, except at two or three places; and we can ride the greatest part.

There was also a change in the vegetation. In the dense damp ravine on the way to Chuka there were still trees familiar from Bogle's experience of Bengal; thickets of

67

bamboo, ragged-bannered plantains, and jack trees with their immense scaly fruit as large as vegetable marrows; the vestiges of perpetual tropical summer. Beyond Chuka the vegetation became even more European than in the temperate pastoral enclave of Muri-jong, and the list of wild plants Bogle rather prosaically made evokes the image of mountain-side woodlands as fresh as those of Savoy or Ticino at the end of spring, for as well as the walnut and the holly, the willow and the ash, there were the primrose and the wild strawberry, the sweet briar and the bramble, and, on the stonier slopes, wormwood and juniper and sage.

The actual journeying beyond Chuka was relatively un-eventful. Each evening they would reach a village of ten or fifteen or twenty large stone houses. The headman would offer a gift of yak butter ('I got as much in presents as would have set me up for a tallow-chandler,' Bogle remarked), the day's porters would be fed at Bogle's expense on the customary Bhutanese meal of rice with pork or dried fish imported from Bengal and would be given some trifling presents. The night would pass in a room that was often smoke-ridden and usually dirty, with drying yak meat smelling high under the rafters. Next morning they would set off with a new crew of porters. On the road there was occasional friction because the arrogance of Bogle's Bengali servants aroused the resent-ment of the Bhutanese, who lived in a society where—despite divisions of wealth—an extraordinary degree of democracy in behaviour existed. On one stage an old woman took up a rock and threatened to knock down one of these presump-tuous underlings, and her action proved more effective than all Bogle's admonishments and punishments, for now the Bengalis realized the temper of the people among whom they had come, and behaved more prudently. Ironically, the one really perilous situation on the whole journey to the Bhutanese capital was brought on by a minor official sent down from Tassisudon by the Deb Raja to facilitate their journey. He met them just beyond Chuka, and almost immediately provoked what looked like becoming an ugly incident.

> Having a dispute about my horse with the head man of a small village, he wanted to strike him, and in endeavouring to wrest a bow from one of the bystanders he hit him a blow in the scuffle. In a moment half-a-dozen arrows were pointed at his breast, and he escaped the fate of St. Sebastian only by getting out of the way.

This official also annoyed Bogle by several times leading him over rough and hilly ground when there was an easier way beside the river. On one occasion Purangir Gosain, who in the meantime had joined the party, was taken with his baggage by the smooth road after Bogle and Hamilton had already been started on one of the more precipitous paths. Later Bogle suspected that this treatment was part of a deliberate attempt on the part of the Deb Raja's people to make his way so difficult that he would decide not to continue.

Curiously, the most important incident of the journey to Tassisudon is absent from Bogle's journal, and is recorded only in the letters he wrote to Warren Hastings after his arrival in Tassisudon. Near the end of the trip, and probably at a village called Lumbulong, Bogle was met by a messenger from the Panchen Lama, who bore 'a Persian letter' to him and another letter to Hastings, and told Bogle that presents would be arriving in the evening. There was yet another letter for Purangir Gosain.

The letters to Bogle and to the Gosain agreed only in attempting to discourage Bogle from proceeding on his journey. The first was written in an unfamiliar character, and Bogle had difficulty in reading it without an interpreter, but he soon gathered the substance.

> He begins with his 'having heard of my arrival at Kuch Bahar on my way to him, and, after some formal expressions of satisfaction, informs me that his country being subject to the Emperor of China, whose order it is that he shall admit no Moghul, Hindustani, Patan, or Fringy, he is without remedy, and China being at the distance of a year's journey prevents his writing to the Emperor for permission; desires me therefore to return to Calcutta, and if I have any effects to carry them with me, but to retain the letter in my hands, and that he will afterwards send a person to Calcutta'. As I cannot make out some of the words at the end of the letter, I beg leave to refer you to the original, which I have now the honour to enclose.

In the letter to the Gosain, it was a delay rather than a cancellation of Bogle's visit that was mentioned, and the reason given was that 'the great distress his country was in on account of the smallpox . . . had obliged him to quit his usual place of residence and return to the northward'. The last statement, as Bogle afterwards found, was true; the Panchen Lama had moved to Namling nearly three years before to escape the danger of the epidemic that raged around Shigatse and Tashilunpo. But the discrepancy between the two versions perturbed Bogle, though he believed there was a single interpretation which embraced them both.

> Teshu Lama was averse to my visit, and the violence of the smallpox, or an order of the Emperor of China, served for a pretence as well as any other. But from what cause this proceeded I could not then discover.

After unsuccessfully questioning the messenger, Bogle decided that his policy must be one of quiet obstinacy while he attempted to recruit the Deb Raja's support as the Panchen Lama's vassal. Accordingly, he refused to accept either the presents of silk which the Panchen Lama had sent or his letter to Hastings, and sent a message to the Deb, who was then in religious retreat fifteen miles out of Tassisudon, announcing his proximate arrival. When the messenger still pressed him to receive the letter to Hastings, Bogle again refused and told him to take it himself to Calcutta; this the messenger said he was not authorized to do, and, on Bogle's insisting on going forward to Tassisudon, he attached himself to the party. Meanwhile, within two days a message arrived from the Deb Raja, explaining the reason for his absence, but welcoming Bogle and telling him that orders had been given for his accommodation.

The next morning the cavalcade set out, inching over the quaking two-chain suspension bridge at Lumbulong, and by evening Bogle and his entourage were straggling down into the little valley, five miles long, one mile wide and wholly surrounded by mountains, where Tassisudon lies, some 7,300 feet above the sea. The travellers looked down on the winding, galloping river with its wooden bridges, the jade-green rice paddies filling the bottom of the valley, the thickly scattered hamlets. On the gentler hillsides waved fields of wheat, and above, on the steeper slopes, reared 'the lofty castles of fakirs', by which Bogle meant the Buddhist monasteries that clung to the crags like massive stone nests. In the midst of the scene the low sun ignited the golden turrets of the great palace which was the centre of government, the residence of both the Dharma Raja and the Deb Raja, the Potala of Bhutan. There was no town even here—only a few scattered houses; but within its great two-storied walls the palace was a miniature city, inhabited by three thousand men (including a thousand maroon-robed monks) and not a single woman. In the midst of the palace rose a solid square tower, gilt-roofed and five or six stories high; this was the residence of the Dharma Raja, the spiritual ruler of the country.

The travellers were accommodated in one of the better houses near the palace. Bogle described his room as a 'wooden balcony', with an excellent view looking out over the river. When he arrived, in mid June, the weather was comfortably warm and the flimsiness of the walls caused no great inconvenience, but as the weeks of waiting in Tassisudon lengthened out, and the nights grew colder, he had to hang the walls thickly with Bhutan blankets to keep out the winds that blew down from the surrounding mountains.

It was weeks before Bogle was able to discuss his difficulties with the Deb Raja. Only on the 4th July did the ruler return from his retreat, and Bogle watched the mediaeval pageantry of his arrival.

> At about ten o'clock the balconies of the palace were covered with priests, who were all clad in red cloth, the manufacture of Bhutan; and 4 long brass trumpets, 6 castenets, 4 tabors, and 4 fifes were sounded at intervals. At eleven, 30 matchlocks were fired on the road he was to pass, and the salute was repeated when he came up to them. The procession consisted of 12 led horses; 120 men dressed in red, with blue solitaires; 30 matchlock men; 30 archers, 30 horses laden with cloths and other furniture; 40 men on horseback, some of them with bushy caps; the chief dewan, with a bushy party-coloured standard; 6 musicians; the Deb Rajah on horseback, covered with a scarlet cloak, a large yellow hat like a cardinal's, a choura burdar [fly whisk carrier] on each side of him, and behind a man carrying a small white silk umbrella with different coloured fringes. As they came near the palace every body except the Rajah alighted; the men with bushy caps pulled them off, and walked up to the gate. At different parts of the road which he had to pass, fires were lighted, and the people prostrated themselves before him. In the whole cavalcade there were about 400 persons.

Two days afterwards the Deb Raja finally sent for Bogle. He walked to the palace, accompanied by his servants, and made for the people of Tassisudon, most of whom had never seen a European before, a spectacle even more interesting than the Deb Raja's cavalcade. The road was lined with peasants, the windows of the palace were crowded with monks and officials. 'I dare say there were 3,000,' Bogle afterwards remarked. He wrote two accounts of the reception, which was his first experience of Himalayan courtly life, one in his journal, and other in a letter to his sister Anne, still in prosaic Daldowie; this is by far the fuller and livelier version.

After passing through three courts, and climbing two iron-plated ladders, I was carried into an antechamber hung round with bows and arrows, swords, matchlocks, cane-coiled targets, and other implements of war, and filled with a number of priests, servants, &c., squatted down in different places. Having waited here about half an hour, I was conducted to the Rajah. He was seated upon a throne, or pulpit, if you please (for that is what it is like), raised about two feet from the ground. At entering I made him three low bows, instead of as many prostrations, with which, according to the etiquette of this court, I ought to have approached him. I then walked up and gave him a white satin handkerchief, while my servants laid my presents of spices, cloths, cutlery, &c., before him; after which I was conducted to a cushion prepared for me at the opposite end of the room. As all this passed in a profound silence, I had now time to get over a kind of flurry which it had occasioned. In the meantime several copper trays, with rice, butter, treacle, tea, walnuts, apricots, cucumbers, and other fruits, were set before me, together with a little stool and a china cup. . . .

The Deb Rajah was dressed in his sacerdotal habit of scarlet cotton, with gilded mitre on his head, and an umbrella with fringes twirling over him. He is a pleasant-looking old man with a smirking countenance. On each side of him his principal officers and ministers to the number of a dozen were seated upon cushions close to the wall, and the rest of the Company stood in the area or among the pillars. The panels of the room and also the ceiling were covered with Chinese sewed landscapes and different coloured satins; the pulpit was gilded, and many silver and gilt vases about it; and the floor all around was laid with carpets. At the opposite end of the apartment, and behind where I sat, several large Chinese images were placed in a kind of niche or alcove, with lamps of butter burning before them, and ornamented with elephants' teeth, little silver temples, china-ware, silks, ribbons, and other gewgaws. Among these I must not forget a solitary print of Lady Waldegrave, whom I had afterwards the good fortune to be the means of rescuing out of the hands of those idols; for it happening to strike some of the courtiers—whether the upholsterer, the chamberlain, or a page, I cannot pretend to say—that Lady Waldegrave would make a pretty companion to a looking-glass I had given the Rajah, she was hung up on one of the pillars next the throne, and the mirror on the other. . . .

In came a man carrying a large silver kettle, with tea made with butter and spices, and having poured a little into his hand and drank it, he filled the Deb Rajah a cup, then went round to all the ministers, who, as well as every other *Boot* [Bhutanese], are always provided with a little wooden cup, black glazed on the inside, wrapped in a bit of cloth, and lodged within their tunic, opposite to their heart and next their skin, which keeps it warm and comfortable; and last of all the cup-bearer filled my dish. The Rajah then said grace, in which he was joined by all the company. When we had finished our tea, and every man had well licked his cup, and deposited it in his bosom, a water tabby gown, like what Aunt Katy used to wear, with well-plated haunches, was brought and put on me; a red satin handkerchief was tied round me for a girdle. I was conducted to the throne, where the Deb Rajah bound my temples with another satin handkerchief, and squeezing them hard betwixt his hands, muttered some prayers over me, after which I was led back to my cushion. We had next a cup of whisky fresh and hot out of the still, which was served round in the same manner as the tea, of which we had also two more dishes, and as many graces; and last of all betel nut.

A great deal of complimentary conversation followed, through an interpreter, but this was hardly the time to bring up the business that was on Bogle's mind, and he accordingly took leave, the Deb Raja throwing over his shoulders two white scarves knotted together. Attired in his silk gown, Bogle visited some of the officers in the palace, and then 'walked home, like Mordecai, in great state to my lodgings'.

The palace was to become very familiar to the travellers during the next three months, as the negotiations and manœuvres relating to their entry into Tibet were carried on. On Bogle's second visit, he insisted that, since he could not accept the Panchen Lama's letter to Hastings, and the Lama's envoys had no authority to take it to Calcutta, it should be deposited with the Deb Raja, and this was granted. But when he asked the Deb Raja's more positive assistance in removing the obstacles to his journey, the Bhutanese ruler advised him to abandon it and return at once to Calcutta, laying even greater stress on the hostility of the Chinese to 'Fringies' [Europeans] than the Panchen Lama had done in his letter. Bogle refused to accept his advice, and on several further meetings with the Deb Raja and his officers he remonstrated with them, and finally wrung from the Deb Raja an agreement to write a letter to the Panchen Lama, 'which was given with so much reluctance that I am not sanguine about its good effects'.

In his desperation, Bogle decided to turn to Purangir Gosain for help, under the theory that, since the journey had been undertaken because of the Gosain's assurances, he might feel bound 'in honour to see it accomplished'. Bogle did not rely entirely on honour; remembering the predilections of these holy men for portable wealth, he 'endeavoured to strengthen this principle by more powerful motives'. On the 15th July the Gosain set off for Tashilunpo, accompanied by the Panchen Lama's messenger. Since they had to take a circuitous route to avoid the area of Tibet affected by the smallpox epidemic, they estimated it would take them twenty days to reach the Panchen Lama in his refuge at Namling, and that it would be little less than two months before an answer could be expected.

The Deb Raja again urged Bogle to return to Calcutta, but he dug in his heels, using the expectation of letters from the Panchen Lama as an excuse to stay in Tassisudon and to find out what he could in the meantime about Bhutan, its people and its possibilities as a source of trade. At first he went about this task with some discouragement, since it was evident that he and Hamilton were being carefully watched. Their servants were not allowed to have any contact with the local people; all purchases had to be made through the Deb Raja's officers. And Bogle found that some of the palace officials who had called before the Deb Raja returned from his retreat were now forbidden to visit him. Yet on the surface there was nothing but courtesy on the part of the Bhutanese, and after the Panchen Lama's messenger departed a relaxation of the watchfulness became apparent.

Bogle and Hamilton occupied the weeks of waiting in taking long walks into the mountains around Tassisudon, and preparing reports on questions of interest to Warren Hastings. They found an unforeseen friend in the Dharma Raja, who was far from being the religious recluse they had expected to encounter; on the contrary, he was extremely interested in the strangers who had arrived from the world beyond the mountains, and, after a first ceremonial visit, he encouraged them to call on him without ceremony, which they frequently did. He was, Bogle remembered, 'a thin sickly-looking man of about thirty-five years of age', devoted to the little Lhasa terrier and the tame mongoose that were always in his company. He would regale Bogle and Hamilton with large meals of boiled rice garnished with butter and sugar, and kid stewed with cucumbers and well seasoned with red pepper. He himself kept strictly to his monkly vows and ate only the vegetarian dessert, 'which consisted of fruits and sour curds cut like pieces of leather, and fried with butter and honey'. The Dharma Raja, Bogle remarked, 'had more curiosity than any man I have seen in the country', and this led to a rather comic incident that might have had serious consequences. 'One day Mr. Hamilton was showing him a microscope, and went to catch a fly; the whole room was in confusion, and the Lama frightened out of his wits lest he should have killed it.' To kill any creature in the presence of a high lama would have been regarded as an unpardonable breach of propriety and, since good relations continued with the Dharma Raja, who presented Bogle with his own yellow satin gown, lined with lambskin, to protect him on the cold autumn nights, we must assume that Hamilton did not succeed in catching his fly.

Bogle and Hamilton, as the Deb Raja insisted, were fortunate to be delayed in Tassisudon during the annual Bhutanese religious festival when all the penlops or regional governors arrived with their feudal followings to bask in the presence of the Dharma Raja. The two East India men were in fact the first British travellers to see and describe the sacred lamaist dances which took place on such occasions. In spite of their political links with the Panchen Lama and the Dalai Lama, the religious leaders did not belong to the

77

reformed Gelugpa or Yellow Hat sect which the Tibetan hierarchs headed, a kind of bland Buddhist Church of England. They adhered to the older Red Hat sects, the Kargyupa and the Nyingmapa, with their pretensions to necromancy and their macabre iconography that recalled mediaeval European fantasies of the Dance of Death and Hieronymus Bosch's landscapes of supernatural terror. When Bogle went into the temple beside the palace monastery, he saw the images of Buddha, 'mostly decent and well-proportioned figures, sitting cross-legged', but he also saw the festoons of human skulls and bones painted on the gallery from which laymen watched the ceremonies. His curiosity led him there, to hear the droning chants of the red-robed monks as the eight-foot-long trumpets boomed like melancholy elephants and the native clarinets, studded with turquoise and coral, added their tenor counterpoint. The sacred dances took place every day of the festival in one of the palace courts.

> About twenty gylongs [monks] dressed in various coloured satin cloaks and gilded mitres, were seated on a bench, with each a large tabor or drum, resting on a stick which they held on one hand, and in the other a crooked rod of iron, with a knob at the end of it, with which they beat time to a priest, who was placed in the midst of them, with two silver cups which he struck against each other. A yellow satin curtain was drawn before the door of the lesser church (the temple), from behind which ran out six, eight, or ten, and sometimes a score of priests in masquerade dresses, with visors like horse's heads, like beaks of birds, or other grotesque figures. They danced and capered with whimsical gestures, the burden of which was to throw down their heads until the red tuft of hair touched the ground, and then suddenly toss it up again.

Far from Bogle's presence at these ceremonials being in any way resented, the Deb Raja approved of his interest and would send for him at dawn or at other more unpredictable hours of the day to witness the services. Yet when he approached too closely the funeral ceremonies of a Buddhist monk who died while he was at Tassisudon, Bogle found his presence unwelcome. Forty monks were chanting prayers in a tent beside a small river, while workmen piled timber into a funeral pyre. The monks objected to being watched by an infidel, and Bogle crossed the rivulet to a bank whence he could look on at a distance.

> When night came on, the body, wrapped in a linen sheet, was silently brought, and at the same instant that it was laid on the pile a shrill pipe, like a cat-call, was sounded. All this passed in the dark. Then a relation of the deceased came with a lighted brand in his hand, and set fire to the pile. Two of the priests fed it with fresh wood; another, dressed in white, threw in from time to time spices, salt, butter, oil, betel leaf, and twenty other articles, and the rest joined in a flourish with trumpets, bells and tabors, while each of these different rites were performing. The fire burned slowly, a heavy shower of rain came on, and I returned home without waiting till the conclusion of the ceremony.

Sometimes Bogle would escape from the overpowering company of monks and monk-trained officials like the Deb Raja, and spend a little time in the company of the more easy-going lay officers, like the Governor of Tassisudon, with whom he went into the country to play a local kind of quoits. He could not compete with the dexterity of his hosts, so he decided to shoot wild pigeon, and among the laymen there was no open criticism of this rather tactless display of British blood sportsmanship. The party ended, as is customary in the Himalayan countries, in an ample picnic, with hard-boiled eggs, rice, boiled pork, pigs' hearts, stewed kid and tea. 'We ate off cloths, and with our fingers, and when the repast was finished had a cup of whisky and some fruit.'

Bogle found a great congeniality in the informal manners of the Bhutanese. They were devoid of Indian caste prejudices, and little burdened with class divisions of the English kind. Even the most powerful people had no pride, 'and live among their servants and dependents on the most familiar footing'. 'The more I see of the Bhutanese,' he told Hastings in October, on the eve of his departure for Tibet, 'the more I am pleased with them. The common people are good-humoured, downright, and, I think, thoroughly trusty. The statesmen have some of the art which belongs to their profession. They are the best-built race of men I ever saw; many of them very handsome, with complexions as fair as the French.' He was especially impressed by the self-sufficiency of Bhutanese life. It was an unluxurious but adequate way of existence, carried on almost without division of labour. The army was a militia raised from the peasantry, and the crafts were practised within the peasant households.

What he did hold against the Bhutanese was their dirt—only the Deb Raja in the whole country struck him as a really cleanly man—and the status of their women (who because even the lay officials were disinclined to marry could only hope to be the wives of peasants and as such were condemned to lives of toil), and the generally priest-ridden nature of the country. Even the Deb Raja, he held, was a kind of state prisoner of the monks.

In fact, Bogle had very contradictory feelings towards Bhutan and the Bhutanese. One side of his nature obviously responded to the rustic simplicity of life in this unvisited mountain kingdom. But, as the representative of a mercantile company, he could not see Bhutan ever becoming an important source of commerce, largely because the Deb

80

Raja tried to control in his own interests what foreign trade went on, and was not particularly anxious for it to increase lest it should slip out of his hands. The best Bogle could do was to arrange with Hastings while he was in Tassisudon a system of passes by which Bhutanese traders would be allowed to cross the frontiers of Bengal to trade at Rangpur and other centres.

The best of Bogle's reports to Hastings was that in which he discussed the military aspects of the Company's relationship with Bhutan. He argued that Captain Jones's war had been too defensively waged, and that if occasion ever came to fight the Bhutanese again, an offensive campaign to seize and occupy all the important Duars should be undertaken. (In the end the British were actually forced to annex the Duars, which remain Indian territory to this day.) But he advised against any expedition in present circumstances, and it is interesting to observe this young civil officer reasoning like an experienced military strategist. A real settlement, he felt, could never be achieved by force.

> The difficulties are insurmountable, at least without a force and expense much greater than the object is worth. This does not arise from the power of the Bhutanese. Two battalions, I think, would reduce their country, but two brigades would not keep the communication open, and if that is cut off the conquest could be of no use. . . .
>
> The objections I have made against an expedition into Bhutan hold good with respect to Nepal and Lhasa, for this sole reason, that a communication cannot be kept open; and should our troops march into these countries, they must consider all communication with the low country out of the question till they return.

A hundred and forty years later, when the British finally did march into Tibet to clear the way for the Younghusband mission, it was precisely this problem of communications over the high passes and the vast uplands that made progress to Lhasa difficult and the city itself impossible to hold for any length of time.

At last, late in August, Bogle was told verbally by the Deb Raja that the Panchen Lama had yielded to the Gosain's persuasive arts and had agreed to the mission entering Tibet; the Gosain was to meet Bogle and Hamilton at the Tibetan border. A few days later 'the Deb Rajah read to me a letter from the Teshu Lama, informing him that he had written to Lhasa, the residence of the Dalai Lama, on the subject of my passports and had obtained their consent to my proceeding on the journey, provided I came with only a few attendants. . . .' By these indirect messages the Panchen Lama's 'face' was carefully preserved; he never wrote an actual letter to Bogle which contradicted that requiring him to stay out of Tibet.

Even now, for motives Bogle could not completely understand, the Deb Raja still tried to dissuade him from proceeding. But Bogle knew, now the Panchen Lama had consented, that the Bhutanese ruler dared not try to halt his journey by force. His departure was in fact delayed six weeks after hearing of the Panchen Lama's consent, but this was because Bhutan had flared into a civil war when the deposed Deb Judhur suddenly appeared in the country and gathered together all those who were malcontent with his successor, including the former governors of Tassisudon and Targa, with two hundred and fifty of their men.

The original plan of the rebels was to seize Tassisudon, and if this had happened Bogle and Hamilton might have found themselves endangered. But the plot was discovered, some monks who had agreed to open the gates of the palace were executed, and Deb Judhir's men retreated to the fortress of Simtoka about five miles from Tassisudon, which they seized without resistance. With the arms and ammunition found there, they felt strong enough to attempt an assault on the palace, and actually came within sight of Tassisudon before they were driven back, and besieged at Simtoka by levies which the new Deb Raja had called from all parts of the country. The fortress was surrounded, but, since there were no cannon whatever in Bhutan, it could have held out indefinitely against the matchlocks and bows of the besiegers. There were only two means of reducing it—by fire or famine. Fire would have been easy, for the roofs and floors of Bhutanese castles are always built of wood, but Simtoka contained a great deal of government property, so the Deb Raja decided to blockade it on three sides and leave one road open to the north. Day after day Deb Judhur watched the forces against him growing steadily, and on the tenth night, by moonlight, he and his men fled up the open road and into Tibet.

On the next day Bogle and Hamilton resumed their journey. It was the 13th October. Before they departed Bogle sent a last letter to Hastings. He sent a slip of rose briar, and the skin of a musk goat, and 'a sentimental cup' which was actually the mounted cranium of a learned lama. A Bhutanese was collecting seeds for him, and plants would be sent on his return when the sap was down. As for yaks, which Bogle called 'cow-tailed cows', there were plenty of them, 'but the weather is too hot for them to go into Bengal'. He was minutely observing his instructions.

# V

## *Into Tibet*

It was a fair-sized cavalcade that set out from Tassisudon on the crisp mountain autumn morning of the 13th October, 1774. Bogle and Hamilton rode on their Tangun ponies, and with them were the Deb Raja's representative, who would assure their easy passage to the borders of Bhutan, and the Panchen Lama's envoy Padma, a tall Tibetan with a laughing ugly face who had taken the Lama's original letter to Hastings, and had now been sent down to usher the East India Company's mission into Tibet. Mirza Settar, the Kashmiri merchant from Rangpur, was also there; Bogle had finally decided to use his services and had written to Hastings asking that he should be recruited. Bickering among themselves were the servants of three nationalities, Bogle's Bengalis, Padma's Tibetans and the Deb Raja's Bhutanese, and the long, straggling and perpetually changing tail of the procession was made up of the porters who were freshly recruited each day as the procession passed up to the frontier and into Tibet; men and women, young and old, dressed in the drab woollen garb of Bhutan, they climbed the high passes and trailed over the bleak uplands with the endurance of animals and the sangfroid of philosophers.

Their journey lay first to the southward, retracing their steps along the banks of the Chinchu until, at Paku, they reached the junction of that river and the Pachu, whose

valley they must ascend to reach Tibet. The recently captured castle of Simtoka lay on this route, and originally they
had planned to take, under armed guard, a difficult way
over the mountains that would have avoided the scene of
fighting, but now the country was in the hands of the Deb
Raja's men, and as they travelled they saw the flames bursting out from villages which had seemed to exist in peaceful
isolation when they first saw them on their way to Tassisudon; now they were being punished for their adherence
to Deb Judhur and his cause.

As they were passing through a village beside the river they
came up with a party of soldiers, and the leader invited them
to share his hospitality. Bogle found they were old acquaintances, for his host was the Deb Raja's secretary who had just
been appointed dewan or chief adviser. They drank a cup
of arrack together, sharing the dewan's rug, while he told
Bogle the story of Deb Judhur's escape, and discoursed on
the politics of Bhutan. He had an appreciative listener, for
Bogle relished the rise to power of this man of humble origin.
'He enjoys the first place in his chief's favour, and his sagacity
and superior abilities entitle him to it. In anything that
relates to the government of his own country, he might be
pitted against many a politic minister. As a philosopher, he
would twist him round his finger. Of a truth, an ounce of
mother-wit is worth a pound of clergy.' A good Scottish
thought, and it found appropriate expression among the
unclassconscious mountaineers of the Himalayas.

Around the dewan stood the soldiers recruited from the
farms and villages, and Bogle for the first time had a chance
to see at close quarters the kind of men who had descended
into Cooch Behar and fought fiercely but futilely against
Captain Jones. Each carried a broadsword with a shagreen
hilt, a round shield of coiled cane and a bamboo bow with

a quiver of reed arrows; a few had pikes, and even fewer had long and clumsy matchlocks. But they had no uniform livery, dressing in the same clothes as they wore in the fields with the addition of such primitive armour as they had been able to acquire. 'Some wear a cap quilted, or of cane and sugar-loaf shape, with a tuft of horse-hair stained; others, an iron-netted hood, or a helmet with the like ornament; under these they often put false locks to supply the want of their own hair, which among this tribe of Bhutanese is worn short. Sometimes a coat of mail is to be seen.' The officers were mounted, and wore caps like great tam-o'-shanters thatched with red-dyed yak-tails.

Leaving this rustic army to its pretence of pursuing the long-fled enemy, Bogle's party continued down the river to Lumbulong of the quaking bridge, and there spent the night in a large warehouse supported on piles. 'A fire was lighted upon a stone in the middle, and as there are no vents, we suffered as much from its smoke as we benefited by its heat.' To relieve their boredom and discomfort, Bogle and Hamilton sent for the women porters who had accompanied the caravan, and in the murky firelight they were entertained with Bhutanese songs. 'There is no giving a description of it; and as I know nothing of music, I could not take it down. It is more like church chimes than anything else. Some of the notes are lengthened out as long as the breath will last, and people used to climbing mountains are far from being short-winded.' It must have been what the Tibetans call 'far-away singing', a kind of falsetto yodelling that is heard for many miles in the clear light air of the Himalayas. The evening ended with a fist fight between the landlord and the Deb Raja's representative; it was the second such fight Bogle had seen since their arrival in Lumbulong that evening, and he marvelled at the democratic contentiousness of the Bhutanese.

The next morning they continued down the Chinchu to its junction with the Pachu, and then turned north-westward into the narrow valley of the latter river. Bogle merely notes rather laconically that the mountains were bare and rocky, and that the only dwellings to be seen were Buddhist hermitages, but the route can certainly have been no better than it was in the beginning of the 1960's, when two modern travellers told how the track up this valley 'climbs the ridges in tight zig-zags so steep that mules pause every few yards to pant. Often the trail crosses high passes broken with rocks and mud pools that have even the mules stumbling; for a distance the route follows the ridge-top until it is time to descend to the warmth of the river bed, and then the whole exhausting process begins again over the next ridge.'* Bogle, who had no mules in any case, does not tell of these particular hardships, but he does relate how—with the onset of winter—the tops of the mountains had become whitened with snow, and how this astonished the servants from Bengal.

> They inquired of the Bhutanese, who told them it was white cloths, which God Almighty sent down to cover the mountains and keep them warm. This solution required, to be sure, some faith; but it was to them just as probable as that it was rain, or that they were afterwards to meet with water hard as glass, and be able to walk across a river.

On the third day they came down into the small fertile valley of Essana, where the people were harvesting rice with toothless sickles, and, leaning in rows against a breast-high beam on the threshing floor, were tramping out the grain. Much of the heaviest work, Bogle noted, was being done by the women, and he saw mothers with newborn infants at their breasts stamping with the rest. Again, he was astonished

* Pradyumna P. Karan and William M. Jenkins in *The Himalayan Kingdoms*.

that, with so hard a life, the people could seem so happy. They appeared to have no fairs, no entertainments, not even the simple and gaudy jewellery of the poor Bengalis, 'and yet I know not how it comes to pass, but they seem to bear it all without murmuring; and, having nothing else to deck themselves with, they plait their hair with garlands of leaves or twigs of trees. The resources of a light heart and a sound constitution are infinite.' After the softness and the love of luxury which had disturbed him among the Bengalis, Bogle's Presbyterian susceptibilities were attracted by examples of contented frugality.

The next day they reached Rinjipu, or Paro, one of the provincial capitals of Bhutan. There was another castle-cum-monastery-cum-palace, smaller than that at Tassisudon, but still impressive in its splendid position on a great crag on the steep side of the valley, with its rooms climbing one above the other up the mountain side, and the crest crowned with richly painted temple towers, looking out over the timbered houses and the groves of prayer flags, over the rich wheatfields and paddies of the wide valley and the white spires of chörtens scattered among them.

Bogle stayed for three days in Paro, living in a room beside the temple as the guest of the governor or Penlop, a cousin of the Dharma Raja who had come back from monastic seclusion into political life, and, after the Deb Raja, was the most influential man in Bhutan. As time went on such regional leaders, with their feudal followings, were to become even more powerful than the hierarchs of Tassisudon, and the present royal family of Bhutan is descended from a Penlop who eventually destroyed the ancient priestly rule and replaced it by secular authority. But such a situation was still far ahead when Bogle travelled in Bhutan.

He paid his visit to the Penlop, who made him a present of

locally woven blankets, which came in very useful as the weather grew colder. He also received a visit from the Deb Raja's dewan who had now overtaken him. The countryside was still in high excitement over the late rebellion, and when Bogle was awakened in his first morning in Paro with gun-shots and eerie Bhutanese warcries, he leapt up with the thought that Deb Judhur had come back to invade the palace; ' . . . but it turned out to be only the head of a rebel, which they were carrying into the palace in procession, with a white handkerchief as a flag before it'.

The difficulty of finding porters prevented Bogle from leaving Paro until the 10th October, and the equal difficulty of keeping them made his days' journeys shorter than he had planned. He stayed one night in a mountain-top castle where hives of bees hung under the windows, and another night in a hamlet of four or five houses, surrounded by turnip fields.

This was Chanon, the last village of Bhutan. Next morning the road began to rise into the Tremo La pass that led into Tibet. It took two days to cross, for the track was steep and the travelling slow.

> High perpendicular rocks were overhead. The Pachu, now reduced to a large stream, running rapidly by: on the other side a high round mountain, covered with silver firs and pines, intermixed with other trees, red, yellow, and all those colours with which a natural wood is variegated towards the close of autumn. The summits of the hills were white with snow. When we got to the highest part of the road, we found the sides of the mountains entirely bare, owing, I suppose, to their being exposed to the north wind.

On the top of the mountain the travellers encountered flocks of small, fine-wooled Tibetan sheep, and herds of yaks, uncouth beasts in Bogle's eyes, which were carrying

loads of sheepskins with the fleeces on them to be sold in
Paro where the wool would be sheared off and made into
coarse Bhutanese blankets. At nightfall they came to an
uninhabited place on the mountain called Gaissar. There
was only a single house, if such it could be called, for it was
no more than a stable without doors, but here they had to
stay, and were glad that the Deb Raja's representative had
insisted they bring fuel up from Chanon, for the mountain was
covered with snow. More fell during the night, so that in the
morning the road was thickly covered, and the stones and
the bridges were hung with icicles as they went on up the
desolate valley, 'which was bounded on the northwest by a
hill between two moderate mountains'. The crest of the hill
was the border, marked by six cairns with flagpoles bearing
banners. Bogle does not tell us so, but we can be sure from
the accounts of other travellers that the Tibetans and Bhutanese who were members of the party made offerings here to
the gods of the mountains, while the two Scots looked down
into the land where no British foot had before trodden:
'plain and open to the north; hilly to the west; behind, to the
east and south, mountains'.

As they rode down the hill towards Phari, the first place
over the frontier, they had a macabre introduction to
Tibetan customs. A small hill stood out on the plain below
them, and they could see a moving cloud of eagles, kites and
ravens circling above it. It was the local funeral ground,
where bodies were not only offered to predatory birds, as the
Parsees do, but actually dismembered, and the bones pounded
into pulp, so that every fragment of the now useless body
might become the food of living beings. This gruesome but
eminently rational ceremony was about to be enacted, for
a funeral party was bearing a body up the hillock as the
travellers rode by, and the birds descended for the banquet.

For once Bogle's curiosity did not delay him; he rode on quickly with a small fear in his mind that the encounter might have been ominous.

A few miles on the fortress of Phari came into sight; it 'cut a good figure' as they rode towards it. 'It rises into several towers with the balconies, and having few windows has the look of strength; it is surrounded by the town.' For Tibet, unlike Bhutan, had places with urban pretensions, and Phari was one of them, a settlement of two or three thousand people huddled beneath the cliff-like walls of the fortress. Recent European travellers who have seen the place have been universal in their expressions of distaste for Phari, a town of epic filth. Spencer Chapman, who travelled through it on his way to Lhasa in the 1930's, found that the streets were 'so choked with the accumulated garbage of centuries that they are many feet higher than formerly and in most cases actually obscure the ground-floor windows'. Edward Chandler, who went as *Daily Mail* correspondent with the Younghusband expedition a generation before, also found these story-high accumulations of filth on each side of the street, and recorded that holes had to be kept open in the rotting piles to give access to the doors.

> In the middle of the street, between the two banks of filth and offal, runs a stinking channel, which thaws daily. In it horns and bones and skulls of every beast eaten or not eaten by the Tibetans—there are few of the latter—lie till the dogs and ravens have picked them clean enough to be used in the mortared walls and thresholds. The stench is fearful. Half-decaying corpses of dogs lie cuddled up with their mangy but surviving brothers and sisters, who do not prevent the scavenging ravens. Here and there a stagnant pool of filth has partially defied the warmth, and carrion, verminous rags, and fur-wrapped bones are set round in broken yellowish ice. In the middle the brown

patch is iridescent. A curdled and foul torrent flows in the daytime through the market-place, and half-breed yaks shove the sore-eyed and mouth-ulcered children aside to drink it.

Both Chandler and Chapman contrasted the squalor of Phari with the splendour of its setting. Chapman, a naturalist, was fascinated by the variety of flowers—delicate and brilliant as arctic blossoms—that studded the austere plateau, and by the number of birds, preserved by the Buddhist respect for wild living things, that inhabited the air. Chandler, with more of an eye to grandeur, told how, 'at the end of every street, hanging in mid-air above this nest of mephitic filth, the cold and almost saint-like purity of the everlasting snows of Chomolhari—a huge wedge of argent a mile high puts to perpetual shame the dirt of Phari'.

Bogle's reactions were more moderate in both directions. Being a pre-romantic, he did not wax lyrical about snow mountains, even about Chomolhari's 24,000 feet splendour, while he detested the 'ruffian wind' that blew in from the north-east, and found even the setting of Phari 'on every account abundantly bleak, and bare and uncomfortable'. On the other hand, perhaps because he already had experience of Calcutta, he did not react to the town with the extreme disgust of his twentieth-century successors. 'The houses', he remarked, 'are of two low stories, flat-roofed, covered with bundles of straw, and so huddled together that one may chance to overlook them. There is little to be said for them. . . . The same style of architecture prevails in the villages upon the road. It has a mean look after the lofty buildings in the Deb Rajah's country; but having neither wood nor arches, how can they help it?' But he has nothing to say of the great walls of filth in the streets, nor will Manning nearly forty years later remark on them, and we can only assume that they accumulated vastly during the nineteenth century. What did disturb Bogle was the prevalence of beggars, and even more the perils of walking after dark in the streets of Phari, for then the people would let loose their fierce Tibetan mastiffs, 'often shagged like a lion, and extremely fierce'.

Bogle and Hamilton were lodged in one of the houses, and learnt their internal disadvantages as well as their external ugliness.

> The ceilings are so low, that I have more than once been indebted to the thickness of my skull; and the beams being very short, are supported by a number of posts, which are little favourable to chamber-walking. In the middle of the roof is a hole to let out the smoke, which, however, departs not without making the whole room as black as a chimney. This opening serves also to let in the light; the doors are full of holes and crevices, through which the women and children keep peeping.

Tibetan children, even at their dirtiest—and one gathers that in Phari they reached the extremity of that condition— are usually gay and engaging, and Bogle, succumbing to their charm, began to give them sugar-candy, and ribbons for the girls; ' . . . but I brought all the children of the parish upon my back by it.'

Even in this first town of Tibet, Bogle began to realize the complicated patterns of power in that country. Generally speaking, at this period, the south-eastern part of Tibet fell under the strong influence of the Panchen Lama, so that, as we have seen, hill states like Nepal and Bhutan turned to him as overlord rather than to the Dalai Lama's Regent in the capital. Nevertheless, the central authorities maintained fortresses throughout the country—even in the town of Shigatse close to Tashilunpo—and the castle at Phari was in the charge of two Lhasa officers. The day after Bogle's arrival their servants appeared at his lodgings with a welcoming gift of butter and tea, and an intimation that they were awaiting his visit. Accordingly he went to the fortress; like all travellers who have penetrated within the gates of this impressive six-storied structure, he found the interior mis-built and depressing. 'The stairs are ladders worn to the bone, and the rooms are little better than garrets.' Here, seated beside each other on carpets, the two officials greeted him. In Tibet it was customary, as late as the flight of the Dalai Lama in 1959, for responsible positions, like the governorship of a castle, to be held jointly by two men, one always a layman and the other a monk official, a man trained to priestly functions who had temporarily abandoned them to serve the state. One of the officials, whom Bogle assumed to be the senior, was dressed 'in a russet coloured tunic of coarse woollen, and a linen cloth folded and laid upon his bare head'; the other in coarse black cloth. The etiquette of drinking tea and arrack and exchanging compliments was much as it had been in the court at Tassisudon, and Bogle's intentions were politely ignored.

How much power these Lhasa officials in their crumbling castle actually wielded it is hard to say, though they had very firmly refused to give up to the Deb Raja the eighty followers of Deb Judhur who had claimed sanctuary in their fortress, a refusal that appears to have stemmed less from partisanship than from a Buddhist desire to minimize the loss of life.

About the standing of Padma, the Panchen Lama's repre-sentative, there could be no similar doubts. Bogle, who previously had regarded him as merely a kind of higher servant, now found that he was considered 'a great man, and all Teshu Lama's vassals endeavoured by their presents and attention to secure his interest at court'. Padma held daily levees, and on the night before the party left Phari he gave a great party, so that Bogle, who had sent for him to play chess, was astonished when his servant returned to report that he had found Padma 'seated under a piece of green silk for a canopy, surrounded by all the peasants and peasants' wives, singing, dancing and drinking, and as great as a prince'.

They set out on the morning of the 27th October, and it was now a considerable cavalcade, for six other members of the Panchen Lama's household had joined Padma, and horses were provided for everyone but a few of the servants. At the head of the procession rode one of Padma's servants bearing like a banner the branch of a tree with a white scarf attached to it.

Imagining it to be a mark of respect to me and my embassy, I set myself upright in my saddle; but I was soon undeceived, for after stopping at a tent to drink tea with the abbot of a monastery in the neighbourhood of Pari-jong, subject to Teshu Lama, we rode over the plain till we came to a heap of stones opposite to a high rock covered with snow. Here we halted, and the servants gathering together a parcel of dried cow-dung, one of them struck fire with his tinderbox, and lighted it. We sat down about it, and the day being cold, I found it very comfortable. When the fire was well kindled, Paima [Padma] took out a book of prayers; one brought a copper cup, another filled it with a kind of fermented liquor out of a new-killed sheep's paunch, mixing in some rice and flour, and after throwing some dried herbs and flour into the flame, they began their rites. Paima acted as chaplain. He chanted the prayers in a loud voice, the others accompanying him, and every now and then the little cup was emptied towards the rock. About eight or ten of these libations being poured forth, the ceremony was finished by placing upon the heap of stones the little ensign, which my fond imagination had before offered up to my own vanity.

95

The object of these devotions was the great mountain of Chomolhari.

That day they travelled only fourteen miles, halting for the night at three o'clock. At that altitude—Phari is 14,600 feet—the Bengali servants found the journey so exhausting that they had to be brought in on the backs of porters. There were not enough horses for all of them, so the next day Bogle hired some yaks, but now the Bengalis preferred to totter on their own feet, for the yak looked suspiciously like a sacred cow, and 'if any accident should happen to the beast when they were on him, they would be obliged, they said, according to the tenets of the Shaster, to beg their bread during twelve years, as an expiation of the crime'. Small wonder that Bogle noted a special memorandum in his journal: 'Inconvenient carrying Hindu servants into foreign parts.'

The next day, a motlier procession than ever, with mounted Europeans and Tibetans, some Indians on ponies and some doggedly stumbling in the name of ritual purity, yaks and porters bearing baggage, they travelled through a country of lakes, already half frozen over, for the winter was rapidly advancing on the high Tibetan plateau. The country was teeming with game. There were hares and herds of antelopes and kyangs or wild asses, and the lakes were densely populated with ducks and wild geese. Bogle's sporting instinct was roused, and he rode out to do summary execution, and killed—as he boasted later to his sister—'three wild geese in one shot'. Padma protested loudly. He regarded the shooting of birds as a crime, he felt it would antagonize the local people with their pious respect for living things, and in any case it was an offence to the holy mountain they had just propitiated. But, like most Tibetans, Padma was willing to reach a face-saving compromise, and it was agreed

96

2. George Bogle

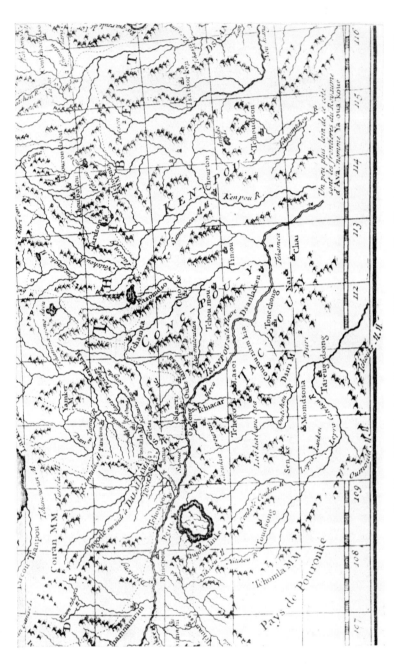

3. The map of Tibet by D'Anville published originally in 1735, which was used by Hastings in planning Bogle's expedition and which accompanied Bogle on his journey

that if Bogle would refrain from carrying out his murderous forays in sight of Chomolhari, Padma would turn a blind eye and a deaf ear when they came to 'solitary and sequestered places'.

At this point in the narrative, after reading Bogle's account of his own vanity at the sight of the white banner born before him, and of his dispute with Padma over the unwritten game laws of Tibet, one is forced to admit a growing impression of a certain self-complacency in his nature. Almost every experience on the journey is seen as it affects him personally; it is all 'I' and rarely 'we', and Hamilton is mentioned far less frequently in the journal than I have mentioned him in this narrative, but he must have been present on many an occasion which Bogle describes as if—from the British side —he were the only actor. Yet Hamilton, though he did not share Bogle's full responsibility, can hardly have been a mere underling with medicine chest and microscope, for later— even when Bogle was still alive—Hastings was to put him in command of two different missions into the Himalayas, and Hastings, if he ever suffered fools, did not suffer them more than once.

So they travel on, Bogle self-involved under his affable exterior, Hamilton his all-too-often invisible and inaudible shadow, and Padma, the dark-faced Tibetan, smiling and diplomatic in the manner of his people, but under all his politeness concealing a firmness that would not yield too far. They skirt the lakes Shem Chu and Calo Chu, and begin to follow the growing stream of the Painam River, one of the tributaries of the Tsangpo, in its turn the Tibetan parent stream of the Brahmaputra. For several days they go by short stages down this river, passing many watermills and bridges, both of which interest Bogle because of their novelty. The mills, he finds, are 'constructed on the simplest plan: a duct is cut in the same manner as in Europe; but the wheel instead of being perpendicular, is horizontal, and turns the upper millstone, which is fixed to its axle, without any other machinery'. The bridges are merely walls built across the river, with openings to let the water through, which are covered with planks or large flagstones. The arch was unknown in Tibet.

> Our route [Bogle narrates] continued almost due north through valleys little cultivated and bounded by bleak and barren hills, between whose openings we saw distant mountains covered with snow. Here and there we saw a few houses, with some spots of rushy ground, or of brown pasture, but not a tree or a plant was to be seen, and the number of ruinous houses and deserted villages rendered the prospect more uncomfortable.

Some of the ruin and desertion was due to a war with the Bhutanese sixty years before, but some was due to the small-pox that came and went ominously in this region. At one village—Kanmur—where their host honoured them by allowing them to sleep in the little domestic shrine room at the top of his house, they found that he had gained occupancy for the grisly reason that all fifteen of the family who owned it had died the preceding year of that sickness.

At Kanmur they were met by a priest from the neighbourhood of Gyantse, the next town on their route; he had come at the command of the Panchen Lama to bear them greetings, and on his own behalf to ask Hamilton for medical aid in some 'inveterate complaint' which the Tibetan doctors with their herbs and spells had not been able to cure. So, with this 'gentle and modest' old man, clad in his tunic of red broadcloth and a brocade cap trimmed with furs, there began a friendship that was to last until Bogle turned homeward from Tibet.

Already, if the splendour of the land did not touch Bogle's imagination, the character of the people touched his heart, and in this part of his journal one is aware of a mounting delight at having discovered a race he found utterly congenial, a delight which rose to a crescendo in those weeks at Tashilunpo that were to be politically so fruitless and personally so rewarding.

The feeling appears when they ride one afternoon into a village called Dudukpai, where the people are working in the fields, stacking their straw and singing as they work. They stayed the night in a polyandrous household, of two brothers married to 'a very handsome wife' and sharing 'three of the prettiest children I ever saw'. Bogle was astonished at the sheer natural happiness of this family, organized on principles so different from those that governed domestic life in Scotland or, for that matter, in Bengal. He entertained his hosts to tea and sugar candy, and after dark the whole family reciprocated by dancing for two hours before their guests to the music of their own voices chanting the folk songs of their region.

Bogle was both surprised and impressed by the ease of existence in these valleys thirteen thousand feet and more above sea level, and compared the life of the Tibetan farmers favourably with the harsher, bleaker life of their Bhutanese cousins. Here the bare and sterile hills were left to nature, and the valley bottoms were cultivated; the roads ran through them, so there was no need to climb mountains. Cattle instead of men trod the corn, water ground it into flour and yaks largely took the place of porters. Bogle granted that Tibetans might be less robust than the Bhutanese, but their life made them more civilized, 'better bred and more affable than their southern neighbours' and far more attentive to women.

In the Deb Rajah's country, whatever a countryman saves from his labour is laid out in adorning his sword with silver filigree work, or buying a square box which contains a little gilt image, and is buckled to his back. Here it is bestowed on purchasing coral and amber beads, to adorn the head of his wife. The head-dress of the women is extremely neat and becoming. . . . But the dirtiness of their hands and faces (many of which deserve a better fate) is a point which, as I cannot attempt to excuse, my partiality to the Tibetans will not allow me to enlarge upon.

I must except, however, our landlady, who kept herself and her family as neat as a Dutch woman, and, saving her black eyes, she had something the look of one.

On the following afternoon—it was the 2nd November—they emerged into the broad valley where Gyantse (which Bogle called Giansu) stands at the junction of the roads which lead westward to Tashilunpo and eastward to Lhasa. As a trading centre and a strategic strongpoint, it is one of the important places of Tibet, and every traveller approaching Lhasa from the south must make his way through it, unless —like the present Dalai Lama in his great trek to freedom in 1959—he commits himself to the perils of journeying through the rugged mountains to the east where the ferocious Khambas still defy the Chinese overlords.

Looking up the broad valley, over fields of wheat and barley and giant radishes, over many whitewashed villages, Bogle and his party saw the fortress as the clear slanting afternoon sunlight threw its features into high relief.

The hills on each side draw close towards the north; between them rises a high and almost perpendicular rock, upon the top of which stands Giansu Castle. It is formed of many walls and turrets. The tower is built at the foot of the rock on the east side; on the west, it is washed by the river, beyond which a monastery and village are built on the declivity of a mountain. Altogether it makes a fine prospect.

They did not go into Gyantse that night; it was controlled by men from Lhasa. Instead, they stayed at the house of the old man who had visited them at Kanmur. It was a typical Tibetan country house, surrounded by willow trees, with small windows and 'little ensigns and written banners' adorning the roof. Once again, they were lodged in the domestic shrine room; it was 'full of painted chests, matchlocks, bows, cushions, and other lumber. One corner was hung with mythological paintings, and below a parcel of little gilt cross-legged images, with a lamp burning before them, from which, as all the family are gone to bed, I have taken the liberty to steal some oil in order to finish this account, hoping that it will not be imputed to me as a sacrilege.'

Here the Gosain joined them, with three other members of the Panchen Lama's household, and they tarried a day. Hamilton treated their host as best he could, and Bogle sat talking to the old man all afternoon, 'and I am sure I drank about twenty cups of tea'. He had sent a message to the castle, asking to visit the Lhasa officials there, as he had done at Phari. The messenger returned with a polite refusal 'on the pretence of one of them being absent'. Bogle interpreted this as a sign of unfriendliness, but it may merely have been bureaucratic caution on the part of an official accustomed to sharing responsibilities with his colleague.

There was no alternative next day but to take the road that led through the town of Gyantse and under the walls of its castle, but they rode straight through without lingering. The people crowded to look at them, with that curiosity about strange things and beings which Bogle had learnt to regard as one of the constant traits of the Tibetan character, but they were not unfriendly and there was no exhibition of hostility from the castle.

Two days through broad valleys and a more populated countryside, with little white towns and villages and picturesque hilltop forts, brought them to the junction of the roads to Tashilunpo and to Namling. They took the latter, climbing northward into the hills by 'a difficult and stony path' and over rushy upland fields where hares were numerous and Hamilton defied local taboos by trying to shoot them; his fowling-piece had got bent on the journey, and the hares escaped, doubtless to Padma's delight. It was in these hills that they encountered a scene that reminds one of El Dorado in *Candide*; it was a flock of twelve hundred large sheep 'with horns extended horizontally', which were being used as pack animals. They had come from far western Tibet carrying salt to Gyantse, and now they were returning with barley and wheat, each sheep carrying 'two bags of grain, which might be about twenty to twenty-five pounds'. They were very obedient to their drivers' whistles, and any of them that happened to get out of the road were easily brought back by the shepherds' dogs.

The travellers were now sixteen thousand feet above sea level, and spent a frugal night in the one house they encountered on these bleak uplands. The next day they rode down out of the hills and came at last to the Tsangpo, long afterwards recognized by geographers as the upper course of the Brahmaputra. Some of the European missionaries had certainly crossed it, but Bogle was the first to write of it in any descriptive detail. It was, at this point, 'about the breadth of the Thames at Putney', and too deep to be forded. Going down to the bank, Bogle performed a personal ceremony intended to balance that which Padma had performed before Mount Chomolhari. He drank from the river, washed his face and hands in it, and then cast a silver rupee into its waters.

In the season of high water the Tsangpo is crossed by large coracles made of frames of willow boughs covered with yak-hides and easy to manœuvre on a swift current. Bogle saw many of them beside the river, one end of each tilted up so that it served as a habitation for the boatman and his family. But in November, when the sources of water in the high mountains were freezing up, the current was not rapid, and it was by ferry boats of another kind that Bogle and his companions crossed the river, taking precedence over the large herds of cattle and flocks of sheep that waited on the bank to be slowly shuttled over.

They [the ferries] are in the shape of an oblong square, about twenty-five feet long and broad. The bottom is a float of thick planks, closed in by perpendicular walls to the height of about four feet, with an opening on each side, cut down to about two feet, which serves for the entrance. The whole is bound together with bars of iron, and painted white. At each end of the boat is a white ensign about a foot square. This large hulk is moved by an oar on each side, which are pulled by two men, pushed by another standing opposite to them, and drawn by a woman, who holds a rope fastened to the end of the oar which is in the water. It is managed at the stern by one man with a large headed oar. In our boat there were twenty-three persons, seven horses, one cow-tailed bullock, and fourteen asses, besides baggage.

They landed on a broad beach that was uncovered in the dry season, and turned northward up the valley of the Siang, another tributary of the Tsangpo, where Purangir Gosain showed an unsuspected sporting spirit by accepting Bogle's challenges and racing him on horseback along the fine sandy roads of the country, an exercise which convinced Bogle that 'the Tibet ponies are much swifter and better blood than I expected'. Farther along, beside the river, they came upon a camp of dromedaries, and as they lingered there a travelling monk came and sat beside Bogle and Hamilton. Up to now they had dealt mostly with the more prosperous and powerful members of the Tibetan hierarchy. Here was one of the many thousands of poor and ordinary monks who filled the great monasteries of Tibet and occasionally went on long pilgrimages, and the incident lingered in Bogle's memory.

> The few words of the language which I was master of were little able to support a varied and entertaining conversation. I understood, however, the priest's caution against sitting on the ground and in the sun. He was dressed in the habit peculiar to his order . . . but it had seen many years of service and was now threadbare. He had thrown off his hose to wade the river, when our snuff-box attracted his notice. Upon this, he loosened a wallet that hung at his back, and after turning over some books of prayers, a yellow cloth coat lined with lambskin, a small parcel of tobacco, and another of tea, he came to a bundle of incense papers, and having presented four of them to Mr. Hamilton, claimed some snuff in return. This exchange being made, and having taken leave by a salutation of thumbs, which is the sign of the superlative degree of comparison, he laid his bundle and hose upon his back, and, wading the river, continued his journey.

On the second day from the crossing of the Tsangpo they came in sight of the fortress which Bogle called Chamnamring; its actual name is Namling, which means Sky Garden and commemorates the fact that the castle stands on a steep rock with gardens at its base. Bogle described it as 'situated on the top of a hill, with a small town under it, built in the form of a square, and enclosed within walls'.

They did not enter the fortress or the town beneath it, for both were in the charge of governors from Lhasa, and Bogle obviously did not wish for a repetition of the rebuff he had received at Gyantse. The Panchen Lama was staying in a small palace of his own at a village called Desheripgay, about two miles from Namling. Accordingly, avoiding the castle, the party crossed the river and on the opposite bank found a group of richly decorated tents raised to welcome them, where they were received by a Gosain who had come to lay white scarves across their hands, and to transmit inquiries about their welfare from the Panchen Lama. They drank tea ceremonially in the tents, and then went up the little cross valley that led from the banks of the Shiang to Desheripgay. 'On the 8th of November, 1774, we rode up to the gate of the palace, and walking into the court, went up the ladders to our apartments.'

# VI

## *With the Panchen Lama*

'I endeavoured to find out, in his character, those defects which are inseparable from humanity, but he is so universally beloved that I had no success, and not a man could find in his heart to speak ill of him.' By the time Bogle had met him, and written these words of adulation, Lobsang Palden Yeshe was only about forty, but for thirty-eight years he had been the second of the great Tibetan hierarchs, assuming his role when, in early childhood, the high abbots of Tashilunpo recognized the signs that declared him the incarnation of the recently deceased Panchen Lama and the earthly manifestation of Amitabha, Buddha of Boundless Light. More than most of the Panchen Lamas, whose role is regarded as spiritual rather than temporal, he had concerned himself with the earthly affairs of the people who reverenced him, and ever since his reign he has been recognized as the greatest of the lords of Tashilunpo, the only one among them who seemed temporarily to overshadow the great incarnation of Lhasa, emanation of the Bodhisattva Avalokiteshvara, Lord of Compassion, known to foreigners as the Dalai Lama and to his people as Kunden, Possessed of All.

The Third Panchen Lama's prestige in 1774, among both Tibetans and Chinese, was largely due to the peculiar situation in Lhasa. The last King of Tibet, heir of a line established by the Mongols in 1642, had been murdered by the Chinese ambans in 1750, and the Seventh Dalai Lama had been restored to the temporal power wielded so effectively in the past by the Great Fifth, the builder of the Potala. He died in 1757, and in the following year the infant hierarch Jampel Gyatso took his place as the Eighth Dalai Lama. Now began the long succession of regencies which was to continue almost uninterruptedly, owing to the worldly incompetence or early deaths of Dalai Lamas, until the Great Thirteenth took power into his own hands in 1895. In 1774 Jampel Gyatso, though in his late teens, was still under the powerful tutelage of the first of the regents, Demo Rimpoche, but Demo Rimpoche was neither in mental power nor in prestige of office the equal of the Panchen Lama, and while the Dalai Lama himself remained a cipher, uninterested in the temporal role which traditionally he possessed, it was inevitable that Tibetans should look for leadership to the incarnation of Tashilunpo.

The situation was complicated by the fact of Chinese suzerainty, for the Manchu overlords in Peking were as conscious as other imperial potentates of the wisdom of ruling by division, and it was their custom, since Emperor K'ang-hi intervened decisively in Tibetan affairs in 1720, to play off the great Tibetan hierarchs against each other. Since in normal circumstances the Dalai Lama wielded more internal power than the Panchen Lama, the Chinese usually sought to foster in the latter an independent attitude. In the 1770's, however, it was Lobsang Palden Yeshe in Tashilunpo who was most respected and loved by the Tibetan people, and who sought for Tibet the greatest possible independence of foreign control; it was one of the reasons for his overtures to the East India Company. This situation meant a reversal of the customary role, and, certainly until the death of the

Panchen Lama in 1780, it was the Regent in Lhasa who was most closely identified with Chinese interests.

But the situation was not so clear-cut as western politicians might have made it, for this, after all, was a region where even in politics the realities were masked behind screens of face-saving protocol, which had the virtue of delaying and usually preventing open conflict. The Panchen Lama still made the gesture of deferring to Lhasa, and maintained relations with the Chinese that were, on the surface, friendly. Because of his prestige among the Mongols and even among the Manchus themselves, he was a potentate whom Peking could not ignore, even less harm. When in 1780 he went to Peking it was not as a subject but rather as the Priest who enjoys the protection of the Prince, in some respects his equal and in others even his superior. It was, in fact, only with the coming of the Republic in 1910 that the Chinese seriously and unsuccessfully attempted the incorporation of Tibet as an integral part of China, and until that time relationships were modelled on those established under the Mongol rulers, when the Emperor was the Protector of Tibet, but in no true sense its ruler. Yet, being Protector, part of his role lay in saving Tibet from a contact with foreigners that might be harmful, and when Chinese armies marched into Tibet, as they did on several occasions during the eighteenth century (notably against the Dzungars in 1720 and against the Gurkhas in 1792), it was less to reinforce Chinese authority there than to save the Tibetans from being dominated by other powers. This fact must be borne in mind when we consider the difficulties which Bogle and his successors experienced in penetrating beyond Tashilunpo.

Against this complicated political background one considers Bogle's visit to Desheripgay and Tashilunpo; that he saw it as more than a frustrating diplomatic exercise was due in part to the personality of the Panchen Lama, in part to the charm of life among upper-class Tibetans, both ecclesiastics and laymen, in part to the fascination of a mediaeval world surviving into the Age of Enlightenment, and not a little to the receptiveness and amiability of Bogle himself.

The Palace at Desheripgay was a comparatively small building, at the foot of a cliff-like hill in a narrow and lonely valley, as good a place as one could find to avoid an epidemic. It enclosed a stone-flagged inner court, and the rooms opened on to wooden galleries, reached by broad ladders. Gilded pinnacles decorated the roof, and great brass discs gleamed on the front wall. Bogle was given a small, neat apartment above the temple, 'and I was entertained with the never-ceasing noise of "cymballines and timballines" from morning to night. But as soon as it grows dark everything is still as death, and the gates are shut about an hour after sunset.'

The Panchen Lama acknowledged Bogle's arrival by sending immediately a procession of servants with a great pot of ready-made buttered tea, a bowl of rice, some arrack, and, a curious present often to be repeated, 'three or four dried sheep's carcasses. . . . They are as stiff as a poker, are set up on end, and make, to a stranger, a very droll appearance.' These carcasses fascinated Bogle, and he went to a great deal of trouble to find out how they were prepared.

> . . . but I could discover no mystery in it. The sheep is killed, is beheaded, is skinned, is cleaned; the four feet are then put together in such a manner as may keep the carcass most open. During a fortnight it is every night exposed on the top of the house, or in some other airy situation, and in the heat of the day it is kept in a cool room. After it is fully dried it may be kept anywhere. In this way they preserve mutton all the year round.

Bogle learnt that the sheep were killed and dried mostly at the end of autumn, when the weather was dry and getting cold, and the grass was diminishing on the pastures. He found the dried mutton more tender than that which was freshly killed, and once followed the example of the Tibetans and tried eating it raw. 'It had much the taste of dried fish.'

Not until the afternoon of the following day did Bogle and Hamilton have their first audience with the Panchen Lama. That morning he was kept busy with a company of Khambas, the fierce warrior people from eastern Tibet, who had come to pay their devotions. They were hard-faced men with, Bogle thought, a touch of the Malay in their features; their heads were shaven and they wore chupas of yellow cloth. None of them, he noticed, went into the presence empty-handed. The richer carried packets of gold dust and little silver ingots; the poorer bundles of tea or pieces of Chinese porcelain.

In the afternoon, when the two East India men, with their servants bearing gifts behind them, were ushered into the presence, the Panchen Lama received them seated cross-legged, supported by cushions, on a carved and gilded wooden throne. He was a rather short, plump man, with a fair complexion for a Tibetan, small black eyes darting merrily out of a smiling face, a trimmed finger of black moustache, a fragment of straggly beard. He was crowned with the mitre-shaped yellow cap of a Gelugpa hierarch, which distinguished him from the leaders of the more ancient and unreformed Red Hat sects of Tibetan Buddhism. He wore a kind of yellow jacket without sleeves, a 'large red petticoat', a satin mantle thrown over his shoulders. On one side stood his physician, with a bundle of incense sticks smoking in his hand, doubtless with the thought of warding off infection. On the other side stood his cup-bearer and favourite adviser, Solpon Chenpo, then a young man in his early twenties.

Bogle presented the letter he bore from Warren Hastings, together with the Company's present of a pearl necklace, and a white silk scarf from himself. His servants laid out the other presents; no list of them survives, but there were certainly some ornamental glass bottles which interested the Tibetans, though their contents have not been remembered. The Panchen Lama greeted Bogle amiably, and seated him on a high stool, covered with a carpet, next to the throne. An abundance of food was placed before the visitors —plates of boiled mutton and rice, dried fruits and sweetmeats, the inescapable sheep's carcasses—and they were urged to eat. Tea was brought and the Panchen Lama drank with them; Bogle noticed the tact with which he refrained from saying a Buddhist grace while entertaining Christians.

The hierarch greeted them not in Tibetan, but in Hindustani; though his father had been a Tibetan, his mother was related to the kings of Ladakh and in her childhood she had lived largely among Indians. His knowledge of the Indian language was sufficient for him to talk to Bogle and Hamilton without an interpreter, and there is no doubt that this helped greatly in shaping their relationship, since they could always communicate directly even before Bogle had learnt enough Tibetan to converse. On this first occasion they talked mainly about the circumstances which had led the Panchen Lama to make his overtures to Hastings. He blamed Deb Judhur for the Bhutanese war, and claimed that he had known of his intentions beforehand and had tried to dissuade him. He considered that Hastings had acted 'piously' in refraining from occupying Bhutan, and he was happy with the cordiality Hastings had shown to Padma and Purangir Gosain who, after all, were 'only little men'.

Bogle replied with a long oration which he had doubtless been rehearsing in his mind ever since he reached Desheripgay. He went into the origins of the war, the reasons for British action, and told how Hastings was 'happy to cultivate the friendship of a man whose fame is known throughout the world, and whose character is held in veneration among so many nations'. Long before he had finished he began to see the smile fade on that animated face, the black eyes shift uneasily, and when the Panchen Lama made no reply he realized that a combination of excessively florid Hindustani and guttural Scottish R's had made him incomprehensible. He rephrased his statement in the simple words the Panchen Lama had used, 'and so we made it out very well'.

Bogle's subsequent meetings with the Panchen Lama were held in an atmosphere of mounting informality. The hierarch would dispense with the yellow hat and silk mantle used on ceremonial occasions, and would receive Bogle sitting in a chair or reclining on a couch covered with tiger skins, clad in his 'red petticoat', a yellow cloth vest, high boots of soft red leather, with a coarse yellow shawl thrown over his shoulders. Usually only Solpon Chenpo would be present at such meetings, though on the 15th November, a week after Bogle's arrival, there was a special gathering to which Bogle was asked to bring his whole party. There the Panchen Lama made a speech expressing his good opinion of England, and then, remarking that the weather was getting rather cold.

he caused me to be dressed in a purple satin gown, lined with fox skins, and trimmed at the neck and cuffs with a scalloped gold lace, which he said had come from Russia; cap of European flowered silk brocade, turned up with sable, and crowned with a red silk tassel; and a pair of large red leather jack-boots. He equipped Mr. Hamilton also in Tartar costume, but his tunic was of blue satin; and all our

4. Buxa Duar

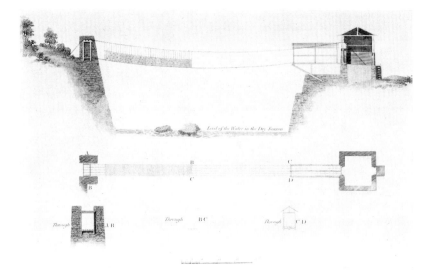

5. Plan, Section and Elevation of the Bridge of Chains at Chuka

6. Chuka

servants, either this day or a few days afterwards, received tunics lined with sheep skins, and boots.

Bogle was doubly grateful for his fur-lined Tibet garb. Before he left Namling the temperature had fallen, at nights, to 3° Fahrenheit, and the water froze in his room even in the daytime, while his new clothes, besides keeping him warm, rendered him less conspicuous in the setting of the Panchen Lama's court.

His intimate conversations with the Panchen Lama at Desheripgay ranged over a wide span of topics. They continued, of course, to discuss the political aims that had brought Bogle into Tibet. The Panchen Lama was well aware of the reasons for the recent decline of trade in the Himalayan regions. He blamed them, justly, on the aggressions by Prithvi Narayan, the Gurkha king, in the valley of Nepal, and on the oppressions and exactions which that ruler had practised against foreign merchants, who had all fled out of Nepal. 'As for me,' he assured Bogle, 'I give encouragement to merchants, and in this country they are free and secure.'

On another occasion, when Bogle raised the question of Tibetans trading into Bengal instead of continuing to use the Bhutanese as middlemen, the Panchen Lama remarked that his people were afraid to go down into the plains because of the heat. Last year he had sent four people to worship in Benares, and three had died on the journey. But there had been a time, he mused, when Tibetans had gone in great numbers to Benares and Bodh Gaya, to study the Indian scriptures and to return after ten or twenty or thirty years to their own country, laden with knowledge. Only after he had been talking for some time in this vein did Bogle realize how far his mind was searching into the past; he was talking about the days, eight hundred years ago, before the Moslems had invaded Bengal, destroyed the Buddhist temples, and forced the Tibetan scholars and pilgrims to flee back over the mountains. Bogle hastened to assure him that, whatever may have happened so long ago, the Company's rule had changed everything. Now 'every person's property was secure and everyone was at liberty to follow his own religion'.

Around the delicate question of when, if ever, Bogle would be able to go on to Lhasa, the Panchen Lama stepped with elaborate evasion. He felt a need to explain his first refusal to allow Bogle to enter Tibet. Many people had advised him against it, though he did not say who. 'I had heard also', he added, 'much of the power of the Fringies; that the Company was like a great king, and fond of war and conquest; and as my business and that of my people is to pray to God, I was afraid to admit any Fringies into the country. But I have since learned that the Fringies are a fair and just people.' Yet this did not lead him to commit himself regarding a definite treaty with the Company, or regarding Bogle's journey to Lhasa, though a few days later he told Bogle 'that he expected one of the ministers from Lhasa in a few days, and that he would introduce me to him, as he wished me to be known to all the principal people in that country. From this I understood that something depended on this man.' Later he talked of representatives of Lhasa being present when he returned to Tashilunpo, and he assured Bogle that then he would discuss the matter of trade with them and with the merchants, and find out what could be done to take advantage of the protection which the Company afforded to traders in Bengal.

'You', said he, 'will also speak with them, and we will see what can be done.' I could have nothing to say against a proposal so reasonable, and I saw plainly he chose not to take any step before he had communicated this to his own officers and to the people at Lhasa.

Thus, during his whole month at Desheripgay, Bogle achieved nothing in a political sense, and all he could send Hastings from there was a brief memorandum on the trade of Tibet, which he found to be much more considerable than anyone who observed the small trickle across the Bhutanese border into Bengal might imagine. Paradoxically, as he realized, the very poverty of the land, its barrenness and slight population, rendered it an ideal trading country, since it manufactured so little, lacked iron, fruit or spices and was prevented by its climate from cultivating such commodities as silk, rice or tobacco. All these had to be brought in, and in exchange the Tibetans had merely a few raw products to offer: gold and musk the most precious, yak-tails, wool and salt the most common, but enough of all to make a considerable trading pattern—and almost none of it tending to the profit of the East India Company! Down from Siberia came the Kalmucks with their camels loaded with furs, red and black 'bulgar' hides, silver and bastard pearls; from China came the coarse tea which the Tibetans loved, brocades and satin, porcelain and glass and tobacco; the merchants from Kashmir, with their establishments in all the important Tibetan towns, were the agents through whom most Indian goods entered the country. As for the Tibetans, there was nothing they better loved than trading among themselves. Clearly it was time Bengal took advantage of the conditions in this country where commerce was an honourable way of life practised by men and women, monks and laymen, with zeal and diligence. Unspoken, this was the obvious implication of the report.

But the weeks passed without any decision, and in the

meantime the Panchen Lama and Bogle began to develop a relationship that was much more than political, and that in the end went beyond mere courtesy to a visitor into genuine friendship.

> Sometimes [Bogle wrote of the earlier days of their acquaintance] he would walk with me about the room, explain to me the pictures, make remarks upon the colour of my eyes, &c. For, although venerated as God's vice-regent through all the eastern countries of Asia, endowed with a portion of omniscience, and with many other divine attributes, he throws aside, in conversation, all the awful part of his character, accommodates himself to the weakness of mortals, endeavours to make himself loved rather than feared, and behaves with the greatest affability to everybody, particularly to strangers.

One is often reminded of a later hierarch, the present Dalai Lama, when Bogle tells of his host's openness of disposition, his merry and entertaining conversation, his flair for telling 'a pleasant story with a great deal of humour and action'.

Most embarrassing to Bogle—who was obviously no adept in Christian theology—were the occasions when the Panchen Lama would question him about religion. 'He inquired if we worshipped the Criss [sic], making a cross with his fingers, and adding that there were formerly some Fringy padres at Lhasa who worshipped the Criss, but they bred disturbances, and were turned out of the country.' He was referring to the Capuchins who had been expelled from Lhasa less than thirty years before. Bogle hurriedly disclaimed any connection with these obstreperous priests, and assured the Lama that the Company maintained complete religious tolerance in Bengal, 'and that we esteemed a good and pious man, of whatever religion he might be. He changed the subject, and I was not sorry for it.' Later, talking about the

Brahminical triad of Vishnu, Brahma and Siva, the Panchen Lama asked Bogle how many Gods there were in the Christian religion.

> I told him one. He replied that he had heard that in my religion God was born three times. I had no mind to attempt an explanation of the mysteries of the Trinity. I felt myself unequal to it. I told him, therefore, that according to my faith God had always existed. He observed, charitably, that we all worshipped the same God, but under different names, and all aimed at the same object, though we pursued different ways. The answer I gave him was in the same tolerant spirit; for I am not sent as a missionary, and after so many able and ingenious Jesuits, dressed in the habits of apostles, and armed with beads and crucifixes, have tried in vain to convert unbelieving nations, I am not so arrogant as to believe that my labours would be successful.

Later, as we shall see, Bogle's disinclination to propagandize for Christianity was to be supplemented by what appears to have been a positive sympathy for Buddhism, and the seeds of this inclination were doubtless sown in these early conversations, when the Panchen Lama would discourse with such rationality that only on rare occasions did Bogle detect anything of the 'marvellous' in his conversations. One of these occasions was when the Lama asked Bogle about the kind of lightning they experienced in Bengal.

> He said in Tibet the thunderbolts are sometimes of stone or iron, and then showed me a knife, with an openworked handle of steel and gold, with several heads carved upon it, and some Chinese characters on the blade which he said had fallen from the clouds.

In fact, even this remark was probably not as 'marvellous' as Bogle imagined, for he almost certainly misunderstood the Panchen Lama. The implement shown to him was a phurba, a Tantric dagger, engraved with *Tibetan*, not *Chinese* characters, and what the Panchen Lama meant to convey to Bogle was not that the complete dagger had fallen from the clouds, but that the three-edged blade was made—as is customary—from meteoric iron.

About once a week the Panchen Lama would conduct public ceremonials, and Bogle always followed them with great curiosity. One day, not long after his arrival, on the 12th November, there was a festival to which three thousand people came to receive the Lama's blessing, and none of them empty-handed; some brought livestock, others sheeps' carcasses, others flour or cloth, and those who could afford nothing more brought a white ceremonial scarf. As the servants received the offerings, they hung silken cords, knotted by the Lama's own hands, around the necks of the donors. The blessing that followed was conducted with a fine discrimination, as the people crowded past the hierarch, enthroned on seven cushions and holding in his hand a stick from which hung a tassel. The monks and noblemen were blessed with the hand. In the case of nuns and slightly inferior laymen, a cloth was interposed between the hand and the head. 'The lower class of people' were merely touched by the tassel as they went by. Bogle was impressed by the Lama's 'dexterity in distinguishing the different orders of people, particularly in knowing the young priests from the nuns, both being dressed in the same habit, and it sometimes happening that they were crowded and jumbled together'. There were, on this occasion, many boys and a few girls dedicated to the monastic life; to consecrate them the Lama with his Tantric dagger cut a lock from the crown of the head.

When he was not in the presence of the Panchen Lama, Bogle was never at a loss for company. 'Being the first

European they had ever seen, I had crowds of Tibetans coming to look at me, as people go to look at the lions in the Tower. My room was always full of them from morning till night. The Lama, afraid that I might be incommoded, sent me word, if I chose, not to admit them; but when I could gratify the curiosity of others at so easy a rate, why should I have refused it? I always received them, sometimes exchanging a pinch of snuff, at others picking up a word or two of the language.'

With some of the officials Bogle established fairly close and friendly relations. One was Solpon Chenpo, the Lama's cupbearer, whom he found an entertaining conversationalist with a great knowledge, through travel, of China, Mongolia and Siberia; by birth he was a Manchu. The other leading member of the court was the Panchen Lama's brother, Chungpa Tulku, whom Bogle always referred to as Chanzo Cusho, and whom he found stiff in manner and uninteresting, completely lacking the engaging manners of the Panchen Lama.

Many Indians lived at the Panchen Lama's court, for his interest in other religions led him to keep an open house for Hindu sadhus and even Moslem fakirs. There were about a hundred and fifty Hindus and thirty Moslems, to all of whom the Lama gave tea, butter and tsampa (roasted barley meal) and who received a present when they departed. Every day the Panchen Lama would spend some time sitting at a window and talking with the holy men about the countries from which they came.

This charity to the pilgrims flows, I imagine, partly from the generosity of the Lama's temper, partly from the desire of acquiring information, and satisfying his curiosity about Hindustan, the school of the religion of Tibet. But the fakirs, in their return to their own country, or in their rambles through other kingdoms of Asia, naturally extol the bounty of their benefactor, and thus serve to spread wide the fame of his character.

Bogle found that, apart from the Panchen Lama, the Tibetans universally disliked the Indian holy men, and he himself regarded them as monumental hypocrites. Many, he claimed, were rich merchants, and used their ascetic garb as a cover for commerce.

They drink plentifully of spiritous liquors, and although directly contrary to their vows and to the rules of their order, above one half of them keep women. In their deportment they mix, by a strange combination, the most fawning and flattering servility with the most clamorous insolence. They intrude into every company, give their opinion in every conversation, and convey what they have to say in a voice of thunder.

For all his disapproval, Bogle was careful to keep on the right side of the holy men, and distributed a great deal of money among them. 'But I will confess I did it from worldly motives, and am far from expecting that it will draw down the favour of heaven upon my constituents, or serve, "to cover the multitude of my sins".'

One of the Moslem fakirs was the cause of Bogle's involvement in a strange and embarrassing scene with Mirza Settar, the merchant who had accompanied him from Rangpur. One morning, before Bogle had summoned the courage to stir out of his bed into the cold air of his room, Mirza came bursting in 'and fell a skipping and dancing in a manner very unbecoming his years and gravity. He then lay down and rolled himself on the floor, and at length, falling upon me, overwhelmed me with embraces. I concluded him mad, and starting up, called for my servants to carry him downstairs.' The cause of this outburst, Bogle discovered afterwards, was the arrival of a Moslem fakir from Lhasa with a message from Mirza's brother. In gratitude Mirza had offered him a share of his apartment, and the fakir in turn had undertaken to cure his host's intermittent fever, which he did by giving him a hallucinatory drug, probably a derivative of hashish. Hamilton administered a vomit, the Panchen Lama administered holy water and Mirza recovered, while the offending fakir was imprisoned in the palace dungeon and released only after Bogle had pleaded for clemency.

Life at Desheripgay was not without interest and occasional excitement, but it was an inactive existence, since, apart from the cold, there was little incentive to stir beyond the gates of the palace, 'where nothing was to be seen but bare hills, a few leafless trees, and a bleak and comfortless country'. Bogle studied Tibetan and played chess and sometimes listened to the travel stories of his only fellow diplomat, the envoy of Cheyt Singh, Raja of Benares. Apart from the interminable services in the temple, and the weekly mass blessings of the people, there was little else to vary the even pattern of a largely monastic life, so that when the Dalai Lama's birthday came, and the palace was illuminated to the music of trumpets and kettle drums, this was a welcome break to be noticed in the monotony that was beginning to envelop Bogle and his companion. They were relieved, at last, when the Panchen Lama announced he was about to end his three-year residence at Desheripgay and return to his capital of Tashilunpo.

On the 7th December they were awakened in the chilly darkness; it was still before dawn when the Panchen Lama walked down the path of yellow cloth that had been laid from his apartment to the mounting block where he got on horseback, and Solpon Chenpo draped him in a yellow fur-lined cloak and put on his head a fur-lined hat which had a black silk flap with fringes to protect his eyes from the sun.

It was a vividly coloured procession with flags and music which set out from the palace that morning, fingers bitten by the early cold. Before they rode out of sight of the palace, they stopped to turn their horses' heads three times towards it, and each time they gave a loud cheer. Bogle carefully noted the order of the procession, and his list, with the images that each line calls up, evokes that world of Central Asian pageantry which one sees from the few films that were made in Tibet during the 1950's, before that amazingly static society finally collapsed under the impact of hostile political forces. This was the line of march:

A Yellow Silk Standard, bound up in two or three places with white handkerchiefs, carried by a man on horse-back.

Eight Kettledrums on horseback.

Four Trumpeters on horseback.

A Set of Bells in a frame on horseback.

About Fifty Horsemen, some with large yellow sheepskin bonnets and red broadcloth coats, others with fur caps and satin gowns.

Four Lamas, or High Priests, in yellow tunics, with brown serge thrown over, and yellow picked caps.

Sopon Chumbo, the Cup-Bearer, or Favourite.

THE TESHU LAMA

A Yellow Satin Umbrella, with strings of coral, carried on horseback.

The Chanzo Cusho

His Cup-bearer          The Treasurer

Mr. Bogle

Mr. Hamilton

Cheyt Singh and other Hindu vakils.

The Pyn Cushos, nephews of the Lama.

About a Hundred Horsemen of different ranks and in various dresses.

The procession drove its way through the crowds that had gathered to see the Panchen Lama. The horsemen at the head of the cavalcade formed a kind of screen so that the spectators were kept at a distance, except for those who were tending little altars beside the road on which fires of aromatic herbs were burning: 'The smoke of these, however disagreeable, served to render the cold less intense.'

The progress of the Panchen Lama's party maintained the leisurely pace to which Tibetan travellers were accustomed. They turned southward out of the little valley where the palace lay and followed the course of the Shiang towards its junction with the Tsangpo. At sunrise they halted on the river bank for tea; tents of white canvas embroidered with blue flowers had been erected, one for the Panchen Lama, another for his brother and a third for Bogle. In the middle of the day they stopped again at a place which Bogle calls Teshu-tzay, where there was a nunnery. The nuns came in procession to receive the Lama's blessing, and Bogle, who had learnt that two of them were nieces of the Panchen Lama, watched them with interest. 'Many of them were young and well-looking; but their dress . . . is very unbecoming, and the loss of their hair is a great want.'

Two miles beyond the nunnery they stopped again for tea, and another mile farther on they came to the Panchen Lama's birthplace, where there was a halt of two days. Bogle found himself lodged 'in a low room in a sorry house . . . the worst quarters I had met with in the country', but a monk who came that evening with fruit from the Panchen Lama reported the fact to his master, and the next day the East India men were transferred to a room in the castle, from which they could look out on the court where laymen were dancing to celebrate the Lama's homecoming. Bogle's description might easily apply to dances that take place to this day in Bhutan and Sikkim and wherever Tibetan traditions still find a refuge.

The court held about thirty dancers, half of them men, half of them women. The men were dressed in different and party-coloured clothes, with their large sheep's wool bonnets, a bit of coloured silk in one hand, and a leather machine, something in shape of, but rather less than, a fiddle at their side. The women had their faces washed, and clean clothes, abundance of rings upon their fingers, and coral, amber beads, bugles, &c., on their heads and necks, and each wore a small round hat, covered with circles of white beads. They formed a ring, the men being altogether, the women altogether, and five men were in the middle of it. They danced to their own singing, moving slowly round in a sort of half-hop step, keeping time with their hands, while the five in the centre twisted round and cut capers, with many strange and indescribable motions. The second part of the entertainment was performed by four or five men, with winged rainbow-coloured caps, who jumped and twisted about, to the clashing of cymbals and the beating of tabors.

Among the rest was a merry Andrew with a mask stuck over with cowries, and a clown with a large stick in his hand. These two were more agile than the others, and between whiles carried on a dialogue, and the grimaces and conversation gave great entertainment to those who understood it. As I was not so fortunate, I was obliged, as I have often been in more polite assemblies, to seek for amusement in the dress and physiognomies of the spectators.

Bogle himself was the object of as much curiosity as the dancers aroused in him; he was visited by the Panchen Lama's two nieces, merry girls whose manner seemed rather inconsistent with their shaved heads and sombre conventual robes, and by the Pyn Cushos, their brothers, two young men of distinctly secular interests who stayed with Bogle the whole day, talking and playing chess and establishing what turned out to be the most pleasant of all his friendships in Tibet.

A day's journey from the Panchen Lama's home the caval-cade halted in a spot where there were no buildings dignified enough to accommodate such an ecclesiastical prince as a Panchen Lama, and, accordingly, an elaborate encampment had been set up, with tents which were a very sophisticated variation on the felt dwellings of the nomads of western Tibet. The Panchen Lama's personal tent, to which Bogle was invited, was naturally the most splendid of all.

> It was round, about sixty feet in circumference, and formed of a number of rods stuck into the ground, and gathered at the top into a hoop, which was covered with oiled paper to let in the light. On the outside it was covered with white cloth, except the top, over which some very beautiful panther skins were spread. The entrance was by a small door. All the inside was hung with crimson satin, and the floor covered with carpet.

But Bogle found that in practice such accommodation 'would have done better for a milder climate'. Even though he had a large fire burning most of the night within his own tent, he observed next morning when he looked at his thermo-meter, which was kept in a linen basket, that it stood just two degrees above zero.

The next day they came to the banks of the Tsangpo, where a crowd of two thousand people watched the Panchen Lama walk on a path of yellow cloth to the landing-place. The river was covered with packs of floating ice, and the horses were ferried over first to give the human beings courage. When the Panchen Lama's turn came, he insisted that Bogle accompany him in the same boat. On the far bank the Kashmiri merchants of Shigatse waited to greet their long absent patron.

They slept another night in tents, and next morning, before they set off, the Panchen Lama sent for Bogle. 'You are to go into my capital tomorrow,' he said; so that his guest should cut a good figure in the procession, he presented him with a yellow satin jacket faced with black fur, and a Tibetan saddle, 'which had a very deep peak of iron, all stuffed, so that it makes one look very lofty'.

The next day they stopped about three miles out of Tashilunpo, where the Dalai Lama's representative and all the local worthies, both secular and ecclesiastical, had come to welcome their lord. A great marquee was set up in full view of the towers and battlements of the castle of Shigatse, which belonged to the Dalai Lama, and here the Panchen Lama sat 'in his sacerdotal habit' upon his cushioned throne, with Bogle seated near him, in rank next to the envoy from Lhasa. They drank tea and ate boiled roots, and 'rice with sugar at the top', while the local dignitaries passed before the Panchen Lama to receive the blessing of hands. Bogle was intrigued by the governors of the fort of Shigatse, who wore their hair plaited and dressed in long gowns which he thought gave them a comically transvestite appearance.

They were dressed like women, but their whiskers and overgrown carcasses left no room to mistake their sex. Their heads were bound with white turbans rolled into a square form; round turquoise earrings, about the size of a watch, hung from their ears, and fell upon their shoulders. They wore slippers, and the rest of their dress was of blue satin, with their arms bare to the elbows.

While the blessing was going on, a light-hearted feeling was given to the occasion by the dancing and singing of monks clad in motley and of the local peasants. Doubtless this was regarded as only appropriate when the great Incarnation returned after so long to the monastery that was his head-quarters.

The atmosphere of joy was preserved as they rode on for the last three miles to Tashilunpo. The peasants lined the road on both sides, clad in their holiday clothes, with groups of them dancing and singing. The great complex of Tashilunpo came into sight, 'built on the lower declivity of a steep hill'. The palace of the Panchen Lama towered massively over the rest of the vast conglomeration of buildings which rose in tiers up the hillside, the gilded ornaments of the temples reflecting the gilded copper roof of the palace itself. It looked like a town, and Bogle used that word to describe it, but it was really one of the largest of those great monastic institutions which existed in many places of Tibet and absorbed a third of the country's male population. Four thousand monks lived in Tashilunpo, and now they were all lined up by the road leading into the monastery; some of them banged drums and clashed cymbals. The sight of them moved Bogle deeply.

> As the Lama passed they bent half forwards, and followed him with their eyes. But there was a look of veneration mixed with joy in their countenances which pleased me beyond anything, and was a surer testimony of satisfaction than all the guns of the Tower, and all the odes of White-head could have given. One catches affection by sympathy, and I could not help, in some measure, feeling the same emotions with the Lama's votaries.

William Whitehead's name strikes a curious note in this context; he was the reigning Poet Laureate, successor to Cibber, predecessor of Wharton, duller than either and perhaps in Bogle's mind a symbol of the emptiness of English regal celebrations, which as a Scot he may have despised, in comparison with the personal devotion that was evident among the Panchen Lama's followers and the warm humanity which the hierarch emanated as he got down from his horse and walked with 'a cheerful look among his people'.

Inside the palace Bogle attended the Panchen Lama to his apartments, and then was conducted to those which were reserved for him and Hamilton in a new building that had been erected during the Panchen Lama's absence. Modestly and inaccurately remarking that he had little success in such descriptions, Bogle proceeded to give a detailed account of his apartment which re-creates admirably the look and the feeling of rooms in prosperous Tibetan dwellings, where cunning craftsmanship, sophisticated architectural sense and a vivid tradition of decoration combined in a visually pleasing combination.

You enter by a door formed of one piece of wood, painted red; the hinges of iron, cunningly gilt, having a large ring of the same workmanship in the middle, with a white satin handkerchief tied to it, so that you may not wear off the gilding in pulling the door after you. The door turns upon two pegs cut out of the planks, and received into two holes at top and bottom. It is fastened by an iron latch and staple, with a lock of the construction of Chinese ones, and about a foot long. The room is about fifty feet long and thirty broad, interrupted by nine square pillars, painted red with white streaks, which make them look fluted. There are two small windows with wooden shutters at the west end, but I never opened them, having enough light from above, for in the ceiling of the room there is an opening about thirty feet long and fifteen wide; and the south side being covered only with loose planks, laid slopingly over, you remove as many of them as you please in the day time, and shut them up again at night. They rest upon a beam, supported by the two middlemost of the nine pillars which are much longer than the others. The walls, which are of plaster, are painted green, broken with a few bands of blue and yellow. The capitals of the pillars, and the beams which form the four sides of the opening I have mentioned, are curiously carved, gilt and ornamented with festoons of dragons and flowers. The floor is of chalky clay, mixed with small pebbles, and formed into a smooth and very beautiful *terrace* which, by the labours of a young gylong, who every morning gets his feet into two woollen cloths, and exercises himself for three or four hours in skating about the room, will, in the course of fifteen or twenty years, acquire a polish equal to the other floors in the palace, which are not inferior to the finest variegated marble.

Even so splendid an apartment, which Bogle thought inferior to none in Tashilunpo, had its disadvantages. During the day, the monks would climb on to the roof and look down at him through the opening where he had removed the planks to give light. And, he remarked with a rueful thought of the disadvantages of office, 'Mr. Hamilton's room is much smaller and warmer than mine.'

Bogle and Hamilton were to stay four months at Tashilunpo. For the most part it was a uniform life, governed by the routines of a great monastery. 'Nothing but priests; nothing from morning to night but the chanting of prayers, and the sound of cymbals and tabors.' The Panchen Lama himself was engaged in a long series of receptions for all the devotees who had come to greet him from as far as Siberia and Mongolia, three months' journey away. The ceremonies were much like those Bogle had already witnessed at Desheripgay, but on a more elaborate scale, as befitted the second of the great centres of Lamaist Buddhism, the York —as it were—of Tibet. The streams of monks and nuns, of broad-cheeked Mongols and fierce Khambas, of high officials and lowly peasants, of bright-cheeked women and laughing children, were longer than ever, and the presents even more varied and elaborate. Now the tea was poured to the high dignitaries, including Bogle, out of a golden pot; Hamilton had to be content with silver. When the sweetmeats were distributed, they were given to the guests in silver dishes, which they were expected to keep. And there were entertainments not available in the rustic solitudes of Desheripgay, such as the troupe of boys in white turbans and 'coloured chintzes and kincobs', who performed an axe dance to the sound of 'hautboys, flutes, kettle-drums and bells', and the religious debates which were conducted between opposing pairs of monks. Bogle's Tibetan had not reached the level of fluency that allowed him to understand the abstruse theological and philosophical points they were discussing, but he enjoyed the gestures.

> They were carried on with much vociferation and feigned warmth, and embellished with great powers of action, such as clapping the hands, shaking the head, &c.

Bogle's increasing sympathy for the Tibetans and their way of life as compared with what was thought civilization in his own country emerged in his ironic remark that the gestures of the debating monks were 'no doubt very improper and ridiculous, because they are quite different from those used by European orators, who are the true standards of what is just and what is graceful'. In fact, on seeing such debates, which are still carried on in Lamaist monasteries in the Himalayas, I have always been reminded of the descriptions of ritualized gestures used in the discussions of the mediaeval schoolmen, which Panurge parodied in *Gargantua and Pantagruel*.

After the first two or three occasions, Bogle stayed away from these great gatherings, and held a kind of court in his own room, where he was visited by a succession of monks and of lay officials 'dressed in their feminine attire' (and even once a general of the Tibetan army), who would usually look inquisitively at his exotic possessions, exclaim, 'Pah-pah-pah Tze-tze-tze,' accept a pinch of snuff and then retire. From most of them Bogle managed to pick some new word or phrase to add to his knowledge of Tibetan, and the Gosains and the Kashmiri merchants were always ready to linger with tales of the marvels seen upon their travels. And there was one very curious figure, Debo Dinji, whom Bogle had already met on the journey to Tashilunpo; he was governor of a castle, and his duty was to save the Panchen Lama from the guilt of having criminals put to death, by confining them without food or drink so that they died of the weakness of their own flesh, without direct human intervention. Debo Dinji looked like 'an overgrown country farmer, smelling strongly of tobacco', and Bogle thought him 'a little crack-brained'. Certainly he was a century ahead of his time by anticipating those Tibetans of Lord Curzon's day who developed a feeling of ardent friendship for the Russians. Debo Dinji's reason for this Bogle found rather startling in the setting of Tashilunpo; he liked Russians 'for their enmity to the Chinese, who were a base, treacherous, and scoundrelly people'. Such a statement verged on the treasonous, and Bogle was surprised by the warmth with which Debo Dinji made it, until he found that the old man had been an adherent of Gyurmé Namgyal, the last king of Tibet, who had been treacherously murdered by the ambans almost a quarter of a century before. In view of his own political aims and interests, Bogle doubtless found it interesting that there were people in Tibet who had such strong feelings against the Chinese, but it was knowledge he would never be able to put to use.

It was the chess-players whom Bogle most liked to encourage, for he had a passion for the game, which he found was shared by the pilgrims from Siberia.

> Their method of playing differs from ours, in the privilege of moving two steps being confined to the first pawn played by each party; in castling and stalemate being unknown; and in the game being reckoned equal when the king is left solus without a piece or a pawn on the board.

Bogle at first found that he usually came off the loser, for a Kalmuck never played alone. He would always get two or three of his fellows to advise him: 'they lay all their great bare heads together canvassing and consulting about every move'. Eventually Bogle found that the Mongols were equally adept at chess, and when he met a Kalmuck in combat he would always engage two or three Mongols to be his advisers, and in this way would usually 'beat them hollow'.

Despite the burdens his sacerdotal duties laid upon him, the Panchen Lama still found time to continue his private talks with Bogle, and even, on the evening after their arrival, to show him the temple in the form of a long gallery filled with images which was part of the new wing where Bogle himself was living. In the centre of the hall there was a great image of the Buddha, probably a hollow figure made of shaped brass plates in the Tibetan manner, and to this the Lama prostrated himself three times. While he did so Bogle had time to observe his surroundings; the ceiling richly covered with Chinese and Mongol and Russian silks; the south wall broken with windows and hung with brilliant thankas, holy paintings; the stacks of pigeon holes at each end of the gallery, filled with long loose-leafed books, each wrapped in yellow or red silk; the long iron grille on the south side of the gallery, where the thirteen lesser images stood; even these were larger than human-size, and Bogle estimated that if they had not been sitting cross-legged they would have stood eight feet high.

They are of copper gilt, holding a pot with flowers or fruit in their lap. They are represented covered with mantles, and crowns or mitres on their heads; and altogether, particularly the drapery, are far from being badly executed. The thrones upon which they sit are also of copper gilt, adorned with turquoises, cornelians, and other stones not of inestimable value. The mouldings and ornaments of the thrones are in a good style. Behind each figure the wall is covered with a piece of carved work, like unto the heavy gilt frames of our forefathers' portraits, or looking glasses. Behind them are china vases, some of them very handsome, loads of china and glassware, the last partly Chinese, partly European, filled with grain, fruit, or gum flowers; a variety of shells, large chanks set in silver, some ostrich eggs, cocoanuts, cymbals, and a variety of other articles, making a most heterogenous figure. Round the backs of the images are strings of coral, ill-shaped pearls, cornelian, agate, and other stones, and their crowns are set with the like ornaments.

The Panchen Lama went behind the iron screen to scatter rice in consecration over these new images. Then he sat down to drink tea with Bogle and explain to him the meaning of the various thankas, some of which illustrated scenes from the Buddha's various lives, while others represented Tibetan deities, or Buddhas and Bodhisattvas in their differing aspects. Afterwards they went from this great private temple by a back staircase to Bogle's own room, where the Panchen Lama curiously examined his possessions, and particularly his English-made chessmen, which were 'drawn up in battle array upon the table', and then liberally sprinkled the room with rice to bring down blessings upon its occupant. He did the same to Hamilton's room, and then departed.

Though Bogle soon tired of the monotony of the great receptions for pilgrims, his curiosity remained active, and whenever anything unusual happened in the monastery, or when the Panchen Lama specially invited him to attend a service, he would always be there. In this way he was a privileged spectator at many ceremonials at which even twenty years ago in Tibet a European would not normally have been welcome. He accompanied the Panchen Lama when the latter made a tour of the various temples within the great complex of Tashilunpo, and would watch from a special gallery sitting among the Tibetan lay officials. In this way he was able not only to hear the ordinary services, with their chanted prayers which in the end he found pleasing and not unmelodious, but also to witness such special occasions as those in which 'a man, dressed in party-coloured clothes, and a cardinal's cap adorned with death's heads, used to come in, and with many strange gestures hop and twist about, pouring out oblations of oil, brandy, rice, &c., and holding a human skull, a bell, a dagger, or an axe in his hand.'

This appears to have been the Shanag or Black Hat dance, one of the most spectacular and sacred of the Tibetan lama dances, celebrating the assassination by a Buddhist monk in the ninth century of King Lang Darma, the Tibetan equivalent of Julian the Apostate, who had sought to set back the clock of enlightenment by reinstituting the shamanistic Bon religion of ancient Tibet and persecuting the Buddhists. It is curious that Bogle goes no farther than describing this dance, without explaining it, since it must almost certainly have been expounded to him by the Panchen Lama or by one of his other Tibetan acquaintances. But there is, over such matters, an evident reticence in his narrative. Even when he tells us that the Panchen Lama interpreted to him paintings or images which embodied Tibetan Buddhist beliefs, he does not record the interpretation. One can only speculate on the reason for such persistent failure to go beyond the mere physical description. That Bogle was not hostile to Buddhist doctrines, like many British officers in India during the evangelically inclined nineteenth century, is obvious. That he shared Hastings's curiosity over strange things there is no doubt. That he may have been enjoined by his informants not to spread the secrets of their religion is a distinct possibility; if this is the case, his observance of their desires may be a sign of more than honourability— it may, in view of indications we shall discuss later, suggest the development of an exceptional sympathy.

One ceremonial occasion that Bogle must have followed with more than ordinary interest was the reception by the Panchen Lama of the delegates who had come from the Dalai Lama and the regent Demo Rimpoche (whom Bogle called Gesub Rimpoche) to congratulate him on his return to Tashilunpo. Bogle knew that on these men rested his hopes of travelling to the Tibetan capital and perhaps beyond it.

The reception took place not in the palace itself, but in a temple outside it yet still within the great monastic enclosure of Tashilunpo. To greet the representatives of the highest hierarch of Tibet, a great company of monks had gathered, sitting tightly crowded together in their tall yellow hats. The Panchen Lama came into the temple, prostrated himself three times before the image of Buddha, and ascended his throne, which for this occasion was raised high upon a flight of wooden steps. While he did this the monks chanted prayers and the novices scurried round with great pots— silver for notables and copper for the commonalty—full of steaming tea well fortified with yak butter.

As soon as the Panchen Lama was seated, the Dalai

Lama's leading delegate walked up to the throne, carrying an embossed silver platter on which were heaped five little piles of rice. He delivered a long harangue, and seemed more than once on the point of breaking down. The thousands of people in the great hall kept completely silent until he had finished. Then the Panchen Lama replied briefly and, taking a pinch of the rice, threw it towards the altar. Then he received the Dalai Lama's letter, accompanied by sacred gifts—small images wrapped in yellow silk, holy books, conch shells set in silver—which he carefully arranged before him on his throne. Then came a procession of servants, bearing first the presents of the Dalai Lama, and then those of his Regent. Bogle kept a close eye on this stage of the proceedings, for he was intent on gathering what clues he could regarding the wealth of Tibet. He estimated that the gifts to the Panchen Lama amounted to 'about a hundred talents of silver, a hundred and twenty pieces of silk and sixty bundles of tea. There were also about six talents of silver, ten pieces of silk, and four bundles of tea given to the Chanzo Cusho.' One special feature of the occasion was the number of petitions which were 'according to the custom, thrown into the church, each being tied to a white satin handkerchief'. The fact that even a mere delegate of the Dalai Lama was in the company of the Panchen Lama suggested a conjunction of mana which pious unfortunate people could not ignore. The monks passed the petitions from hand to hand, until they were all piled at the foot of the throne and then handed to the Panchen Lama. 'I am told they are principally desiring prayers for sick people, or for the souls of those lately dead. The Lama read over one or two of them, after which he said a short prayer for himself, and was followed by another by the gylongs. Then everyone departed.'

Afterwards Bogle was to have much closer dealings with the Dalai Lama's delegates, but that is part of the story of his efforts to reach Lhasa, which lasted until he left Tashilunpo in the spring, and I shall discuss it in the next chapter.

Meanwhile, after the Christian New Year had passed, that of the Tibetans approached. It was a variable lunar festival, taking place in 1775 on the 26th January according to the Gregorian calendar which Bogle observed. It was preceded by ceremonials starting a week beforehand, and followed by the Monlam, the Great Prayer, a strange mixture of religious services and saturnalian games intended to discourage the powers of evil and hasten the coming of the Maitreya, the Bodhisattva of the future who will emerge out of the west.

These festivals brought to Tashilunpo a great number of the Panchen Lama's relatives, some of whom Bogle found extremely congenial company. They were accommodated in a house in a grove of old trees near the palace, and in a Kalmuck tent that had been put up beside it, and they included the Panchen Lama's sister-in-law, Chum Cusho, and her two daughters, the merry nuns whom Bogle had already met on his journey from Desheripgay. Their two brothers also appeared, full of gaiety and delighted to find the East India men still in Tashilunpo. The most formidable of these family visitors was the Panchen Lama's half-sister, a great hierarch in her own right, and the only woman in Tibet who belonged in the same class of high and powerful incarnations as the Dalai, Panchen and Sakya Lamas. Under the name of Dorje Phagmo—which can be translated somewhat unedifyingly into English as the Thunderbolt Sow—she reigned, as her successive incarnations did until 1959, over the great monastery by the Yamdrok Tso Lake on the road to Lhasa.

Since Bogle's supposed relations with Tibetan women were later to become the subject of curious speculation and controversy, it is interesting to consider the evidence to be gained from his own papers that have survived from this period of his travel.

Bogle's account in fact suggests that Hamilton, whose medical skill was called upon successfully by both Chum Cusho and Dorje Phagmo, was much more intimate with the women who came to Tashilunpo for the New Year's festivals than his superior, for Bogle sought in preference the rather wilder male company of the Pyn Cushos. Hamilton, indeed, was making a name for himself at Tashilunpo by his lucky cures, and since in societies where Shamanism lingers the physician and the magician are hardly distinguished, the young Doctor was visited by a succession of Siberian pilgrims, each of whom presented him solemnly with a white scarf, and then whispered urgently in his ear.

> They told him, that having heard of his great skill in the occult sciences, they were come to have their fortunes told, and at the same time stretched out their hands for that purpose. While he was hesitating whether to carry on the joke a little farther, they desired him first to tell what had happened to them last year, and then to proceed to unfold their future destiny. This would go far to prove skill in fortune-telling and was a test Mr. Hamilton was unable to undergo.

As the incarnation of a great Tibetan deity, Dorje Phagmo doubtless regarded herself as sufficiently versed in occult lore, but she appreciated Hamilton's more material abilities to the extent that they became very friendly, and he would visit her every day. Unfortunately Hamilton left no record of this most interesting relationship between an East India man and a Tibetan female reincarnation of deity, a relationship that in the nineteenth century might have become the material of some Rider Haggardish fantasy. All we have is Bogle's unromantic record of his own visit to the Thunderbolt Sow. She received him sitting cross-legged on a low cushion and without her sacerdotal finery; she wore merely the maroon robe of a nun, and her arms were bare to the shoulders.

> She is about seven-and-twenty, with small Chinese features, delicate, though not regular,¹ fine eyes and teeth; her complexion fair, but wan and sickly; and an expression of languor and melancholy in her countenance, which I believe is occasioned by the joyless life that she leads. She wears her hair, a privilege granted to no other vestal I have seen; it is combed back without any ornaments, and falls in tresses upon her shoulders. . . . After making my presents and obeisances, I kneeled down, and stretching out her arm, which is equal to 'the finest lady in the land,' she laid her hand upon my head.

Tea was served, boiled mutton and broth and fruit, but the Thunderbolt Sow had little to say, and Bogle obviously regarded the visit as one of his less pleasurable duties.

Chum Cusho was quite a different matter. She was a widow of forty-five or so, with a ruddy complexion, the remnants of handsomeness, a disposition 'as merry as a cricket', and something of a past. Originally she had been a nun, and while in that condition she had encountered the Panchen Lama's brother, himself a monk, and 'they happened somehow to form such a connection together as put an end to their state of celibacy'. The incident created a major scandal even in easy-going Tibet, and the Panchen Lama refused to receive his brother for many years. After her husband died, Chum Cusho reverted to religion, put aside the rich gold and turquoise and amber ornaments of a Tibetan noblewoman, took up again her vows of chastity, and set out, as enthusiastically as the Good Wife of Bath, on a round of pilgrimages through Tibet, Nepal and parts of India, with all the Chaucerian delight which such exercises still inspire in the hearts of Tibetans.

Bogle enjoyed Chum Cusho's company, but he seems to have done so only on relatively few occasions, and the same was evidently the case with her daughters, the two unnamed nuns. The older of them was twenty-seven or twenty-eight, and Bogle remembered her as 'dark-complexioned and hard-featured'; clearly she did not stir his special interest, though he granted she was merry and good-humoured enough. And indeed there was nothing in the dress of either of the girls to do more than repel masculine interest. Their heads were shaved, they wore jackets and skirts of coarse red material, 'and red woollen hose soled with leather, and gartered under the knee', while the only ornament allowed to them was the few beads of coral that hung from their rosaries. Yet such a bald head and a dress of red frieze had not prevented Chum Cusho from acquiring a lover, and Bogle obviously found the younger of the daughters more pleasing than her sister. She was about nineteen, 'remarkably fair and ruddy', and Bogle records an occasion when the two girls came to visit him in the company of their brothers, the Pyn Cushos, and, in an atmosphere of general amusement, they asked to see his 'Fringy dress', and the younger sister was per-suaded to put on his braided coat. 'We had a great deal of laughing and merriment. But who can repeat the little un-important trifles which gladden conversation and serve to while away the time?'

And that is as far as Bogle's own account of his relationship with Tibetan ladies takes us. He went to the trouble of buying some coral beads to give to Chum Cusho and her daughters, which they accepted only after great persuasion. But that is not enough to suggest that Bogle—and his Tibetan friends equally—were doing anything more serious than whiling away the time with 'unimportant trifles'.

Yet, as Bogle's final regret at leaving Tashilunpo shows more eloquently than his protestations of tedium can deny, these occasions of merriment and congenial companionship built up into the vision of a pristine kind of existence that could not be lived in the world from which he had come. And no-one contributed to that impression more thoroughly than his young friends the Pyn Cushos, who, when he tried to include them among the recipients of his coral beads, refused for a whole hour. 'You are come from a far country,' they said. 'It is our business to render your stay agreeable; why should you make us presents?' Bogle was so touched by the incident that in his journal he wrote that it 'set the character of the Tibetans in a stronger and more favourable light than if I were to write volumes on the subject'.

His sentiments are understandable when one reads in his narrative of the attentiveness and generosity with which these high-spirited young men provided for his entertainment during the New Year celebrations and even afterwards. They would take him and Hamilton out to little encampments of gay tents set up in the countryside around Tashilunpo, where they would amuse themselves with horse races, peasants would be brought in to dance and sing, and a great picnic feast would feature 'every kind of flesh and fowl they could think of', and, after dining, tables covered with fruit would be carried in, and rich chupas and Mongolian horses be presented to the protesting guests. The entertainment would end merrily in the drinking of chang, or barley beer, served by handsome waiting girls.

Beyond a nominal respect for the pieties expected in the holy environs of Tashilunpo, the Pyn Cushos had no more inclination for the monastic life than any young English squire of the same period, and when they left their uncle's palace at the end of the New Year celebrations to return to their country house two days' journey to the west, Bogle was delighted to receive an invitation to accompany them. He needed a change. Not only had he been subjected to a surfeit of collegiate ceremonials; he had also been working on a commission from the Panchen Lama to prepare an account of life in Europe. He set to work conscientiously, describing what must have struck his host as a curious variety of institutions, from parliament to travel by stage coach, from the custom of duelling to the hospitality of European inns, including French as well as English examples. Working with an interpreter, he translated the account in Tibetan, and the result 'afforded a great feast to the Lama's insatiable curiosity'. Doubtless the curiosity was compounded by astonishment, and one may perhaps find in this startling account of the barbarities of European civilization—as it must have seemed to its Lamaist readers—one of the reasons why, in the generations that followed, the Tibetans were reluctant to allow these strange people too far into their country.

Rinjaitzay, where the Pyn Cushos lived, lay in a little valley on the north side of the Tsanpo, and the little cavalcade, which included a dozen servants of the Pyn Cushos, and only one servant for Bogle and Hamilton, who had decided 'to live like Tibetans', spent the first night—the 11th March*—in the headman's house of a little village

* There is a discrepancy between Bogle's various accounts. The date above is given in his journal, but in a report to Hastings he says that he left Tashilunpo with the Pyn Cushos on the 25th February and returned on the 2nd March. Even if we were to suppose that he slipped into the use of the recently obsolete Julian calendar, it would not account for fourteen days' difference in the date of departure, since the discrepancy between Julian and Gregorian calendars was only *eleven* days.

overlooking the great river. The meal was rustic, in a very
Central Asian manner, consisting of varieties of meat in
various stages of rawness.

> A cup of hashed mutton, not unlike a greasy curry, another
> of boiled rice, a third of raw beef beat into a jelly, and
> highly seasoned with salt, turmeric, and other spices. It is
> far from unsavoury, when one can get the better of
> European prejudices. There were also a joint of mutton
> well boiled, and another just scorched on the outside but
> raw within. It requires no conjuring to find out on which
> I made my dinner.

After dinner there was smoking of pipes, and then archery,
a sport beloved of the Tibetans, at which Bogle competed
without distinction, and afterwards an evening sitting
around a blazing fire lit in the centre of the room, drinking
chang, and singing, to the tune of Tibetan mandolins. The
entertainment was gargantuan; when Hamilton and Bogle
retired to their apartment, they found yet another dinner
prepared for them, this time in the English manner, of eggs,
fish and roast chicken, just in case they had not relished the
Tibetan food. Of this, 'as I can always eat at any hour of the
day or night', Bogle partook freely, and he did not diverge
from this pattern throughout the days of gluttonous ampli-
tude that followed.

Leaving the next morning, after having been dutifully
honoured with the customary presents of sweetmeats and
dried sheep's carcasses, the party continued to the banks of
the Tsangpo. The ferry boats were all on the other side of the
river, and the crossing was difficult because of the packs of
snowy ice that clogged the current, so that it was two hours
before they were embarked, but Tibetans are comfortable
travellers, and tents were pitched and tea served, while
Bogle astonished the Tibetans and amused himself by sliding

on a frozen pool, a Daldowie pleasure for which Bengal had given no scope.

On the other bank they rode briskly along the beaches, where the whirling winds whipped the sand into high moving columns, until they reached a holy cliffside painted over with red ochre, where the Pyn Cushos offered a branch with a white scarf tied to it. Here they were on a kind of eminence, with the Tsangpo broad and glistening below them. 'You have a view of its windings for a great way up and down, and the prospect would be very fine if there was anything besides bleak bare hills to look at.'

Leaving this austere prospect, they turned northward up a side valley, halted to drink tea and eat 'excellent mutton puffs' with the steward of a house on the way belonging to the Lhasa Regent, and, about an hour after dark, reached the house of Rinjaitzay, 'having, by our stoppings and tea drinkings, taken a complete day to perform a journey which might easily be done in six hours'.

Bogle and Hamilton, as the honoured guests, were given what is regarded as the best quarters in a Tibetan house, the room occupied by the domestic shrines, and occupied also, in evidence of the Pyn Cushos' sportsmanlike predilections, by 'matchlocks, bows and arrows, swords, shot-bags, &c.'. Here the hosts and guests sat down to dinner, which, as Bogle remarked, was the sixth time he had taken meat that day. Even for Tibetans, who are more lax in these matters than Buddhists in other lands, the Pyn Cushos were remarkably addicted to the flesh of slaughtered animals.

And, indeed, once away from the holy environs of Tashilunpo, they had little objection to the actual killing of living beings, provided they could be sure it did not come to the ears of their uncle. The five or six days that followed contained a variety of bloodsports that would have satisfied any

English country gentleman of the time. The Pyn Cushos ordered hares to be caught, so that they could be released and coursed by dogs. They competed with Hamilton in shooting partridges, and, indeed, it was Bogle who on one occasion showed the more Buddhist compassion, for some birds which his hosts had caught for him to shoot turned out to be so tame that he could not bear to kill them, and he let them go; for this the servants at least regarded him as a pious man.

While many wild animals in Tibet were mostly immune from persecution and slaughter, cupidity had become the enemy of one particularly attractive species. This was the musk deer, or musk goat as Bogle called it, a creature in fact more akin to an antelope than to either deer or goat.

This animal was sought for the valuable product which gave it its name and which formed one of the most important articles of export from Tibet, and one method of hunting was to take it in nets. One day the Pyn Cushos took Bogle and Hamilton out on an expedition of this kind. They rode about three miles from Rinjaitzay, and stopped in one of the ubiquitous decorated tents, while the servants went off to reconnoitre in the hills. After drinking tea and playing chess for two hours, Bogle became restless, and went riding with the dogs over the hills, until, just as the whole party was about to return to the house, a servant came with the news that one of the animals had been sighted asleep in a quarry. What followed makes painful reading, and shows that other side of the Tibetan character, the curious coldness which would put a man to starve to death in a dungeon rather than sign his death warrant.

> The people with the toils went along the side of the mountain, and above the place where the game lay, while we followed slowly after. The toils are made of cords,

formed into a number of nooses hung close to one another, on a rope which is extended at about three feet from the ground, and supported by rods stuck in the earth at intervals of about ten or twelve feet. There is another row of nooses similar to this placed parallel to it, and at a distance of about five feet. When these double toils were set all round one side of the quarry, and at about a gunshot from it, we spread ourselves, encircled the other side, and with shouts and stones at length awakened the musk from his profound sleep. As soon as he got upon the brow of the hill, he boundingly made towards the toils, and having twice attempted to leap over them, thrust his head into one of the nooses. When we came up to him he was quite breathless with struggling, and all the skin, which is very tender, was torn off his neck with the cord. We carried him home, and put him in a closet adjoining to my room; but he died before morning.

Less valuable animals were often treated with greater consideration; the Pyn Cushos had a whole menagerie of them confined at various points in and about the house, including a wolf and a tiger cat, and these animals were the cause of the only real scare that the travellers experienced during their whole journey in Tibet. They and all the household had gone to bed on their last night at Rinjaitzay, when they were awakened by a fearful barking and howling among the great 'parcel' of dogs that inhabited the house, and very soon the whole household gathered—for safety—on the roof. A strange company they appeared in the starlight, Bogle and Hamilton clad only in their shirts, and the Tibetans of both sexes, who slept naked, draped inadequately in a variety of blankets.

Some said it was thieves; but as I could not think anybody would be so wicked as to attempt to rob the Lama's family, I had nothing for it but to conclude it was the devil. In the meantime a most extraordinary yelling began

146

just under our nose, which being totally different from anything I had ever heard, would certainly have served to confirm my notion, had not the whole family, to our utter astonishment, burst out into a fit of laughing; and, Paima having managed to light a lamp with his tinder-box, we had the satisfaction to see Mr. Wolf, whose breaking loose had occasioned all this disturbance, pinned down by the tiger cat, with her claws fixed in his cheeks. And so, having remanded him into confinement, each of our motley group, after looking a little at one another, returned laughing to bed.

Early next morning Bogle and Hamilton took their leave. Down in the Tsangpo valley they encountered one of the great dust storms that sweep over the Tibetan plateau, and rode on through it as quickly as they could, resisting the suggestions of their servants that tents should be set up for tea, and by nightfall they were in Tashilunpo, having completed in one day a journey which in the amiable company of the Pyn Cushos had taken two. It was the day when the whole monastery was illuminated in memory of the late Panchen Lama, but the storm blew out the lamps, and the monks chanted special prayers far into the night to avert the misfortune that this unruly wind portended.

# VII

## *The Mirage of Lhasa*

Bogle returned to Tashilunpo to find the grip of winter loosening, the ice melting 'faster than it froze', and the noons bringing a comfortable heat. He returned also to the final withering of his hopes to reach Lhasa, the great objective of his journey.

Perhaps it had all been a series of misunderstandings. Certainly, as his original instructions made clear, Hastings had been unaware of the distinction between the Panchen Lama's government in Tashilunpo and the Dalai Lama's in Lhasa, and had assumed that if Bogle did visit the Panchen Lama it would be in the capital of Tibet. With that understanding Bogle had started on his journey; he carried with him a letter from Hastings to the Panchen Lama, but none to the Regent in Lhasa, and he bore only enough presents to do honour to a single hierarch.

It is true that Hastings had adopted a very flexible attitude towards the whole mission. However far Bogle got, as long as he entered some new territory, there would be an extension of knowledge that could not fail to be useful to humanity in general and to the Company in particular. In August, when he did not yet know that the Panchen Lama's refusal of permission to proceed into Tibet had been withdrawn, Hastings was busily thinking of how best to draw some small victory out of apparent defeat.

I shall be happy to learn that you are allowed to proceed
[he told Bogle] but entertain small hopes of it. If it is
true that you cannot pass without an order from the
Emperor of China, perhaps you might still be allowed to
leave some persons with the Rajah till such a licence could
be obtained. . . . Having engaged in this business, I do
not like to give it up. We should both acquire reputation by
success. The well-judging world will be ready to class it
with other wild and ill-concerted projects if it fail. . . .
Leave no means untried, but hazard neither your person
nor your health by an obstinate perseverance. If you
cannot proceed, return, but . . . do not return without
something to show where you have been, though it be but
a contraband walnut, a pilfered slip of sweet briar, or
the seeds of a turnip, taken in payment for the potatoes
you have given them gratis.

When Hastings learnt that Bogle had finally received permission to enter Tibet, he had no doubt that this meant a
passport to Lhasa. The letter he wrote to him from Calcutta
on the 8th September makes that abundantly clear.

I have just received yours of the 20th ultimo, and read
in it with infinite pleasure that you had surmounted all
your difficulties, and were preparing to proceed to Lahassa.
I feel myself more interested in the success of your mission
than in reason perhaps I ought to be; but there are
thousands of men in England whose good-will is worth
seeking, and who will listen to the story of such enter-
prises in search of knowledge with ten times more avidity
than they would read accounts that brought crores to
the national credit, or descriptions of victories that
slaughtered thousands of the national enemies. Go on and
prosper. . . . Remember that everything you see is of
importance. . . .
Be not an economist if you can bring home splendid
vouchers of the land which you have visited.
The superior council and judges are not yet come; I
expect them about November. You shall not suffer by

your absence; I am your vakeel [advocate], and will take care to seize every occasion for your advantage. Your fellow-traveller has my good-wishes, and God bless you.

By the time Bogle reached Desheripgay, he realized that the Panchen Lama did not rule in Lhasa, and his first interviews with that dignitary made it quite clear to him that a free passage to Lhasa depended on the good will of the Dalai Lama's Regent. It was therefore with a peculiar interest that he watched the reception of the Dalai Lama's envoys. The envoys expressed a desire to see him, and he met them after his first intimate talk with the Panchen Lama in Tashilunpo. The hierarch had talked about his idea of founding a Tibetan monastery beside the Ganges near Calcutta, and Bogle had assured him that this wish would undoubtedly be met. Then the Panchen Lama had gone on to say that he was writing to the 'Changay Lama' (Changkya Tulku, the current head of the Lamaists in Peking) to say that the Fringies who ruled in Bengal had showed him special favour, and suggesting that he send some of his people to visit the religious places in India. The Changay Lama, he assured Bogle, had great influence over the Emperor of China.

Though Bogle did not realize it at the time, the Panchen Lama was rather obliquely preparing him for the disappointments of his meeting with the Regent's delegates, who called on him shortly afterwards. Already, in Desheripgay, the Panchen Lama had told Bogle that the Regent, in reluctantly agreeing to allow the East India men into Tibet, had insisted that they should not be allowed to visit Lhasa. At the same time it had been hinted that this refusal did not spring entirely out of Demo Rimpoche's fear of 'Fringies'; it was not unconnected with the jealousy that existed between him and the Panchen Lama, whose intent was to persuade the Emperor to allow the Dalai Lama to assume power and in the process to deprive the Regent of authority. Now the Regent's representatives had expressed a desire to see the Company's representative, and that in itself seemed a minor victory.

It remained nothing more. The delegates were in the usual Tibetan bureaucratic tandem, a monk official dressed in maroon robes, and a lay official clad in what Bogle still persisted in calling feminine attire. They came with about twenty attendants, and brought with them the Regent's presents, mysterious barrels and boxes which Bogle and Hamilton afterwards opened with interest and, it is evident, with disappointment. They consisted of bamboo vessels of Chinese whisky (presumably rice spirit) 'stronger and better than that of Tibet'; some small Chinese cakes of very fine flour, 'but not half baked or even kneaded', some dried mushrooms which they found very useful to give a savoury flavour to their food, and some small dried fish which they 'could never find out how to dress'. To anyone reading the language of presents in Asia, and noticing the lack of a single precious gift, the course which the conversation followed would have been predictable.

The layman acted as spokesman, and this again was ominous, since in Tibet it was always the monk official who claimed seniority. It was not, the spokesman told Bogle rather haughtily, customary for delegates sent from the Dalai Lama to the Panchen Lama to wait upon a visiting stranger, but since Bogle had come so far, and represented 'the chief of the Fringies', the Regent had ordered them to call. They expressed the Regent's satisfaction that Hastings had made peace with the Bhutanese and had restored their country. Bogle, talking hard to make the best impression, enlarged on the essentially peaceful intentions of the British towards their neighbours to the north. The monk official kept his silence. The lay official nodded his head curtly, and then went on to say that the Panchen Lama had written to Lhasa about merchants. The Tibetans, he declared in a refrain that had already become familiar to Bogle, were afraid of the heat in Bengal; their ancient custom was to take their goods to Phari, whence the Bhutanese carried on the trade as middlemen. That ancient custom would continue to be observed. Bogle protested that formerly there had been a great direct trade between Tibet and Bengal, whose decline the Company regretted, and that he trusted the Regent and his government would accede to his proposals for facilitating a revival of this commerce.

> They answered, that Gesob Rimpoche would do everything in his power, but that he and all the country were subject to the Emperor of China. This is a stumbling-block which crosses me in all my paths. The Lhasa people took their leave. I offered to return their visit. They seemed not to wish it, but said they would come to see me again.

No mention had been made of Bogle's travelling to Lhasa, and he realized that all he could now do was to try to use the rivalry between the two Tibetan governments to reach some kind of agreement, with Tashilunpo if not with Lhasa, over the trade between Tibet and Bengal. He consoled himself with the thought that in any case, without presents for the Dalai Lama, the Regent and the four ministers of the Kashag, the Tibetan cabinet, he could not properly represent the Company and its Governor. The reasoning was specious; since Hastings had allowed him to spend freely, he could easily have obtained in Tashilunpo the kind of presents customarily offered by envoys in Tibet. He was in fact saving his face before whoever might read his journal, for the second visit of the Regent's envoys left no doubt at all of his unwelcomeness in Lhasa.

He had in the meantime carried his problem regarding trade between Tibet and Bengal to the Panchen Lama, and the latter had promised that in a year or two, after the expansionist intentions of the Gurkhas had been curbed by the Tibetan army sent to oppose their attack on Sikkim, he would see about opening direct trade. As for the Regent, he remarked, 'his heart is confined, and he does not see things in the same view as I do'.

The Regent's envoys called again on the 30th December, and Bogle asked them to take a letter from him to the Regent. Perhaps the envoys had heard of his conversations with the Panchen Lama since their last meeting, for their manner was curter than ever when they answered that they would take the letter if it merely conveyed thanks for the presents Bogle had received, but that if it made any reference to business or to anything that might cause trouble for the country they must refuse it. Bogle replied that the Panchen Lama had advised him to write, and expressed concern that they should imagine him capable of writing anything harmful. He had come into the country with a 'pure heart', and wished only happiness to Tibet and its Regent. They asked to see a copy of the letter he intended to write. He offered to show it to the Panchen Lama and to stand by his judgement. He added that he was concerned over the suspicion with which the Regent seemed to regard him, and was anxious to know what had given rise to it.

Their answer was that they were come to take leave of me, that much conversation was not the custom of this country, and so wished me a good journey to Bengal. I endeavoured to get them to listen to me. I wished to introduce the subject of trade, but it was to no purpose; so we parted.

The behaviour of the Regent's envoys was so out of character with the politeness and geniality to which Bogle had become accustomed in his dealings with both Tibetans and Bhutanese, that he was naturally perturbed, and he immediately repaired to the Panchen Lama's apartments. He expressed himself with a great deal of warmth, and the Panchen Lama set out to soothe his hurt feelings. Of course, he said, the Regent did not understand the true character of the English. But in a year or so the Dalai Lama would be of age, and then everything would be different. Bogle then read out the draft of the letter he intended to send to the Regent. The Panchen Lama smiled and nodded. 'Every country', he said quietly, 'has its particular manner of writing. If you like I will write a letter for you.' With that he called in a scribe, and dictated in Tibetan a letter on Bogle's behalf. After the customary compliments, it ran, as Bogle remembered:

> I have received the Chinese wine, fish, mushrooms, biscuit, &c., that you were so good as to send me in great abundance, and all very good of their kinds. May your country enjoy tranquillity and yourself happiness. I request, in the name of the Governor my master, that you will allow merchants to trade between this country and Bengal. I have sent you a gun, a piece of broadcloth, and a handkerchief, which you will please accept of.

This letter Bogle sent by a servant of the Panchen Lama to the Regent's envoys, with a message to say how concerned he was over what had passed between him and them. 'They returned me an answer that they were sorry and ashamed of what passed at our last meeting; that they would deliver the letter and would faithfully mention what I had said. From this I found that the Lama had spoken to them.'

This was the last communication Bogle had with the official envoys from Lhasa. They left early in January; the Regent never replied to the letter they carried. But even before they departed a curious comedy bearing on Bogle's relations with Lhasa had already begun. On their first visit the Regent's representatives had warned him to take no notice of a Nepali who called himself the Chauduri (which was usually the title of the minister of a petty state) and who would probably be calling on him. They refused to enlarge on the point.

The next day the Chauduri appeared on a visit of ceremony, and later he came to talk privately. He said that he had come recently from Lhasa, where he was in the Regent's confidence, and that the latter had specifically asked him to visit the East India Company's representatives. In reality, he whispered in his oily, intimate voice, the Regent was extremely pleased with the way the Company had made peace with the Bhutanese, and was anxious to cultivate Warren Hastings' friendship. Bogle listened with some surprise, in view of the attitude of the official envoys, and he was no less amazed when the Chauduri said that he had in fact been appointed the Regent's vakil and been told to accompany Bogle on his return to Calcutta, carrying a letter and presents to the Governor.

All this puzzled Bogle a great deal, but though he suspected that the Chauduri was going beyond his commission, he 'had no doubt of his having some commission'. But, maintaining stoutly that 'it was the custom of the English to deal plainly and openly', he insisted on mentioning the matter to the Panchen Lama. The Chauduri was reluctant at first, but finally agreed, and, when the Lama had been enlightened, he came again to Bogle and began to make even more sweeping assertions. The Regent was anxious to do everything that

Hastings wished. He was willing to grant permission for the Company to set up factories in Lhasa (a favour Hastings had not even thought of asking); he was even thinking of introducing Bengali rupees into Tibet. Comparing these flowery promises with the dour reticences of the official delegates from Lhasa, Bogle found his suspicions magnified. But the Chauduri continued, saying that in ten or twelve days he was going to Lhasa, and that there he would get a favourable answer from the Regent to all Bogle's proposals regarding freedom of trade. Then, bearing the Regent's letter and presents, he would return to Tashilunpo and accompany Bogle to Calcutta.

Bogle thought of making the Chauduri some presents, just in case his stories were true; there was, after all, the curious fact that—as Tashilunpo gossip asserted—the Regent had made the Chauduri a present of four or five thousand rupees and one 'could hardly think he would be so generous to a man he had only seen once, merely for his *beaux yeux*'. But Scottish prudence prevailed; Bogle kept his purse closed and opened his mouth as little as possible.

Meanwhile, the Panchen Lama had written to Lhasa, and received an answer from the Regent, who denied that he had given the Chauduri any commission to visit Bogle, that he had talked of sending him to Calcutta, or that he had any connection whatever with him. He asked that the Chauduri be sent immediately to Lhasa, and the plausible little Nepali was taken off under escort to the capital. Consistent in his prudence, Bogle was careful not to see him before he went, but sent a message by a friend promising to reward him if indeed he succeeded in putting the Company's case favourably to the Regent.

Nothing more was heard of the Chauduri in Tashilunpo until, about a week before Bogle's departure, he returned, and kept discreetly out of the way until Bogle sent a message saying that he was surprised not to have seen him. Then the Chauduri appeared. His story had changed. There was no doubt, he still insisted, of the Regent's friendship towards the Company, but he was afraid of the Chinese. Nevertheless, he still thought of sending him—the Chauduri—to Calcutta after the summer rains. Bogle thought of upbraiding the Nepali for his deceptive promises. 'But it would have served no good purpose; and as I had not and did not intend to give him anything, what right had I to upbraid him? I therefore took leave of him with fair, but guarded words.'

Bogle was still puzzled as to how he could account for 'this strange intrigue'. There were two possibilities. Either the Chauduri had invented everything with the aim of ingratiating himself with Bogle and getting presents from him. But this did not seem to fit in with the Regent's having himself given the Chauduri a large present. Therefore, Bogle decided, the most likely explanation was that the Regent, 'jealous of my visit to the Lama, and desirous to know my errand, had employed the Chauduri to sound me; at the same time, as he could not avow this, that he disclaimed any connection with him, and summoned him to Lhasa on pretence of punishing him; but, in fact, to know what had passed between him and me. Be it as it may, the whole matter ended in smoke.'

And in the same smoke, elusive as a puff of incense, ended Bogle's hopes not merely of ever getting to Lhasa, but even of reaching any understanding with its rulers.

# VIII

## *Return to Bengal*

As the winter passed into spring, the urge to go on journeys
touched many hearts in Tashilunpo. Dorje Phagmo, successfully cured at last, set off with her entourage for the great
abbey she ruled on the way to Lhasa. The Pyn Cushos
arrived from Rinjaitzay, but only to take their mother and
sisters back to the convent at Teshu-tzay. Bogle parted sadly
from them all. Chum Cusho gave him many blessings and
much advice as to how to conduct his life according to good
Buddhist precepts, and the young nuns gaily extracted from
him promises to write to them and send them parrots and
looking glasses from Bengal. But, as he tells us, it was his
parting with their brothers that was the hardest task. 'I
never could reconcile myself to the thoughts of a last farewell, and however anxious I was to return to Bengal and to
the world, I could not take leave of my Tibetan friends with
indifference. . . .' He did not see those amiable Tibetan
Gemini, the Pyn Cushos, again. Within a year they had both
died, one a few days after the other, just after they had
finished a long joint letter to their British friend.

It was time for Bogle and Hamilton to make their own
departure, and in the early days of April all their acquaintances in the palace began to visit them with pots of tea and
little gifts. On the 3rd April Bogle took his public leave of
the Panchen Lama. In a private conversation beforehand

the Lama reverted to the question of his relations with the Emperor of China. He was obviously distressed that Bogle should have come so far and failed to achieve his main aim of going to Lhasa, and he had shrewdly understood that the Company was intent on using any advantage it might get in Tibet to further its trade in China. Once the Regent was removed, and the Dalai Lama was in power, he suggested, everything would be well, 'and then I shall have no difficulty in carrying any point that the Governor pleases, and hope to settle it so with the Emperor that the Governor may send his people to Peking, and, if he pleases, establish English factories'. From all Bogle knew of the Chinese government's obstructiveness at Canton, he must have realized that the hopes thus held out were chimerical, but he also recognized the friendliness that made the Panchen Lama spin such amiable fantasies.

The Lama then asked Bogle if there was anything he could do for him. Bogle asked for some musk deer and shawl goats to satisfy Hastings' fondness for strange animals, and the Lama promised they would be sent down in the cold weather when they would be likely to survive the journey. He also promised, when Bogle asked it as a personal favour, to obtain from the Lamas in Peking a list of all the records of comets in Chinese history from the earliest times. Then he produced his letter to Hastings, allowing Bogle to read it before he sealed it.

> After giving me presents of some silks, purses of gold dust, silver talents, &c., and clothing me in a fine khilat, he took a bit of red silk, and tying a knot upon it himself, he threw it about my neck with his own hands.

This was the public leave-taking. Actually Bogle called on him in private every day until his departure four days later and in these last conversations their talk ranged over a variety of subjects from the difference between the tenets of Catholicism and Protestantism to the political relations between Russia and China; and from the treatment of small-pox to the images the Panchen Lama was going to put into the temple he wished to build at Calcutta. The Lama showed Bogle and Hamilton his collection of watches, whose mechanism fascinated him, requested that a crocodile and two lions' skins be sent to him from India, and asked to hear some English poetry, whereupon Bogle recited the 'Elegy in a Country Churchyard'. And he returned once again to the question of China, and promised to try to get permission for the English to visit the Emperor in Peking. Bogle accepted this assurance with gratitude, meant as it was in kindness to himself, but he could not help balancing it against the Panchen Lama's last request, that when the Company's next envoy were sent, he should be a Hindu and not an English-man, to avoid a repetition of his difficulties with the Regent.

It must have been evident to Bogle at this moment that his expedition had really pushed the door into Tibet no wider than it had been before. And yet, for all his lack of any spectacular political success, he had learnt and seen and recorded things that none of his countrymen had known before, and he had found a people and a way of life from whom he was departing with a heavy heart. 'Although my days have been spent without business or amusement, they have been passed without care or uneasiness,' he wrote to his sister, 'and I may set this down as the most peaceful period of my life. It is now almost over, and I am about to return to the hurry and bustle of Calcutta.'

On the morning of the 7th April, he bade farewell to the Panchen Lama, who promised him his prayers, threw a white silk scarf over his neck in the Tibetan gesture of speeding the parting traveller, and, laying his hand upon his head, gave him the blessing accorded to those of the highest rank. Then he took from his own neck a triple necklace of blue and green glass beads and of cornelian and chalcedony, and gave this to Bogle, telling him that any lady on whom he bestowed it would be protected from evil. Moved almost beyond the power of speech, and showing his emotion so obviously that the Panchen Lama consolingly remarked that he hoped they would meet again in Tashilunpo, Bogle retired hurriedly, and, mounting his horse, joined the cavalcade that awaited him.

It was a considerable party. Mirza Settar and Purangir Gosain were accompanying Bogle and Hamilton back to Calcutta. So was an old rascal of a sadhu, who had made a fortune in forty years of pilgrimages which had carried him 'from the banks of the Indus to the plains of Siberia', and had obtained permission to accompany the travellers so that he could enjoy their protection of his wealth through the mountains of Bhutan. Padma, and the monk who used to bring Bogle his morning tea, were instructed to accompany the party to Buxa Duar on the borders of Bengal, and, besides the Bengali servants who had come all the way from Calcutta and endured the cold of a Tibetan winter, there were ten Bhutanese servants. Finally, the Kashmiri merchants of Shigatse had all arrived to see the travellers fairly on their journey.

Bribing their way through a clamorous cordon of beggars, they rode slowly southward over the plain until, at midmorning, they came to a great tent that had been erected for their entertainment, and there they drank tea, and took their last look at the place that had been their home for four frustrating yet beguiling months; 'the palace and town, the monastery of Teshu Lumbo with its copper-gilt roofs; the castle of Shigatse, with the town below it and the high surrounding hills . . .'

Since they were not returning by way of Namling, it was no longer necessary to cross the Tsangpo, and their journey took them in a south-eastward direction until they joined their original route at Painam, on the river of the same name. Though the hardness of the winter had broken, the landscape was still bleak and barren in appearance, 'for not a single blade of grass had yet sprung, nor a tree budded'. Yet it was a rather hilarious first day's journey; Padma and the other Tibetans had drunk heavily with their friends before leaving Tashilunpo, and had not abstained as they travelled on to their first halting place, a kind of hermitage, kept by a monk, with the life-size image of a former Lama gracing the room where Bogle slept. At Bogle's suggestion, the more drunken of the Tibetans lit perfumed torches before the image to 'deprecate its wrath'.

If the road from Painam was the same, the people—as always in Asia—were various and interesting, and one gains from Bogle's sketches of them a mental pageant of the pre-mechanical travelling life rather like that evoked by the European picaresque writers. He meets a general whom he knows, on his way to visit the Panchen Lama before going to fight against the Gurkhas in Sikkim. 'He was preceded by his wife and her female attendants, mounted astride on horseback. She had her face half covered, like the Armenian women.' At Painam, a blind beggar and his young wife come into the courtyard to serenade the travellers. 'He played on the fiddle underhandwise; she sang; and both, assisted by a young boy, beat time, hoppingly, with their feet.' Snow had fallen, on the road and in the hills, and the beggars everywhere came shivering to take advantage of the pity their appearance aroused, trailing after the riders and lamenting their cold and hunger in a shrill, plaintive and professional whine.

The most interesting of these mendicants were a group of wandering monks of one of the ancient Red Hat orders.

It may be necessary to state [Bogle explains, demonstrating the knowledge he had acquired since he first arrived in the lands of Buddhism] that there are two sets of clergy in Tibet, distinguished by, and classed under the names of, Yellow Caps and Red Caps. The Dalai and Teshu Lamas are at the head of the Yellow Caps; the Red Caps have their own Lamas and monasteries. In times of old there were violent disputes between them, in which the Yellow Caps got the victory, as well by the assistance of the Tatars as by their superior sanctity. But as I adhere to the tenets of this sect and have acquired my knowledge of religion from its votaries, I will not here say much upon this subject, lest it should be thought spiteful. I may be allowed, however, just to mention two things, which must convince every unprejudiced person of the wicked lives and false doctrines of the Red Caps. In the first place, many of the clergy marry; and in the next, they persist, in opposition to religion and common sense, in wearing Red Caps. The priests who now visited us were of this last sect. There might be about eight of them. Each held a staff in one hand and a rosary in the other. They formed into a circle, and began to chant their prayers, which, as I understood they were put up for my welfare, I was in no haste to interrupt. At length, to show them that, however hostile to their principles, I bore them no personal grudge, I dismissed them with a few small pieces of silver.

There is obviously heavy irony in this passage; Bogle is jesting at the insignificant points that mark off to the world the differences between various schools of religion. Yet at the same time one senses his contempt for the beggar monks of the older sects as compared with the more urbane and more intellectually polished representatives of the Yellow

Hat Gelugpa order which it had been his good fortune to encounter. And there is a haunting, slightly puzzling sound to the statement: 'I adhere to the tenets of this sect and have acquired my knowledge of religion from them.' Is this merely a sarcastic sally? Or does it suggest that Bogle, having observed the good effect of Buddhist precepts on the life and temperaments of his Tibetan companions at Desheripgay and Tashilunpo, had developed at least a genuine sympathy towards this religion? Its essential rationality, partly concealed by its crowded Lamaist pantheon and exotic liturgy, may have appealed to his eighteenth-century mind, which quite evidently had little use for the complexities of Christian theology.

Hurrying through Gyantse, the travellers stayed once again with the old priest in his house south of the city; thanks to Hamilton's medicines they found him in fine spirits. At Dudukpai they revisited the polyandrous household of the woman married to two brothers, and spent another gay evening watching the children dance, and listening to the songs of the men and one of the maidservants. Bogle no longer felt a stranger, as he had done on first arriving at this place. 'As I could now make it out without an interpreter, I had much more satisfaction in these parties, and when one is travelling there is nothing like making amusement out of everything.'

They crossed without incident the pass from Tibet into Bhutan and before the end of April had reached Paro. After resting there a couple of days, they went on to Tassisudon, which they reached on the 8th May. The two rulers—the Deb Raja and the Dharma Raja—were absent when they arrived; they were staying at Punakha, in the winter palace of the Bhutanese rulers to which the whole court migrated at the onset of the bad weather; it was a low valley where, as Bogle was told, 'the climate is so much hotter that it produces mangos, pine-apples, &c. and they say cassia'. On the 16th May the two rulers returned, and on the 17th Bogle paid his ceremonial visit to the Deb Raja.

In the meantime a letter had arrived from Hastings, congratulating Bogle because his visit 'has proved so acceptable to the Lama', but it was obvious that the Governor wanted the mission to end with gains more concrete than had been won in Tibet. 'The great object of your mission', he reminded Bogle, 'is to open a communication of trade with Tassisudon, and through that place to Lhasa and the most distant parts of Tibet.' During Bogle's absence in Tibet, Hastings had been busily writing to the Deb Raja to point out the advantages to him of such an arrangement, and now Bogle was to build on this foundation. 'I recommend you to use your utmost endeavours during your stay at Tassisudon to settle conditions with the Rajah for the establishment of an entire freedom of trade between his country and Bengal.' To achieve this end, Bogle was authorized to remit the 'tribute or duty' levied on the annual trading caravan that came out of Bhutan to Rangpur. Hastings noted that the caravan had in the past brought the government of Bengal about 2,000 rupees a year, but with a realistic eye to the corruption inherent in Asian administrative practices, he added that 'it is probable that the right of levying it may serve as a cover to much greater exactions, and that the surrender of this privilege may therefore be considered by the Rajah as considerable. This is to be the ground work of your negotiations. You will build such improvements on it as your own judgment and occasion may dictate.'

Bogle tried his best. He made much—perhaps too much —of a request that the Company be allowed to establish in Bhutan factories staffed with Englishmen. The Raja refused to consider the idea, and Bogle did no better in his efforts to gain permission for Tibetan merchants to travel through Bhutan.

Bogle would have liked to stay on and wear down the Deb Raja by negotiation, but he fell sick and did not want to delay returning until the rains set in. Accordingly at the beginning of June, he left Tassisudon. He was conscious of how little that was specific and tangible he had achieved in either Tibet or Bhutan, and he feared that his commission would 'gain me but little credit with the world' though he felt that its eventual result might be a great increase in the trade between Bengal and the Himalayan kingdoms.

Padma and the Deb Raja's representative travelled with Bogle to the border of Bhutan, and said farewell at Buxa Duar; the priest whom the Panchen Lama sent had already succumbed to the sicknesses of a strange land. By the 9th June Bogle was in Cooch Behar, reporting to Hastings on his failure to achieve his political objectives. He then set out through Dinajpur to Calcutta, where Hastings waited to hear his report in person.

It is certain that Bogle wished to see Tibet again. His premature death was to prevent it when the opportunity did arise a few years later. But he retained his interest in the country, and kept in contact, through Purangir Gosain and in other ways, with the Panchen Lama and his other friends in Tashilunpo. He may even have established a more direct link with that idyllic interlude by bringing with him into Bengal a Tibetan wife.

Bogle's Tibetan marriage, if it ever existed, is the one totally mysterious strand in a life that otherwise appears as open and clearly cut as the character of the man who lived it. I can only present what evidence exists on this most elusive of relationships and suggest its possible implications.

The first reference I encountered was by Hugh Richardson in *Tibet and its History*, where that distinguished Tibetologist included in his brief reference to Bogle's journey the following statement:

> He married a Tibetan lady, described as a sister of the Panchen Lama, by whom he had two daughters. The girls were later educated at Bogle's ancestral home in Ayrshire and there each married a Scottish husband. All reference to Bogle's Tibetan wife seems to have been suppressed when his papers were edited for publication; but his descendants, of whom several survive in Britain, now look back to that ancestry with pride.

As Dr. Richardson remarks, there is no statement or hint in the Bogle journals as published by Clements Markham in 1875 that might suggest a marriage, or any intimate link with a Tibetan woman. But the papers Markham used, then in the possession of Bogle's grand-niece, Martha Brown, had been 'judiciously sorted' by a friend of the family, a Mr. Gairdner of Kilmarnock, and they were certainly incomplete. I had searches made in the India Office Library, the British Museum, the Public Record Office and the National Archives of India in New Delhi, all of which contained papers relating to Bogle's journey, including versions of his journal. Nowhere was there any reference to a marriage or to children.

When I wrote to Dr. Richardson, he told me that the source of his information was a Mrs. Heathcote who claimed to be the great-great-grand-daughter of Bogle and his Tibetan wife, and who had come to his attention when she wrote a letter to the *Sunday Times* about Bogle and his Scottish ancestry. According to the information Mrs. Heathcote provided, the family traditions had it that Bogle's wife was named 'Tichan' and that she was indeed a sister of the

Panchen Lama; one romantic feature of her story as it had developed over the two centuries since Bogle left Tibet was that she had 'waded a river to follow after him'.

There was no mention of Tichan, whoever she may have been, coming to Scotland, or of when she died or what happened to her after Bogle's death. But the family tradition was emphatic about the children. There were two of them, bearing Bogle family names—Martha and Matilda. They were brought up—as Richardson says—in Ayrshire, though he is incorrect in saying that the Bogle family home was in that county. However, the discrepancy adds a touch of authenticity, for only one of Bogle's brothers and sisters married and would have been able to give a home to the two children; this was Martha, who married Thomas Brown, and lived at Lanfine, in Ayrshire. It was, significantly, to Martha—rather than to his dearer sister Anne—that Bogle left the necklace he had been given by the Panchen Lama. The tradition also relates that the two Bogle children were well brought up, with servants, a governess, a carriage at their disposal and that each married a Scottish gentleman; from Martha, who married William Browne, were descended Mrs. Heathcote, Richardson's informant, and a certain Amelia Sturrock, Martha's grand-daughter, who apparently passed on the details of Tibetan ancestry to Mrs. Heathcote.

Richardson had no doubt that children by Bogle did exist and were taken to Scotland and brought up by his family. This seems possible, but not much more, since there is a curious absence of documentary proof, even in the very large collection of Bogle family papers which is held in the Mitchell Library at Glasgow; not even among the papers relating to Bogle's estate is there any reference to children.

On the other hand, these papers establish quite clearly that Bogle—although he is consistently described as a 'bachelor'

—did, according to the custom of India Hands in his time, establish a relationship with an Asian woman who actually went by the name of Bebee Bogle, and survived him by more than half a century, dying in 1838. There must have been feeling and even a sense of permanence in the relationship, for in his will Bogle left a fund out of which she was to be paid twenty-five rupees a month for the rest of her life, which continued too long to please the executors.

Yet there is no clue to the identity of 'Beebee Bogle'. Since Bogle expressed freely and often his dislike of Bengalis and his approval of Tibetans and Bhutanese, it is likely that she belonged to one of the hill peoples. That she was a sister of the Panchen Lama is not only unlikely but impossible, for the Lama's only sister, according to Bogle's own account, was the incarnation Dorje Phagmo, the Thunderbolt Sow, and it requires the imagination of a Rider Haggard to suppose that this living semi-deity would elope with a visiting East India man; even if she had any such inclination, Hamilton would have been a more likely recipient of her favours than Bogle. There was, indeed, the sister-in-law, Chum Cusho, but Bogle referred to her affectionately as an 'old lady'. There remain, among the Tibetan women Bogle mentioned, only the two young and merry nuns who were daughters of Chum Cusho. Bogle certainly found the younger of them both likeable and attractive, and enjoyed with her that easy, joking kind of relationship which one quickly establishes with young Tibetan women, who are accustomed to a social freedom far greater than that of most other Asian women. But Bogle tells us that he had seen both girls departing to their nunnery before he himself left Tashilunpo, and we can hardly believe that one of them broke away from the escort of her brothers or fled many miles from the convent itself to follow Bogle's departing caravan, accompanied as it was by officials of the Panchen Lama. Besides, if Bogle had seduced one of the Panchen Lama's nieces from her religious duties, it is unlikely that he would have remained *persona grata* with the Tibetans, in view of the Lama's sustained anger at his own brother for having lapsed in a similar way; yet we find that Bogle maintained good relations with the Panchen Lama until the latter's death. In any case, a relative of the Panchen Lama would hardly have been pensioned off at the cheap rate of twenty-five rupees a month.

Even the possibility of Bogle's having established during his journey a relationship with a Tibetan woman outside the Panchen Lama's family is difficult to envisage. In Tassisudon, in Desheripgay, in Tashilunpo, he lived in monastic and masculine societies where the establishment of any relationship with a woman would immediately have rendered him unwelcome. In other words, even if Bebee Bogle were Tibetan or Bhutanese, Bogle must have established his relationship with her in India and not in one of the Himalayan kingdoms. The whole romantic story of Bogle's Tibetan princess and his half-Tibetan children whose descendants still live in Scotland remains a legend until there is more convincing proof than has yet been brought to light.

# IX

## *Pressing on the Door*

If Bogle's expedition did nothing else in a political sense, it revealed to Hastings and his advisers the realities of the situation within Tibet and Bhutan. They knew now the true structure of government in the country; they were aware of the opposition of interests between the Panchen Lama and the Regent; they realized the double role China played in the situation, as a military power whose armies could and sometimes did repel by force the attempts of other nations to interfere in Chinese affairs, and as a paper dragon which the Tibetan and Bhutanese rulers were in the habit of using to conceal their own motives; they understood how far their conquests in Bengal had made them feared in the countries round about, so that neither the Tibetans nor the Bhutanese were anxious to allow Europeans to see very much of their territory. Moreover, with an adeptness which anyone who has had close dealings with modern Tibetans and Bhutanese will find familiar, both the Panchen Lama and the Deb Raja had carefully avoided committing themselves definitely on the vital question of free trade, which would have allowed the Company to infiltrate their countries in concealed ways.

Hastings was the kind of political realist who welcomed such exact knowledge of the kind of difficulties he was likely to face. At the same time he was optimist enough to see in the personal trust established between Bogle and the Panchen

Lama a promise of wider co-operation in the future, and he reassured Bogle by expressing his 'perfect' satisfaction with his envoy's conduct and the results of his mission. The scientist in Hastings was even more pleased with the observations on Tibetan and Bhutanese life that made Bogle's journal so memorable. 'Its merit shall not be lost where I can make it known,' he declared, and kept his word, for in August, 1775, he sent a copy to that Grand Lama of the English literary world, Dr. Johnson.

> I confess I received great pleasure from it [he told Johnson], and I assure myself that whatever originality you may discover in the description of the countries and inhabitants of which it treats, you will at least be pleased with the amiable character of the Lama. I am afraid it may look like an ill compliment, after having desired your acceptance of this production, to tell you that I have endeavoured to prevail on the writer to put it into a more connected form, and to send it, with some additional materials, to England for publication. If it would not be assuming too great a liberty, I should request to be favoured with your opinion upon the propriety of this intention.

If Johnson replied, his opinion has not been preserved. But in April, 1777, James Stewart, a Fellow of the Royal Society who had recently returned from India, produced an account of Bogle's mission which was read at a meeting of the Society. This was the only occasion on which Bogle's achievements were made public until the printing of his journal ninety-eight years afterwards.

Meanwhile a briefer twilight fell in India upon Hastings' plans for closer links with Tibet and upon Bogle's personal career. By the time Bogle returned to Calcutta in the midsummer of 1775, Hastings had become the first British Governor General in India. It was a change in title only, and any increase in power it may have implied was negated by the arrival of a new Council whose majority, led by Philip Francis, was hostile to Hastings and to his policies. The deadlock in the government of Bengal continued until September, 1776, when Colonel Manson, one of the hostile faction, died, and Hastings gained a majority on the Board.

While Francis was in the ascendant, the protégés of Hastings lay under a cloud of hostility. Bogle's friend, Alexander Elliott, left for London to counter the misrepresentations regarding Hastings which Francis had assiduously spread. Bogle found himself virtually without employment, except as a kind of casual clerk in Hastings' office. It is true that the Council made him a grant of 15,000 rupees in recognition of his services on the mission to Tibet, most of which he sent home to pay off the debts his family had incurred in unwise business ventures. But all Hastings' efforts to give him employment commensurate with his talents and achievement were assiduously blocked.

> The other day [Bogle wrote to his brother Robert at the end of 1775], Mr. Hastings proposed me for a high office. He was seconded by Mr. Barwell, but it was carried against me by the three other members. So that at present, when I expected to reap all the fruits of my labours, I am disappointed. . . . As I am not called at present to act in any public employment, I propose to dedicate my time entirely to the service of Mr. Hastings, and to improving myself in Persian. The factions in Calcutta render society, beyond the circle of one's intimate friends, very unpleasant and I intend, therefore, to lead a quiet life, and see what turn things will take.

He even appears to have been accused of financial irregularities, and in particular of having given presents too generously, for in the Hastings papers in the British Museum is a rather moving unsigned statement by Bogle pointing out that he received as much in presents as he ever gave, and

173

that the hospitality of the Panchen Lama at Tashilunpo was so great that in four months he and Hamilton lived on about forty rupees. As for the gifts in gold dust and silver talents and other valuables which he received in Tibet, all these, except for a few trinkets, he claimed he had given away 'in the same manner as I got them'.

Things took no turn at all, so far as Bogle was concerned, until the end of 1776, when, in November, he was appointed, with two colleagues, to form a commission directed to re-forming on a more scientific basis the revenue structure of Bengal. Shortly afterwards, he was appointed Commissioner of Lawsuits, and by 1779 it was clear that Hastings intended to put his talents and his special knowledge to full use, for he was then appointed Collector at Rangpur, which meant that he would take charge of any commercial arrangements the Company was able to establish with the Bhutanese.

Meanwhile the links established with Tibet had not been allowed to die entirely away during the period when Hastings' ascendancy was most bitterly and effectively opposed by the Francis clique. The indefatigable Purangir Gosain passed to and fro bearing messages between Hastings and the Panchen Lama. One of them, which reached Calcutta in July, not long after Bogle's return, emphasized the unsureness of the Panchen Lama's position.

> As this country is under the absolute sovereignty of the Emperor of China, who maintains an active and unrelaxed control over all its affairs, and as the forming of any connection of friendship with Foreign Powers is contrary to his pleasure, it will frequently be out of my power to dispatch any messengers to you. However, it will be impossible to efface the memory of you from out of my mind, and I shall pray always for the increase of your happiness and prosperity—and in return—I hope you will frequently favour us with accounts of your health.

There is no doubt that in Lhasa annoyance was felt at the length of Bogle's stay, and it appears that the Chinese ambans had not been willing to allow the Regent to deal with this situation on his own. A Chinese mission was expected in Tashilunpo, and its presence would inevitably restrict relationships between that court and Calcutta.

Hastings was not content to leave relationships in this indefinite condition, and in November he sent Alexander Hamilton, Bogle's former companion, on a mission ostensibly to visit the Deb Raja of Bhutan, but really with the hope of strengthening the link with Tashilunpo. Hamilton tried to enter Bhutan from the western side of Cooch Behar, by the Lakhi Duar, which would have taken him by an easy route to Paro and thence to Tassisudon, but the Bhutanese insisted that he travel, as before, through the Buxa Duar. There he found a messenger awaiting him with a friendly message from the Deb Raja. He proceeded to the winter palace of Punakha, and accompanied the court when it returned to Tassisudon in May, 1776.

Hamilton's immediate task was to examine the claims of the Deb Raja to certain border areas, and he appears to have reached an amicable settlement, by which the Deb agreed in return for the surrender of these disputed territories to reduce his transit dues on goods proceeding through Bhutan from Tibet to Bengal. But in his major task Hamilton failed completely. He established contact through messengers with the Panchen Lama, but the Chinese embassy had now reached Tashilunpo, and the Lama insisted that this made it quite impossible for him to receive an Englishman. Hamilton reported to Hastings in May that because of the situation in Tashilunpo, and 'the unreasonable jealousy of the Lassa Government, the expectations which I had formed of visiting Tibet are now at an end'.

Hastings did not cease to press on the tantalizing door to Tibet. He punctiliously carried out the agreement with the Panchen Lama regarding the temple near Calcutta. The land was loaned in 1776, and, after the temple had been built and Purangir Gosain installed there, the site was given in perpetuity to the rulers of Tashilunpo. Guest houses were built under Bogle's supervision, and a trickle of Tibetans began to find their way into Bengal and to use the temple as a base from which to make their pilgrimages to Bodh Gaya and Sarnath. Neither side in fact was willing to abandon entirely a relationship that might eventually be profitable, and the Panchen Lama at the end of 1775 sent an envoy with presents to Hastings, gold dust and silver ingots, while in 1777 another mission arrived to pay compliments to the Governor General and offer sacrifice on behalf of the Panchen Lama at the historic sites associated with the Buddha. In 1777, when a new Deb Raja took power in Bhutan, Hastings used this as an excuse to send Hamilton a second time to Tassisudon, ostensibly to congratulate the recently installed ruler, but also to probe again the possibilities of proceeding into Tibet. Hamilton went in July, a hard time for travel, but his trouble was fruitless, and in September he was back in India with nothing achieved and his health much deteriorated.

Shortly afterwards the situation in Tibet changed. The old Regent, Demo Rimpoche, died, and a new Regent was invested in office by the Panchen Lama, whose power in Tibet now seemed unchallenged. It seemed a good time to redeem from him some of the promises he had made with an eye to such a situation, an opportune time indeed for the Company, since an increase of trade with Tibet would be beneficial to the economy of Bengal, while it also seemed desirable to make some kind of direct contact with the

Imperial Court at Peking, since at Canton the Company
was experiencing ever greater frustrations in its dealings with
petty officials and with the merchants officially allowed to
trade with Europeans, who owed debts in the neighbourhood of two million silver dollars which the Company's
Select Committee had not been able to collect either in cash
or in kind.

Accordingly, early in 1779 Hastings decided that another
full-scale mission be sent to Tashilunpo, and that Bogle
should lead it. The appointment was made in April, and in
July, having heard from Purangir Gosain that the Panchen
Lama intended to leave shortly on an eight months' journey
to visit the Emperor of China in Peking, Bogle thought that
this might be the time to call on the Lama to redeem old
promises and get him a passport to Peking so that he might
be present when the Emperor met the Tibetan hierarch.
The Panchen Lama sent a message suggesting that, even if
Bogle could not be allowed to accompany him from Tibet,
he would try to get him a passport to go via Canton. In a
memorandum to Hastings, Bogle proposed that he should
make the journey to Peking in whichever way the Panchen
Lama could arrange. If he could go only via Canton, he
would send Purangir Gosain to accompany the Panchen
Lama overland, and then meet him at Canton for the last
lap of the journey to Peking. In Peking he felt that he would
have no difficulties because his knowledge of Tibetan would
enable him to converse without an interpreter with the
Changay Lama, head of Mahayanist Buddhism in the
Chinese capital. Bogle was optimistic enough to insist that
presents of the kind that might be acceptable in Peking
should be got ready; he suggested 'large pearls, large coral,
some best birds' nests, some Arabian horses, and some
muslins'.

But the Panchen Lama set off without arranging for Bogle to accompany him, and when Purangir Gosain reached Tashilunpo with a message from the East India man he found the hierarch already departed, and set off in pursuit. Having left in the late summer of 1779, the Panchen Lama decided to spend the harsh Tibetan winter at Kumbum, the great abbey on Lake Kokonor. Here the Gosain overtook him, and distributed the presents he carried, particularly to Solpon Chenpo, the cup-bearer, who—Bogle hoped—would make sure that the Panchen Lama spoke well of him and Hastings to the Emperor of China.

The party proceeded into Mongolia, and it was already August when they reached Jehol, the summer residence of the Emperor. There the Panchen Lama and his entourage stayed until the onset of the autumn, when they accompanied the court on its return to Peking. Twice—once in Jehol and once in Peking—the Panchen Lama is said to have urged the merits of Warren Hastings, and on each occasion the Emperor is said to have replied that he would establish contact with the East India Company. But the only records of these conversations are to be found in the narrative of Purangir Gosain, who had already shown himself a subtle double agent, and of Solpon Chenpo, who, activated by the Tibetan inclination to mould the truth to the desires of others, may have felt he must send a report that would be agreeable to Hastings his benefactor and Bogle his friend. The Chinese accounts, which otherwise deal quite copiously with the Panchen Lama's visit, are silent on this point, and the one witness whose word would have settled the question —the Panchen Lama himself—died in Peking on the 27th November, 1780. Ironically, the disease that slew him in a swift three-day bout was the smallpox which he had kept away from Tashilunpo for three years to avoid. He died, according to the records, in prayer and in great tranquillity, supported between two pillows, his back to the wall.

Later, the rumour-mongers got to work, and it was reported in the bazaars of Central Asia and Calcutta that the Panchen Lama's death had not been natural: that, indeed, he had been poisoned at the order of the Emperor because of his independent policy and his friendship for the English. There is no evidence for such a charge, and no hint of it in the account of Amiot, the Jesuit missionary who happened to be in Peking at the time. Even if the Chinese themselves remained little affected by the death of this hierarch from the barbarian mountains, the Manchu rulers were genuinely sorrowful, and there is a ring of obvious sincerity in the quotation Amiot gives from the letter the septuagenarian Emperor wrote to the Dalai Lama when the remains of the Panchen Lama, embalmed by boiling in butter and enclosed in a golden coffin shaped like a Buddhist temple, were sent back to rest among the bodies of his predecessors in the monastery of Tashilunpo.

> Although I am well aware that to come and go are but the same thing to the Panchen Lama [wrote the Son of Heaven to the Lord of Compassion] yet when I reflect that he made a most long and painful journey for the sole purpose of doing honour to me, and that after having fulfilled that object it was not his fate to return in tranquillity, as I had hoped, to the place of his usual abode, this reflection is distressing to me beyond all expression.

Hastings' plans for the reunion of Bogle and the Panchen Lama were doubly doomed, for by the time the news of the Tibetan hierarch's death had reached Calcutta, Bogle himself was dead. The past two years had seen a steady progress in his career. When it was realized that he would be unable to accompany the Panchen Lama into China, he had received his appointment as Collector at Rangpur, so that he might be near to Tibet (he was within sight of the hills of Bhutan, as he told his sister), and while he was there he established an annual fair for the traders from Bhutan. The first fair took place in 1780, and Bogle reported that 'there was a great concourse of Bhutan merchants, who, having been excused all duties and left to the freedom of their own will in buying and selling, went away very well satisfied'. He thought of making a trip into Bhutan and perhaps beyond, though, as he told his brother Robert, 'I shall regret the absence of my friend the Teshu Lama, for whom I have a hearty liking, and should be happy again to have his fat hand on my head.' Instead of going north into the healthy mountains, Bogle was called south to the unhealthy plains. Hastings had more than once lamented the absence of Bogle at Rangpur, since it robbed him of the services of an able writer of despatches with a fine touch of legal casuistry, and in January 1781 the Governor General wrote the fatal letter which recalled Bogle from Rangpur to take his place in a Committee of Revenue that would be in charge of the collection of taxes in all the provinces of India. 'If you are pleased with your appointment to it, come immediately to Calcutta. If you are not, stay where you are, and I will nominate another; but I shall be sorry to lose you.' Bogle's loyalty to Hastings overbore his desire to remain at Rangpur; he returned to Calcutta, and on the 3rd April, immediately after his arrival, he died of cholera, not yet thirty-five years of age.

The deaths, so close together, of Bogle and the Panchen Lama closed a chapter in Anglo-Tibetan relationships, and revealed the fragility of the contacts made up to the present. Whatever *rapprochement* had been made between the Company and Tibet had been founded on the liking and trust which two exceptional men of alien backgrounds had inspired in each other. Hamilton had died before Bogle, and now, apart from the equivocal Purangir Gosain, the Company lacked any representative with either a knowledge of Tibet or an acquaintance with the people with whom he might have to deal there. From the Company's side everything must begin anew.

On the Tibetan side, the death of the Panchen Lama had meant a complete dislocation of the delicate balance of power. In Tashilunpo there could be no ruler until the high abbots of the great monastery had located by esoteric signs the infant who would take the place of the departed (rather than deceased) Lobsang Palden Yeshe. Meanwhile the power at Tashilunpo fell into the hands of the late Panchen Lama's brother, who became Regent, and of Solpon Chenpo, neither of whom were men who could wield the power that had formerly emanated from Tashilunpo. In Lhasa, on the other hand, the Eighth Dalai Lama, though of age and awaiting formal installation, showed virtually no interest in temporal affairs, and the real power—in so far as it was not exercised by the Chinese ambans—remained in the hands of Tsomoling Nomenkhan, the Regent who had succeeded Demo Rimpoche; his policy, like that of all the Regents, was timid and conservative, aimed principally at the preservation of his own power, and the prevention of an independent policy on the part of the Panchen Lama and his followers. Always, in Tibet, the Regents and the ambans were natural allies, intent on preserving an appearance of tranquillity and of avoiding the attention of the Peking authorities.

But Hastings had no intention of abandoning his policy of seeking a closer link with Tibet, in the obstinately sustained hope that this might lead to a trading connection with western China and a political link, through Lhasa, with

Peking; when, in February 1782, Purangir Gosain returned from China via Tibet with messages of friendship from the Regent of Tashilunpo, and, shortly afterwards, the news reached Calcutta that the incarnation of the Panchen Lama had been found in a small child, Hastings resolved to send as quickly as possible a mission to Bhutan which would seek entry into Tibet with the avowed aim of congratulating the Panchen Lama on his return in a new body.

# X

## *Turner's Mission*

Not until the beginning of 1783 was Hastings ready to assemble the second or—if one counts Hamilton's two abortive journeys—the fourth British mission into Tibet. To lead it he chose Samuel Turner, a Lieutenant in the military service of the East India Company; Turner was also Hastings' first cousin, the son of his wife's sister, but nepotism seems to have entered into the appointment only in so far as Hastings may have been influenced by the Indian inclination to trust a kinsman more than a stranger, for Turner, if one can judge from the style and substance of the account he wrote of his journey, was intelligent and not lacking in the tact that is needed in diplomatic missions everywhere, but especially in the East. Hastings, who was a good and objective judge of character, considered Turner to be Bogle's equal in 'patience and understanding', and if, when the expedition set off, he remarked: 'I expect no great things from Turner's Embassy, but it will at least satisfy curiosity', this was not because of any sense of Turner's incapacity, but because he realized that the situation at Tashilunpo, while the Panchen Lama was still an infant, was not likely to be productive of great immediate results. The important thing was not to let what has been gained slip away, and Turner was certainly competent to achieve this.

What Turner appears to have lacked was Bogle's power of

183

empathy, for though he found the Tibetans as genial as his predecessor, he never experienced the same emotional attachment towards them. Also, though he had a clear and observant eye, his interests were not so varied as Bogle's, and his power of generalizing from details and assessing patterns of politics and trade was not so great. He combined, with an interest in the exotic, some of the dash one expects of a young officer in the Indian service, and there is a brittle Anglo-Saxon detachment about his narrative that differentiates it from the warm involvement which enters into Bogle's journal almost as soon as he crosses from Bhutan into Tibet. But in justice one must admit that Turner was at a disadvantage from the very fact that for the greater part of his journey he was following the path taken by his predecessor, so that one has the feeling on reading his *Account* that he is merely filling in with detail the outline sketched out by Bogle. Yet it is only fair to remember that for many years Turner's was the sole English account of Tibet available to the general public, and that all British conceptions of the country up to 1876 were shaped by what he had to tell.

To accompany Turner, whose commission was issued on the 8th January, 1783, Hastings picked two companions. Remembering Hamilton's success with the Thunderbolt Sow, Hastings evidently realized how much trust could be built up through the presence of a medical man who was willing to put his skill at the service of dignitaries along the route; Dr. Robert Saunders was chosen for this role. The other member of the mission was Lieutenant Samuel Davis, a military engineer, and, like so many of his kind in the eighteenth century, an excellent topographical artist.

To take advantage of the dry winter weather, Turner and his companions set out from Calcutta soon after they had received instructions, and made their way north by water and land to Rangpur, where they awaited the passports from the Deb Raja which they needed to enter Bhutan. As soon as these arrived, they travelled through the Buxa Duar, by the same route as that used by Bogle. Following Hastings' instructions, Turner kept a detailed journal of events and observations, noting carefully the number of miles from village to village, while Davis took observations of the sun to determine latitudes and sketched assiduously as he went. Thus the very fact that it was led by military men rather than by civilian officers gave the journey a professional character from the beginning. This did not go unnoticed by the Deb Raja's representatives, who accompanied Turner from Buxa Duar; given the suspicion which scientific observations of their countries have always aroused in Himalayan rulers jealous of their isolation, it was not surprising that Davis's observations should later influence the course of the expedition. Bogle had behaved less obtrusively, more prudently.

In Tassisudon, Turner negotiated with the Deb Raja— —the same as Hamilton had met in 1777—over the final cession of the disputed lands discussed during the last mission, and then corresponded by messenger with the Regent in Tashilunpo, who was Chanzo Cusho, the brother of the late Panchen Lama, who had left Bogle so unimpressed. While the arrangements regarding the party's entry into Tibet were being laboriously determined, the Bhutanese showed their chronic turbulence by staging a revolt similar to that which had taken place during Bogle's visit ten years before. This time a chieftain in the valley of Punakha attempted to overthrow the reigning Deb Raja. Though the centre of the revolt was only 24 miles from Tassisudon, the mountainous terrain protected the capital, and after a few weeks of disorganized fighting the chieftain's fortress was captured, and Turner and his companions were allowed to visit Punakha.

Finally, after three months, the embassy set off for Tibet. Only Turner and Saunders were allowed to enter the country; Davis was kept out on the nominal grounds that the authorities in Tashilunpo could admit no more Englishmen than on the previous occasion, when Bogle had been accompanied only by Hamilton. In fact, it was Davis's too obviously displayed talents as a topographer and military engineer that closed the frontier to him. Once again, Purangir Gosain accompanied the party.

They left on the 8th September, and followed in reverse the route Bogle had taken on his return in 1774. They reached Tashilunpo on the 22nd September after two weeks of pleasant autumn travel. On the way, in the valley of the Painam, they had been shown a white house just visible through a screen of unusually large willow trees. It was the birthplace of the infant Panchen Lama, and when Turner and his party rode past it the child hierarch was still living there with his father and mother. Though there is no necessary connection between blood relationship and the incarnations of Tibetan Lamas, the fact remains that the incidence of such phenomena tends to run in families; the new Panchen Lama was the cousin of the Dalai Lama.

Turner and Saunders stayed in Tashilunpo more briefly than Bogle; they departed on the 2nd December, after less than ten weeks, during which they had long and interesting but ultimately frustrating discussions with the Regent and with Solpon Chenpo, the former Panchen Lama's cup bearer, who retained his influence under the new régime.

There was an obvious reluctance on the part of the Regent to allow Turner to see the young Panchen Lama, who he assured him was the same person as his predecessor, but incapable of action because of the infant body in which he found himself. Shortly after the arrival of the British mission, the young ruler was brought, with great pomp, from his home in the Painam valley to the monastery of Terpaling, west of the main road to Gyantse and about two days' journey to the south of Tashilunpo. Turner and Saunders were not allowed to accompany the Regent who had gone to bring the Panchen Lama to his new home; this may well have been because of the presence of Chinese envoys.

Turner was more impressed than Bogle had been by the power of the Chinese in Tibet, and there does appear to have been an increase in their numbers and activities during the intervening decade. The Chinese envoys who had taken part in the ceremonials at Terpaling returned by way of Tashilunpo, and while they were there Turner could not help being impressed by the ambivalence which the Tibetans exhibited towards them. Every Tibetan hesitation or timidity of conduct was blamed on the authority of the Chinese. At the same time, while the British envoys were entertained in the Panchen Lama's palace at Tashilunpo, the Regent would not allow their Chinese counterparts even to sleep within the walls of the monastery, and Turner noticed the great secrecy with which everything that concerned local affairs was concealed from them. When the Chinese departed, everybody in the little court at Tashilunpo seemed relieved, and the relations between Turner and his hosts became much more relaxed.

Turner discovered that it was not only Chinese influence that posed a rivalry to the Company's ambitions in Tibet. He detected the beginning of that Russian interest in Tibet which a hundred and twenty years later was to be the excuse for the Younghusband Expedition to Lhasa. The Regent and Solpon Chenpo told him that the Russians had on several occasions attempted to open trade connections with northern Tibet, but neither Lhasa nor Tashilunpo had encouraged them. However, these overtures had led to a certain knowledge of Russia among Tibetans, for whom Catherine the Great occupied the same mysterious eminence as Queen Victoria in a later generation. The Russians, perhaps understandably in view of their territorial drive into northern Asia, had paid more attention to Mongolia than to Tibet, but since the Mongols were adherents of the Gelugpa sect, the hierarchs of Lhasa and Tashilunpo felt a special responsibility for them, and inevitably became involved when the Taranatha Lama, the ranking hierarch of Urga, wrote to the late Panchen Lama for advice. He sent on the presents he had received from Catherine; one of them, which Turner saw, was a Bible illuminated by Russian icon painters. The Panchen Lama had advised the Taranatha Lama to limit his concessions to the Russians to a minor trading post. There is no sign that either Turner or the Tibetans in Tashilunpo regarded the Russians as the kind of threat they became long afterwards in the mind of Lord Curzon. But that was before the Tsarist armies had made their drive southward into Central Asia, before the great mysterious cities of Bokhara and Samarkand had fallen into their hands, and before their power, extending to the Pamirs, stood divided only by Kashmir from the western marches of Tibet.

Like Bogle, Turner had not been without the ambition to proceed from Tashilunpo to Lhasa, where he would have liked to represent Hastings at the forthcoming installation of the Dalai Lama, who had now come of age. But the impossibility of this was soon evident; though, in the Tibetan manner, the Regent at Tashilunpo clothed refusal in consolatory statements. The Dalai Lama himself was really very friendly to the English; the trouble was the new Regent who was even more jealous of foreign intervention than his predecessor. As for himself, there was little he could do against the obstinacy of Lhasa and the threat of the Chinese, but when the Panchen Lama became of age, it would be another matter. Meanwhile, Solpon Chenpo, talking separately to Turner, magnified the difficulties in securing consent to admit the English even as far as Tashilunpo.

It was obvious that the Regent and Solpon Chenpo wished to maintain an independent centre of power in Tashilunpo, and for this reason were anxious to maintain their links with the British. But neither had the personality or the influence of the late Panchen Lama, and so the whole tale of their meetings with Turner leaves one with a deep sense of inadequacy, and not on the Tibetan side alone. Never—at least in Tashilunpo—occurred a complex of sympathetic encounters like that which endeared the Tibetans and especially the Panchen Lama to Bogle. Perhaps Turner was more reserved; possibly he was more insensitive. Yet at the very end of his stay in Tibet there was an extraordinary intrusion of emotion—even a touch of the marvellous—that forms the high point of his narrative.

During his stay in Tashilunpo Turner had been allowed to wander freely in the grounds of the great monastery, where he attended ceremonies as Bogle had done and visited the tomb of the late Panchen Lama. He was also free to wander in the immediate environs of Tashilunpo, but not to visit the young Panchen Lama in Terpaling on the grounds that the Emperor of China had sent a special message on the occasion of the discovery of the infant incarnation, enjoining the Regent to conduct his education in complete privacy and to give strangers no access to him.

When Turner left Tashilunpo, however, he evidently protested that he must have at least one opportunity to wait on the young Panchen Lama if only to lay before him the presents which Hastings had sent; the Regent appears to have given a reluctant consent, though he was careful not to be

189

present on the occasion, doubtless calculating that in this way he would avoid blame in Lhasa and Peking.

Turner and his party left Tashilunpo on the 2nd December, reaching Terpaling on the evening of the following day. The next morning they had their audience with the child Lama, then eighteen months old. He was seated on a throne, dressed in miniature as a Gelugpa hierarch, with his father and mother standing beside him. Turner was immediately struck by his beauty and by the peculiar intelligence and earnestness of his glance as he watched the presents being laid out before him: a jewelled watch, pearls, coral ear-rings, Russian cloth and silver cups filled with spices from Hastings; gold brocade from Turner himself. Turner had been told that the child, though he could not yet speak, understood perfectly what was said to him, and, as if addressing an adult ruler, he spoke to him with an air of solemn respect, telling how:

> ... the Governor-General, on receiving news of his decease in China, was overwhelmed with grief and sorrow, and continued to lament his absence from the world until the cloud that had overcast the happiness of the nation was dispelled by his reappearance, and then, if possible, a greater degree of joy had taken place than he had experienced of grief on receiving the first mournful news. The Governor anxiously wished that he might long continue to illumine the world by his presence, and was hopeful that the friendship which had formerly subsisted between them would not be diminished, but rather that it might become still greater than before; and that by his continuing to show kindness to my countrymen there might be an extensive communication between his votaries and the dependents of the British nation.

It was a scene that had all the makings of farce—the young British officer in his braided uniform addressing in orotund and formal phrases the tiny child in his incongruous robes, yet none of the witnesses thought it ludicrous, nor did Turner himself, so extraordinary he found the young Lama's response. 'The little creature looked steadfastly towards me, with the appearance of much attention while I spoke, and nodded with repeated but slow movements of the head, as though he understood every word, but could not utter a reply.' His impression of the Panchen Lama's precocity was so strong that when he later told Hastings of it, the Governor General was so impressed that for a moment he wondered whether there was not a shadow of truth in the Tibetan belief that the deceased Panchen Lama, with all his intelligence, had indeed been reincarnated; on consideration, he decided to consider it an extraordinary instance, of a kind never seen in the west, of 'the effect of education on the infant mind'.

As for the Tibetans, they were delighted by the obvious emotion of Turner and his companion, Dr. Saunders, which they erroneously attributed to an awakening of belief. Their record, presented by Schuyler Camann in his *Trade Through the Himalayas* (Princeton, 1951), gives an interesting, if rather oblique, view of the occasion.

> Although (the visitors) were not knowers of the niceties of religion, by merely gazing (at the young Panchen) an irresistible faith was born in them. And they said: 'In such a little frame there are activities of body, speech and mind, so greatly marvelous and different from the other.' Thus they spoke with great reverence.

Turner's behaviour won him a friend in the Panchen Lama's father, a great sportsman, with whom, in the discussion of shooting and archery, Turner established something like the rapport which Bogle had established on a rather less mundane level with the late Panchen Lama. The father promised to use his influence in the English cause, but it was obvious that he possessed little.

After a further audience with the Panchen Lama, Turner and Saunders set off on the 7th December on their journey back to India, bearing a letter and presents from the Regent. They followed the route by which they had come, staying for a few days with the Deb Raja at his winter palace of Punakha, and, after inconclusive conversations, leaving on the 30th December. Travelling via Rangpur, they proceeded up the Ganges to Patna, where, in March 1784, Turner submitted his report to Hastings.

Turner added little in an exploratory sense to Bogle's achievement (except for his small divagations to Punakha and Terpaling), and in diplomatic terms he added nothing at all, gaining no important concession, and, at best, merely sustaining the goodwill Bogle had established. Undoubtedly the situation in Tibet, divided between the rulers of Tashilunpo and Lhasa and more dominated than before by Chinese influence, was inimical to any hope of profitable contact, yet Turner had few of the modest misgivings which Bogle had displayed on returning from his mission, and talked as if the establishment of trade would be 'the sure basis of an intercourse with China'.

This was the last of the East India Company's official missions to Tibet, but interest did not end there; in fact, for a brief period there was a stimulation of activity, revolving around the personality of Purangir Gosain, who now came into his own as the leading envoy of the East India Company. Clearly, Hastings at last took notice of the late Panchen Lama's remark to Bogle that it would be better if a Hindu were sent than a European. Out of four missions led by English and Scots, two had not even been allowed to enter Tibet, and the other two had got no farther than Tashilunpo and had returned with no definite agreement regarding the future relations between Bengal and Tibet.

7. Tibetan Yak

8. The Mausoleum of the Panchen Lama who entertained Bogle

Hastings decided to try what could be done through non-European channels. It was Purangir Gosain who represented the Company in October 1784 when the young Panchen Lama was installed in his abbey at Tashilunpo in the presence of the Dalai Lama, the Lhasa Regent, the Chinese ambans, and the abbots of the great Gelugpa monasteries, and who on that occasion brought back presents from the Tashilunpo Regent and assurances of a desire to continue friendly relations. It was Purangir Gosain who led the 'adventure' of Indian merchants which Hastings had set about organizing in 1784 immediately after Turner's return, to try whether a non-European trading caravan would actually be allowed to enter Tibet. The merchants were guaranteed exemption from duty, and a respectable number of them set off in 1785, loaded with a miscellaneous cargo of cloth, cheap watches and clocks, smelling-salts and scissors, conch shells, corals and indigo, pieces of amber, and the imperfect pearls which the Tibetans preferred to the perfect ones. They were allowed to pass through Bhutan and to proceed into Tibet, and returned, after good trading, with yak tails and wool, silver and gold dust and musk.

It was the only 'adventure' of its kind. By the time Purangir Gosain returned at the end of 1785, Hastings had resigned as Governor General and returned to England. Macpherson, who replaced him temporarily, appears to have been interested in developing the Tibetan trade, but Cornwallis, who arrived as Governor General in 1786, was mainly indifferent to the prospect of trade with Bhutan and Tibet. Still Purangir Gosain flitted between Tashilunpo and Calcutta, and the idea of Tibet as a way to China made fitful and mirage-like appearances in the minds of East India men. When Colonel Cathcart was instructed to go to China in 1787 there was talk of sending him through Tibet; there was a never-realized scheme in 1789 to send Purangir Gosain that way to Jehol; in 1792 the idea of the Tibetan route again cropped up in connection with the mission of Lord Macartney to Peking.

By this time, however, events in the Himalayas had killed the possibility of developing in any meaningful way the relations between the Company and the rulers of Tibet. In 1788 the Gurkhas invaded Tibet, and the Regent of Tashilunpo wrote to Cornwallis requesting his help. One cannot in hindsight judge what Hastings would have done, but it is hard to believe that he would have replied quite so crudely as Cornwallis, who promised merely that he would take neither side in the war, and remarked that if he had been in contact with Peking he might have acted differently. The implication that he was placing a price on his assistance was obvious. But by the time he wrote it was already too late; the Tibetans had bought peace at the expense of a large indemnity. In 1791 the Gurkhas attacked again and sacked Tashilunpo; this time a Chinese army marched westward and roundly defeated them.

As a result of these events British credit in Tashilunpo disappeared and any friendliness Bogle created vanished with it, while the Chinese established themselves more firmly than ever as the overlords of Tibet. In the years that followed, the East India Company was occupied with winning and consolidating its great empire in India, at the expense of Moghuls, Mahrattas and Mysore, and interest in the Himalayan region declined so far that in 1811, when an Englishman appeared with the intent of travelling into Tibet, he received only lukewarm assistance from the authorities in Calcutta, and when he returned, having done what Bogle and Turner had failed to do, his achievement was virtually ignored. He was Thomas Manning, who reached Lhasa.

# Part II

# LHASA  ATTAINED

# XI

## *The Unlikely Hero*

When Bogle started on his journey, Thomas Manning was
not yet a year old. Like so many Englishmen whose achievements echo in the long tunnel of the imperial past, he was
the son of a country clergyman, born in the Rectory of
Broome, in Norfolk. He grew up to become a man of many
promises, and his friend Charles Lamb told Crabb Robinson
that he thought Manning 'the most *wonderful* man he ever
knew, more extraordinary than Wordsworth and Coleridge'.

When Crabb Robinson, in 1824, noted in his journal
Lamb's opinion on Manning, he added a revealing comment: 'Yet this Manning does nothing. He has travelled
even in China, and has been on land from India through
Tibet, yet as far as is known he has written nothing.' It is
hard not to share Robinson's bewilderment at this man of
talent who might have been so many things, yet, except for
his single achievement of travelling to Lhasa, enters history
only as the shadow of greater men.

A brilliant student at Cambridge, Manning left the university degreeless because—though he was not a dissenter—he
found the oaths and religious tests that were required two
centuries ago repugnant to him. Living afterwards as a tutor
in Cambridge, he published a brilliant *Introduction to Arith-
metic and Algebra*, and then abandoned a career as a mathe-
matician to follow the passionate interest which he developed

round about 1800 in the Chinese language and the general culture it represented. Over many years of study he was to gather a vast knowledge of matters Sinological, yet in the end he produced as evidence of this vast labour a most negligible mouse in the form of a series of translations of Chinese jokes which in 1826 he published in the *New Monthly Magazine*. He became the friend of Charles Lamb, provoked him to write his most eloquent letters and through him moved in the most influential literary circles of his time, making the acquaintance—and never quite acquiring the friendship—of Coleridge and Wordsworth, of Hazlitt and Godwin. Yet he remains a puzzling background figure in the literary London of the immediately pre-Victorian age, represented in print—apart from a few brief and uninteresting fragments—by his Tibetan journal, published only in 1876, and his letters to Lamb, published only in 1925, long after his death; the letters disappointingly revealed the inspirer and hero of Lamb in the character of an irritating and facetious pedant.

There is in fact, for all Manning's promise and all his opportunities, only one reason to recall him from oblivion: his achievement in reaching Lhasa. And that achievement—ironically—was a failure in Manning's eyes, for the Tibetan capital was the point at which he was turned back from his great objective, the imperial city of Peking. That objective he did gain, five years after his return from Lhasa, when he went there with the embassy of Lord Amherst, but it was in the end a victory so diluted by humiliating circumstances that Manning never afterwards found it a reason for boasting. He ended his life a disappointed, embittered man, withdrawing into an eccentric isolation that was darkly shadowed by paranoia, and the one feat by which he is remembered as something more than the friend of Charles Lamb seemed to him in the end—and perhaps even at the time—of negligible importance. Perhaps that is one of the reasons why he must be counted among the true travellers; he regarded no place as a real destination.

Manning's interest in China, which led him to Tibet, appeared while he was still acting as a tutor at Cambridge, a young man of yet untested brilliance and of clear-cut intelligent features, which appear on the portrait painting now in the possession of the Royal Asiatic Society. Whence the interest emerged we cannot tell, but it is certain that by the time he met Lamb he was already sufficiently engrossed in his Chinese studies to be aware that he could not follow them adequately in England. As early as August 1801 Lamb was rallying him on the intention he had expressed to travel into the Orient.

> I *heard* you were going to China, with a commission from the Wedgwoods to collect hints for their pottery, and to teach the Chinese *perspective*. But I did not know that *London* lay on your way to Pekin. I am seriously glad of it, for I shall trouble you with a small present for the Emperor of Usbeck Tartary, as you go by his territories: it is a fragment of a 'Dissertation on the state of political parties in England at the end of the eighteenth century,' which will no doubt be very interesting to his Imperial Majesty.

The reference to the 'Emperor of Usbeck Tartary' suggests that even at this early date Manning had been speculating on the possibility of travelling to China overland through Central Asia.

In fact, in November 1801 he did leave England. He went, not to China, but to France, to study under the distinguished Sinologist, Dr. Hagaz. 'I am learning the Chinese language,' he told Lamb. 'I expect next spring to set off on my voyage to China.' In the autumn of 1802 he went on his first real travels, if one excepts the brief cross-channel journey to Paris, and toured Switzerland, north Italy, Savoy and the Midi before returning to Paris for a winter of study. His comments on Switzerland, in which he compares the scenery of the Alps with that of the much lesser mountains of the English lakes, which Lamb had just visited, form an interesting anticipation of his later reactions to the Himalayas.

So you have really visited the Lakes. Your Eye has reposed on the silent forms of the Mountains & on the limpid bosom of Derwentwater. You have done well—you have seen the choicest spot in Europe, compared with which the scenery in Switzerland is clumsy & graceless. In the wildest part of Switzerland you have precipices & rocks in your path, a deep deep hollow beneath you, along which a torrent falls with ungovernable fury, dashing from rock to rock with the Vilest uproar; & looking up among the Clouds, & above them, your eye is struck with the cold dazzling of the never-melting snows. This is what you cannot see in the north of England; & tis what many people even who visit Switzerland see but little of. But for the rest, the north of E. is far more interesting.

Manning could not start for China in 1803, for that year the brief peace of Amiens was broken, and Britain was at war again in France. He appears to have been unmolested in France and, indeed, treated with some respect, for his studies in Chinese had aroused the interest of Carnot and Talleyrand, and finally, in 1805, they obtained a passport for him to leave France, on his promise that he would proceed to China and carry on his researches there. The story that permission was granted by Napoleon himself after having conversed at length with Manning, is untrue, though Manning did, as part of the correspondence relating to his departure, write to the Emperor what the editors of his letters describe as 'a very humble note'.

Manning spent most of 1805 in Cambridge and later in London where, by the autumn, he was taking a rapid course in medicine at Westminster Hospital. 'Manning's come to town in spectacles, and studies physic,' Lamb told Hazlitt, 'is melancholy, and seems to have something in his head, which he doesn't impart.' The 'something in his head' was doubtless the sustained intention of reaching China; he was studying medicine to acquire the knowledge that would—according to the lax standards of the day—pass him off as a physician when he reached Asia. 'Manning is not gone to China,' Lamb communicated to Hazlitt in February, 1806, 'but talks of going this Spring. God forbid!'

Manning hoped at this time, as Mary Lamb revealed in one of her letters, to make his way through Russia into China, 'but he found so many difficulties in the way that he gave up the idea'. He therefore decided to reach China by ship, and to do this in the beginning of the eighteenth century it was imperative to arouse the interest of the East India Company, since they had the power to dictate who should go from England to the part of Canton to which Europeans were restricted, and on their favour depended a passage on the East Indiamen, the great sailing ships that brought the tea from China to Europe and returned loaded with trade goods for India and Canton.

Lamb was a useful if rather unwilling contact with the East India Company, but more was needed than the recommendation of a humble clerk in the Company's employ, and in March, 1806, Manning approached Sir Joseph Banks, President of the Royal Society, known for his willingness to assist scholars who were anxious to carry on their studies abroad. Manning told Banks that he wanted the opportunity to live among the Chinese, faithfully adopting their dress and manners, so that he could learn to speak their language exactly. Banks transmitted Manning's wishes to the Company's Court of Directors, adding his own recommendation of 'this very amiable young man, both on account of his mild character and the energies of his mind'.

Manning's plea was accepted by the Company, and early in May he sailed by the *Thames* East Indiaman, to Lamb's great sorrow. 'I didn't know what your going was,' the essayist exclaimed in a letter sent to intercept Manning at Portsmouth, 'till I shook a last fist with you, and then 'twas just like having shaken hands with a wretch on the fatal scaffold, and when you are down the ladder, you can never stretch out to him again.' 'I am not dead nor dying,' Manning replied from Portsmouth; 'some people go into Yorkshire for 4 years & never come to London all the while! I go to China. What's the difference to our London friends?'

It was, as always before the advent of steamships, an exasperatingly slow journey. Manning reached the Cape of Good Hope in August, and Canton late in 1806. There he was allowed to stay in the English factory, to practise medicine among such as chose to demand his services (and there appear to have been few of them), to use the excellent library which the East India Company provided, and to learn Chinese as best he could. To amuse himself, he started to grow a beard in that age when beards, among Englishmen, were out of fashion, and in April 1807 he boasted to Lamb that it was already five inches long. In his more serious avocations he was less successful. The tightly restricted compound in which the European factories and their inhabitants were kept by the Manchu authorities left little scope for mingling with the Chinese, apart from a few servants and the handful of merchants who were allowed to trade with foreigners. Except for a few villainous streets immediately around the factories, Canton was out of bounds to foreigners, and among the many regulations the mandarins imposed was one that forbade Chinese under dire penalties to teach their language to the red-haired foreign devils who lived on sufferance among them. It is true that there were means of learning Chinese under these unpromising circumstances, particularly during the winter season when the Europeans moved en bloc to the Portuguese colony of Macao, where intercourse with the local Chinese was less inhibited, and in these conditions some notable works were actually carried out, such as the Chinese grammar and the Chinese–English dictionary compiled by Robert Morrison, who arrived shortly after Manning to become the first Protestant missionary in China.

What Manning learnt—and in March 1808 he was able to tell Lamb 'I begin to talk a little China'—was probably gleaned in Macao, for the unnamed Chinese who later accompanied him to Lhasa came from there, but he found such opportunities insufficient, and as early as the autumn of 1807 he was trying to get into China itself.

> I have been petitioning Mandarins for leave to go to Peking as ASTRONOMER AND PHYSICIAN (not astrologer & quack Doctor). They refuse as yet to send my petition to the
>
> EMPEROR
>
> but I have not given them up; they shall hear from me again shortly. I have made them speak: & that's something.

Something perhaps, but not enough, for by the following spring Manning had abandoned his hopes of entering China directly from Canton, and had obtained permission to join a surveying ship, the *Discovery*, commanded by Lieutenant Ross, which was sailing from Macao to the coast of Cochin-China, where he hoped to land in the Annamese robes with which he had provided himself, and to make his way to Peking. 'I shall soon see the Emperor & shall perhaps feel his pulse!' he told Lamb.

The trip to Cochin-China was a total failure so far as Manning's aims were concerned. He blamed Lieutenant Ross for arriving too late on the coast of Cochin-China for him to make his travel arrangements, and in default of them he was forced to accompany the *Discovery* on its survey trip in the Paracel Islands, almost two hundred miles off the coast of Cochin-China.

> A grievous bore, to say no worse of it [he told his father]. We found the Paracels in all their hideous deformity— breakers—sandbanks—coral rocks &c &c, turtles, shell- fish, wailing sea-birds so unused to man that they would not rise from their nests. Fishermen from Hainan visit these places for the sake of Turtle, Biche de mer, & other sea productions—what is very curious, the first object we saw on the very first Islet we came to (& that was before we put into Turon) was a large China Vessel wrecked, and a surprisingly numerous crew in great distress on the shore. We saved them all; they amounted to 561 souls. Their Gratitude was unspeakable. Our ships were noisomely crowded with them. We made for Turon directly, where we landed them all. Their original crew, on leaving Amoy (a Port to the eastward of Canton, in the next province), amounted, they say, to about 700; partly poor passengers, going out to seek a livelihood at Batavia, or other European settlements. Some had been drowned. Some had gone off in their boat. . . . I saw a little of the Villages of the coast of Cochin-China, but that was not my object. I lost my time—I can hardly bear even now to think of it with patience.

They returned in July, 1808, and Manning represented himself then as struggling hard to make up for time lost. 'The veil'd Mysteries of the Chinese language gradually open

upon my view.' There were times when he sank into enjoy-
ment of the high living that was a feature of the English
factory at Canton. 'I've dined, & am ruined,' he ended a
letter to Lamb in 1809. 'My ideas are obtundaded, fattened,
oil'd, quenched, overlaid, stuffed, greased, spoil'd!' Yet the
desire to enter China and make his way into the presence of
the Emperor continued to provoke him. What led him to
decide on Tibet as a route of access is not certain. It may
have been Turner's *Account*, which had reached the library
of the Canton factory by 1809, and which we know he read.
It may have been merely a process of eliminating the routes
that had already appeared impossible. Whatever his in-
spiration, by the beginning of 1810 he was on his way to
Calcutta with the intention of undertaking the vast journey
to Peking through Tibet.

He carried with him a letter from the Company's Select
Committee in Canton, addressed to Lord Minto, the
Governor General.

> The object of this gentleman's visit to China has been to
> qualify himself, by studying the Chinese language and
> customs, to explore the country. In these pursuits he has
> made considerable progress, but finding his ultimate views
> impracticable from this quarter, he proceeds to Calcutta,
> and will personally explain his further plans. As we con-
> sider Mr. Manning eminently qualified for the task he has
> undertaken, we anxiously hope your lordship will not con-
> sider it improper to afford Mr. Manning every practical
> assistance in the prosecution of his plans, and this we beg
> to solicit in his behalf.

In the steamy height of June he reached Calcutta.

# XII

## *The Way to Lhasa*

'Just going to leave Calcutta for God knows where!'
Manning wrote to Lamb on the 11th October, 1810. 'Very
strange in mind—cannot write. Give one of these boxes of
India Ink to Mary & the other to my brother Edward when
you see him. I'll write to you before I am out of the bounds
of civilization.'

In fact, it was almost a year before Manning got 'out of
the bounds of civilization', for it was in September 1811,
as we know from his own records, that he left Cooch Behar
on his way into Bhutan. The time since he reached Calcutta
—more than a year—had been spent urgently soliciting the
aid of the East India Company, and behaving in a way that
effectively cancelled out his solicitations.

I cannot help explaining in my mind (as I often do),
[noted Manning in his diary just after he had crossed the
pass from Bhutan and was waiting for events at Phari]
what fools the Company are to give me no commission,
no authority, no instructions. What use are their embassies,
when their ambassador cannot speak to a soul, and can
only make ordinary phrases pass through a stupid interpreter? No *finesse*, no *tournure*, no compliments. Fools, fools,
fools, to neglect an opportunity they may never have
again!

The outburst was typical of the man, in its immoderate-
ness, its injustice and at the same time its underlying truth.

If Manning was referring to the envoys who had gone before him, it is true that Turner never gained a great knowledge of Tibetan, and that Bogle began to speak the language fluently only after months at Tashilunpo. But Manning himself was in this respect no better equipped than they, since he knew no Tibetan to begin with, and learnt far less than Bogle by the time he returned to India. What he could offer was only a fluency of reading and a halting power of speech in *Chinese*, the language of the overlords, not the natives of Tibet. Yet there was obviously an urgent sense of purpose in Manning when he arrived in Calcutta which the Company's officers did not utilize as fully as they might have done, and the fact that Manning went off to Tibet with no commission from the Company, and attended only by a single companion, is a fact curious enough to demand an explanation.

That explanation is not to be found entirely, as Clements Markham and other critics of Hastings' successors have suggested, in the small-mindedness of petty men in office. Lord Minto, incumbent Governor General, was a man not inferior to Warren Hastings in the breadth of his vision; one remembers the encouragement he gave to Stamford Raffles, the founder of Singapore, and there is no doubt that initially he regarded Manning's project with interest and goodwill. To the Select Committee's letter of recommendation he replied on the 16th June, 1810, 'We shall not fail to pay due attention to your recommendation of Mr. Manning by affording him every practical assistance in the prosecution of his scientific pursuits.'

It is, of course, one thing to provide facilities for a man's scientific pursuits, and another to turn him into an official envoy. Manning was, to begin with, unfortunate in the time he chose to arrive in Calcutta, for during the whole of 1810 and 1811 Minto was preoccupied with the problem of countering and finally destroying the power which Napoleon had gained in the Far East by acquiring, as a puppet realm, the empire which the Dutch had built up in the Indonesian archipelago. The Company's trade with China was in peril while French vessels could use Java as their base, and through 1810 Minto was occupied with building up in Malaya the forces needed to mount the great amphibian operation that led to the British capture of Java in 1811. It is not surprising that he and his subordinates did not choose to revive the interest in Tibet that had faded so completely since Cornwallis mishandled the situation created by the Gurkha war almost twenty years before.

Nor did Manning behave in a way that can have furthered his case. He chose to appear in Calcutta society, where for a time he was lionized, as an eccentric, and a rather contentious one. H. T. Prinsep, the pioneer archaeologist who first interpreted Ashoka's inscriptions and established the identity of the Greek kings of the Punjab, remembered Manning in 1811 with some amusement, for the visitor from Canton went around as if he were already embarked on his expedition, wearing 'a fancy dress, which he said was that of a Tatar gentleman' though, as Prinsep remarked, 'with his broad English face and full flowing beard', he looked 'as little like a Tatar as any son of Adam one might meet in London'. In this strange guise he would visit the Hindu temples and ostentatiously prostrate himself before the images. The ladies crowded around Manning in admiration of his beard, that forerunner of Victorian symbols of virility, but the men regarded him with growing distrust as he indulged in paradoxical conversation better suited to Lamb's London chambers than to a Calcutta drawing-room, and set up a carping criticism of their manners, their dress and

9. Thomas Manning (artist unknown)

18 The Potala at Lhasa. This illustration, from Kircher's *China Illustrated* (1667), is based on Father

their military customs. To us, who live after the sahibs, it is more amusing than it can have been to listeners in Fort William to dwell upon his barbed comments, such as the following passage from one of the vast footnotes to his journal.

When I was in India I used frequently to rally the absurdity of the English dress, by gravely observing how lucky it was the Russians had no settlement there, for their fur dresses would be an intolerable nuisance to them. The persons to whom I addressed it could not say, 'Oh, they would leave them off,' because they would be aware that I should say, 'No more than your neckcloth.' The warmth and thickness of a European's coat is not so great an evil, though evil enough in a hot climate, as the tightness of his clothing, which occasions throbbing, and a stifling sensation of heat and sweat, and probably may be very injurious to the health. He will deny, I know by experience, that his clothes are inconvenient, but his natural efforts to relieve himself betray the contrary. When he comes home in the evening, though he is not going to bed for an hour or two, does he not take off his neckcloth and unbutton his breeches' knees, with a pleased, inarticulate expression, denoting that he is somewhat relieved—that his blood has room to circulate? . . . The military gentlemen I have conversed with in India seem still more certain of the absolute necessity of wearing tight uniforms. They reject with scorn and contempt the idea of making any change, and consider the man that proposes a change as very ignorant of the duties of a soldier.

Imagine such men in uniform, being lectured by a bearded jester who boasted of the superiority of the loose oriental robes in which he paraded his originality through the best houses of Calcutta! It is unlikely that they would be inclined to regard him as fit to represent either the Honourable Company or His Majesty King George III among the grand hierarchs of Tibet. Manning claimed the jester's privilege, to mock his hosts; he earned the jester's reward, to be dismissed with laughter.

And so he set off to Tibet with no official commission, and with a minimum of assistance from the authorities, though they probably helped him more than he chose to admit, for the British representative in Cooch Behar certainly assisted him with introductions to the Bhutanese, without which he could not have crossed the frontier. He left Calcutta accompanied by a Chinese from Macao, a Catholic convert whom he refers to never by name, but sometimes as his 'servant' and more often as 'Munshi' (interpreter); the relationship was quite obviously something more than that between master and servant, and by the end Manning was to have had his fill of his companion's intractability. Together they travelled by the route which Bogle and Turner had both followed, by way of Dinajpur and Rangpur to the town of Cooch Behar. Here, having established his contacts with the Bhutanese, Manning abandoned the route followed by his predecessors and struck westward to enter Bhutan through the Lakhi Duar, a route never before taken by any European traveller, but chosen, it appears, because Manning had heard of its greater ease of ascent.

On the 7th September he entered Bhutan. Two of the English from Cooch Behar accompanied him as far as the borders of Bhutan, and on the other side of the frontier the official in charge of the little settlement of Cantalbary (or Kathalbari) sent out an escort to meet the travellers with music and bring them in on horseback, 'and I had a strange entry into Cantalbary, where I spent a great deal of money'. Here all his Indian servants left him except for one Chaprasi, and this did not entirely surprise him, for he noticed how the Bhutanese lorded it over the Indians who lived in this lower part of the Duar. Even the servant who had been attached to him 'was imperious, but it might be because I travelled by authority'. The first days, in the foothills, were pleasant enough, for it was still possible to travel on horseback, and he spent the night of the 10th September as the guest of a 'Bhutan friend', in 'a village on a hill about six miles from the mountains, pleasantly situated among orange and lime trees'.

It was the last day of easy travel for a long time ahead. Next day the way rose into the mountains, following the ravines through which the Tursa river found its way into the plains. The travellers reached a torrent, and there they were told the horses could go no farther. The headman of the next village came to guide Manning. 'I walked with him through water and over cruel stones above a mile, which brought me to a wretched pigsty of a place, and they said I was to stay there that night.' As it was still only midday, Manning refused, engaged porters and a guide, and started off for the next settlement, Tazigong, which was high in the mountains.

> The road passed over the bed of a torrent with cruel stones, and I was sometimes up to my middle in water.
> . . . I was tired when I arrived at the foot of the hill, and it was steep and stony, and my feet were sore, but we could not stop more than half an hour. I toiled up slowly, and with considerable difficulty. When I got to the top, my servant had palpitation, sweated profusely, eruption broke out, and next day he said his skin peeled away. I told him it would do him good, and prevent fever.

This was a wilder land than any Manning had seen before, wilder even than Switzerland, and for a man who had spent the last five years in the narrow setting of the Canton factory and under the punkahs of Calcutta houses, it was a hard beginning to the journey. Little wonder that when Manning

records those early days there is no mention of scenery and
very little of the people he met on the way. At Tazigong—
where Manning could see only one house—his last Indian
servant left him, and he was alone with his Chinese companion among strangers. He hired porters to carry them in
chairs on the day he left Tazigong, and for the next few days
tells only of the swinging bridges he crossed and the big,
three-storied houses in which he slept. The weather was bad;
there were rains as they went up through the mountains, and
at Matakah, near the head of the valley of the Tursa, which
Manning reached on the 19th September, he arrived wet
through, and let his clothes dry on his body.

> Afterwards, upon walking the room, I was seized with a
> violent palpitation. The insects disturbed me all night. I
> saw a lad gnawing a turnip, and called to him immedi-
> ately, and, showing it to my conductor, asked the name,
> and told him to give me plenty of it. I thus got an excel-
> lently well-dressed stew with turnips.

Beyond Matakah they had to climb on a high ridge, rising
to about 12,000 feet, before they came down into the Pachu
Valley and reached Paro. It took them two days, and in the
night they slept on the bare mountain, because there was no
village, nor even a house. 'Wet, wet, always rain.' The second
day they climbed still higher. 'I find going up hill does not
agree with me,' Manning noted with dark whimsicality,
'perhaps because naturally I am going down hill. Wet
above, wet below; hard stones all the way.' The travellers
were exhausted when they finally crossed the high bridge
over the river into Paro. Manning had managed to hire
a horse on the way down, and crossing the bridge he was
frightened lest the animal shy and fall into the rocky stream
below.

In Paro, which they reached on the 22nd September,

there was a delay during which it is obvious—though
Manning does not tell us so explicitly—that the Bhutanese
were deciding whether to allow him to continue on his
journey. They kept him closely under observation. He was
lodged 'in a guardhouse, with no window, and much smoke'.
For several days he was not allowed to go out, or to visit
the bazaar at Paro, and he complained bitterly because,
though the river flowed close by, the Bhutanese would not
let him have any fish. He was evidently unfamiliar with the
fact that the Buddhist peoples of the Himalayas, unlike the
Buddhists of Ceylon and South-East Asia, do not eat fish,
partly on the grounds that to do so involves the killing of
more living beings than if one remains content to eat the
flesh of large animals like cows and yaks.

It is likely that the Bhutanese had from the beginning seen
through the flimsy disguise Manning assumed, for he himself
was never very explicit about the role he played, representing
himself vaguely as 'a man from Calcutta', and all the time
proudly displaying his great beard. His case appears to have
aroused the attention of the authorities in Tassisudon, for he
was not allowed to go on his way until, on the 15th October,
three weeks after he had arrived in Paro, the Munshi, who
must have gone with a message to the Bhutanese capital,
returned with a lama sent by the Dewan 'to see how we
were, and whether everything was right'. The next afternoon, after great delays on the part of the servants and
porters, whom Manning was completely incapable of organizing, they set off in the late afternoon, Manning on horseback,
and at evening stopped in a hamlet four miles up the Pachu
Valley. Here occurred an incident that aroused the paranoia
always latent in Manning's mind. He found that his two
silver spoons had vanished and pewter ones had been substituted. The Munshi and the Bhutanese guide were, he

suspected, in league to rob him. He insisted that the Bhutanese go back for the spoons. Nothing was done that night
and the next morning Manning obstinately refused to go on
without his spoons. The Bhutanese went back and returned
with one silver spoon.

> I swore I would have the other, or go back myself and
> speak to the magistrate. This frightened my rascal: he
> sent the slave again, and he brought back the other. It was
> not the value, but the example. I am in bad, bad hands.

So they continued, the Munshi sulking until Manning
decided that 'a spaniel would be better company', and
Manning himself dispensing rupees and looking-glasses to
officials along the road, noting the presence of 'plenty of
priests and monks like those in Europe', observing with
pleasure the snow on the hills, delighted by the change to
clear, bright weather, and finding himself, perhaps as an
effect of the altitude, in a curious emotional condition.

> Strange sensation coming along: warm and comfortable.
> Horse walking in a lane between two stone walls. The
> snow! Where am I? How can I be come here? Not a soul
> to speak to. I wept almost through excess of sensation,
> not from grief.

Before leaving Bhutan, Manning called on a Lama and
arranged for prayers to be said for his welfare, 'going and
coming'. Then he crossed the pass into Tibet, an experience
which he described with remarkable economy of statement.
'Uphill. In a deserted house at night: could not sleep for the
insects and rats. Good-for-nothing horse.'

On the 21st October he reached Phari, where the temperature had fallen below freezing-point, and he and his companion were 'lodged in a strange place, but so are the natives',
a cryptic reference to the squat and ugly houses Bogle had
described. He had hardly arrived, when the two governors

of the town appeared to visit and to inspect him. Manning revealed himself as a somewhat tactless traveller. 'I took them for idle fellows (by mistake), and paid no respect to them.' This was clearly taken for foreign ignorance, which it was, rather than ill manners, which it also was, and when Manning went to the castle three days later, a collection of 'miserable galleries and holes', the magistrate who received him was the essence of politeness, presented him with a dried sheep and some rice, and urged him to call again for a longer visit. His experience with the monks of Phari was not so pleasing. He went to sell them some broadcloth he had brought with him for trading, using as interpreter a woman who spoke a little Chinese, but at the end of the transaction he found that the holy men had been the better traders and had roundly cheated him.

Yet on the whole he had reason to be content with his reception at Phari. It was clear that he enjoyed an advantage in going as an individual rather than the representative of the Company. There was no question of high policy involved in his presence, and the Tibetans appear to have been content to accept him as some strange kind of Asian, without attempting to state the suspicions they must have harboured. Perhaps, in any case, the local officials had decided to leave the whole embarrassing question to be settled by the Chinese mandarin—a high military officer—who was to reach Phari in a few days.

The general's entourage arrived by instalments. First came a batch of soldiers; Manning was turned out of his lodging to make way for them. 'The new room had dirty floors, and was rather cold. We cook for ourselves. Dirt, dirt, grease, smoke. Misery, but good mutton.' Three days later the general's Tibetan interpreter arrived, and the next day the general himself. This was the 31st October. That evening the general's cook appeared, obviously instructed to take a look at Manning, whom he observed curiously, and then asked if he were a Moslem. Manning was delighted with the visit, and his remark on it—which Bogle could never have made—reveals the great rift that exists between Sinophils and Tibetophils. 'Chinese politeness, even in the common soldiers, forms a great contrast with the barbarians of the place,' he wrote, and two days later he added, with great satisfaction, 'things are much pleasanter now the Chinese are here'.

In the meantime he had made the acquaintance of the general, presented him with two bottles of cherry brandy and a wineglass, and received a promise to write immediately to the ambans in Lhasa asking for permission for him to proceed. It was obvious that things had changed, and the Chinese grown more open in their use of power, since Bogle's day, for now there seems to have been no question of consulting the Tibetan authorities in the capital. Manning had fallen, by sheer luck, among friends, for the news that he was a physician spread rapidly among the Chinese soldiers, and his ability to give quick relief in some of the cases made him so popular that several of his patients suggested he should be allowed to accompany them to Gyantse, where he could wait in more comfort for the permit from Lhasa. The general invited him to join his party; on the 5th of November, before daylight, a gun went off to announce departure, and Manning and the Munshi set off after the main party in the company of the two Tibetan interpreters. 'We mounted at dawn of day, and scampered over the plain. Snow all round on the mountains—a strange sight.'

There was a strong streak of the manic-depressive in Manning. Good fortune raised his spirits immoderately, and one sees the effect in his journal, which suddenly becomes expansive, almost verbose, filling out the details of the journey with an interest and a vividness that give the illusion of an entirely different personality having taken charge from the laconic and depressed complainant of the days in Bhutan.

Eventually they caught up the official party; Manning salaamed to the general, and rode on in his company. They passed a Buddhist shrine, a cairn of stones with projecting stakes from which hung festoons of prayer flags. 'A raven sat crouching on top of one of the stakes. The mandarin alighted and prostrated himself to the ground, as did some of the soldiers, others not—we not.' Manning mistakenly assumed that the place was the tomb of a holy man; in fact it was probably the cairn where Padma had paid homage to the great mountain Chomolhari on Bogle's journey to Tibet, and the general was performing—with the pragmatic ease of the Chinese—an act of diplomatic respect towards Tibetan beliefs. Why Manning, who had so freely bowed down before Hindu images in Calcutta, did not do the same in this instance is not evident; perhaps he was trying to live up to the role of Moslem which the Chinese cook had invented for him.

His Chinese companions behaved towards Manning with a consideration he noticed they did not show to the Tibetans, towards whom he felt their attitude was very similar to that of the British towards the Indians. The general honoured him by having a special tent erected for him at each stopping place, and sent him meals of boiled mutton. Yet he found the journey over the high plateau as trying in its own way as the struggle up through the rainy mountains into Bhutan. It was so cold that the ice beside the running streams would bear the weight of horses, and as the day went on:

The sun became obscured, and a terrible cutting wind blew upon us. I was not sufficiently clothed against this.

217

I had a thick heavy cloak on, which one of the soldiers had lent me. The aide-de-camp had also lent me a sheepskin under-cloak, which I thought too much, and had packed up with my things. I was so bruised and bit and cut by this wind, that when we came to our resting place I was in a slight fever. I lolled on the cushions before a good fire, but could not recover thoroughly till next day.

Yet, with his journey unfolding promisingly before him, Manning could now be attentive to his surroundings, and draw a curious chiaroscuro picture of the village people gathered 'in the dirt around the fire', while the local scribe allocated their shares in the cost of providing food for the general and his party (Manning and the Munshi included), which was imposed as a kind of tax upon them.

It was a curious scene. A shoe-shaped pan, with a bit of cotton lighted in the bottom, and two or three lumps of tallow laid over, was the lamp. The clerk held the paper in one hand and the pen in the other. One man flared the light as close to him as he could, sloping it, and shoving in the tallow with his finger as the light grew dim. Another put the inkstand in his way when he looked about for a dip. They were eager and noisy. Afterwards they introduced the dice, using their hands for a box, and gambled for their shares and perhaps for money.

The next day, which everyone had prophesied would be just as cold and windy, turned out to be warm and pleasant, and even uncomfortably hot when they rode through narrow defiles in the mountains. But Manning was the kind of helpless traveller whose misadventures must have caused a great deal of mingled amusement and annoyance to his companions. In particular he was a bad horseman, and this, combined with an ill-tempered horse which he was given on the second day of the journey, led to an experience that at one moment he feared might prove the end of his journey.

[My vicious horse] happened to have remarkably bad furniture. In lengthening the stirrups they made them so long that I could scarcely reach them with my toes. I mounted him without his playing any tricks, and thought myself secure; but whether it was the unusual length of legs he felt at his belly, and the unusual mode of riding that made him impatient, or whether it was his natural temper alone, I do not know; he grew headstrong, and would not keep his place, but pressed forward. He fatigued me very much. A soldier offered to change with me, but I thought he would be a good goer after he had had a little run. I put him ahead, and gave him two or three notices with my heels that he might go his own pace. He changed his form instantly; set his head and ears, and at once sprang forward in a full runaway gallop, with the most furious and awkward motion I ever experienced. I could not have imagined he had ever been so fleet. The bridle was of little use. I pulled and sawed at it as hard as I dared; I could easily have broken it. I expected every minute my stirrup leather would break, though I pressed as lightly as I could; but what was worse, the road, which at first was tolerable, grew worse and worse, and I saw we were coming to the fearful bog we had passed the day before, which was full of concealed holes, frozen knobs of earth, flakes of ice, and had proved troublesome to walk our horses over. I reckoned upon a serious fall, but I believe he had had enough. A man driving cattle stood still, in his way, upon my clamorously invoking his assistance, and my horse made that a pretence for falling into a trot. I turned his head towards my companions, who were now nearly a mile off. When they came up they insisted on my changing, which I refused, until I saw they were a little angry, upon which I dismounted and exchanged for a quiet creature, who was as willing to keep behind as the other was to run ahead.

Most of the time the horses did not even trot. The caval-cade proceeded at a slow walk of three miles an hour, and moved according to the general's caprice, sometimes ten miles in a day, sometimes fifteen and occasionally as much as thirty, from dawn until evening, when Manning would be totally exhausted from the discomfort of the Tibetan saddles and would often end the day riding side-saddle. Every now and again there would be a halt by the wayside, when they would take tea and eat cold meat, Manning using the wooden bowl which, like a Tibetan, he carried tucked into the bosom of his gown. They passed frozen lakes where the ducks were fat and tame because no one hunted them, and houses 'looking like ruins of villages, as the Tibet houses often do', and stayed the night in hamlets where they were put to sleep in buildings which Manning, with his romantic flair for depicting dark and gloomy scenes, described as 'strange caverns', which were 'low, long, dark, narrow, black, windowless, and full of smoke'. Going inside, he would find a room supported, in the Tibetan manner, by posts and beams, with the side aisles crammed with untidy packages, and at the end 'cushions and a good fire, and the good woman of the house preparing the pot'. So many people would crowd in that he imagined several families shared these houses, and at night he would lie down without troubling to undress, since there was little room to lay out his bedding and 'the smoke was so thick that the slightest exertion made me breathe quick and almost suffocated me', and 'all was dirt and dust'. What most interested Manning, as he confessed in that journal written without intent of publication, were the women and girls who would come in, make up their beds, and then nonchalantly undress. 'I now and then took an impertinent peep, but the smoke was so thick and the light so bad, that I could discern nothing.'

The party continued, through barren valleys where deer grazed unmolested, 'seeing no diversity, but the ever-varying shapes of the still more barren mountains, whose colour, where it was not actually sand, slate, or granite, was a melancholy pale mouldy green, produced no doubt by the scaly covering of dried stems and withered herbage'. The greenest thing he saw for a long time, Manning remarked, was 'a pot of young growing onions' in a cellar where he and the Munshi stayed one night, waited on by a humbler Chinese with the improbable name of 'Sid', who had been currying favour by offering Manning cups of stewed lights in the hope of being engaged—as eventually he was—to accompany him to Lhasa.

There were variations in the monotony of the route, things to see and wonder at, such as steaming medicinal springs, and 'a strange straight between the mountains, where the water seemed to flow uphill', and a point where the road widened 'into a little area, filled with religious piles of white stones, and with a sort of open temple in it, where was carved a strange gigantic figure'. From the latter point they descended to the Painam river, where there were trees to refresh the eye, and 'a pleasant sunshiny village' in which Manning and the Munshi were given a room opening on to a flat roof.

> I was now so eaten up by little insects, which I shall not name, that I was compelled to set aside shame, and sitting down on a terrace buttress in the sunshine, dismiss as many of my retinue as I could get sight of. . . . I suffered a great deal from these little insects, whose society I was not used to. I shall say no more of them than that I did not get thoroughly rid of them until some time after my arrival in Lhasa.

The following day Manning entered Gyantse in the general's company, and since his patron was met by the resident Chinese officials and by one of the Tibetan governors his own good standing was made manifest in official eyes, and he and the Munshi were given their share of the 'very palatable viands' which had been brought out to entertain the general. Like Bogle and Turner before him, Manning was impressed by the splendid appearance of Gyantse from a distance, but found that when he came near to it 'the handsome white stone houses are converted into dirty white walls, and the windows into belfry holes'. The road was half inundated with water, and nothing was growing in the fields. 'Like every place I have seen in Tibet, it appears a little area surrounded by mountains without any visible outlet.'

Once again, the presence of the Chinese was visible to a degree far exceeding anything Bogle had observed thirty years before. They had set up a kind of tribunal in a building where, as Manning remarked, the appearance of everything was 'perfectly Chinese'.

> The same neatness, the same folding doors and paved yard, the same figures of mandarins in ancient dresses smugly painted on the folding doors, the same Chinese characters pasted up, the same style of building, and, in short, an exact conformity to the Chinese model.

Even the little lodge in the courtyard of the house which the general assigned to Manning had the Chinese look. 'Two tomb-like brickwork structures against the wall, with good thick cushions on them, were the places to lay our beds on, and here I slept much more comfortably than I had done for a long time; while the cold was much less', which was an advantage, since it enabled Manning—well wrapped in his Chinese robes—to live most of the time without a fire, and so avoid the smoke that was giving him asthma. Otherwise, life in Gyantse was relatively easy, since Manning's reputation as a physician had accompanied him, and the Chinese who wished to gain his favour kept him well supplied with food and drink, and with such necessities as pens, ink and candles.

He began his stay in Gyantse with a round of visits to the high officials, beginning naturally with the general, who showed enough whimsical interest in Manning and his disguise to advise him to assume a complete Chinese dress, which he did by adding to his gown the Chinese boots he had brought with him from Canton. The general was full of admiration for Manning's beard, and—if we are to believe its vain owner—never tired of discussing it.

> He named such and such a mandarin, such a one he thought had better moustaches; in fact, I had kept mine cut short in India, for convenience of eating soup and drink, and they had not yet full grown. Afterwards, when I had combed my beard and adjusted it properly, and he saw its tapering shape descending in one undivided lock, he again expressed his admiration, and declared he had never seen one nearly so handsome. The General likewise approved of my countenance and manner; he pretended to have skill in physiognomy and fortune-telling.

The junior mandarin, a rather awkward but sensible man who had risen from the ranks, pleased Manning greatly by inviting him to 'a pastry breakfast', which consisted of a variety of Chinese dumplings and noodles, washed down with good wine. His visit to the castle, where he called on the senior Tibetan governor, was a much more formal affair. The Munshi had, from some caprice, refused to accompany him, and he went with one of his Chinese patients, who understood Tibetan.

> I was ushered into a very large lofty room, with an immense window to the south, full of papers and records, and scribes. The mandarin after a few minutes came in, and tea was brought. We sat together on cushions, and discussed Calcutta and Tibet, for about half an hour, when I took my leave. He intimated that he would call on me the next day, and would send me some eatables. I had

made him a trifling present. He sent some rice and a useful piece of cloth, but did not come himself. Another mandarin came in his stead (inferior, I believe), and made some apology; I forget what.

Here, again, Manning shows how little he had acquired in the way of knowledge of Tibetan affairs, for the official who visited him was obviously the other member of the pair of governors, and it is unlikely that any slight was deliberately intended. However, there is no doubt that during his journey up to Lhasa the Tibetans kept aloof from Manning, and this was not surprising, since his ready acceptance of the general's protection and his sympathy for the Chinese obviously identified him in native eyes with the unpopular overlords.

Even among the patients Manning acquired, at least in Gyantse, there appear to have been no Tibetans; all were Chinese. He made a few successful cures by the application of drastic remedies like antimony, opium and Fowler's Solution of Arsenic, and he rightly tried to persuade his patients not to drink the polluted water of Gyantse, but to pay the little cost of importing it from a distance. What with seeing his patients and rolling pills for them, Manning did not even have time to get out the skates he had brought with him in anticipation of winter sports in the Himalayas. The leisure he had was taken up eating great feasts of noodles and other 'farinaceous food' with his grateful patients, and entertaining the general, who would often stroll over to Manning's courtyard where the two of them sat in chairs and smoked while the general's attendants stood in the background.

The general was not stinting in his hospitality, and one evening, hearing of Manning's interest in Chinese music, of which he himself was an aficionado, he arranged a concert for him, playing himself on several instruments, and accompanying on the Chinese guitar when two of his soldiers acted

out a scene from a Chinese opera. Manning was more impressed than many travellers of his time. 'The Chinese music,
though rather meagre to a European, has its beauties, and
has, like most other national music, its peculiar expression,
of which our musical notation, which we vainly imagine so
perfect, conveys no idea whatever.' The difficult part of the
evening came when the general handed Manning a Chinese
flute and demanded that he play some 'Calcutta' music on
it. After many protests, Manning performed some English
country dances, but realized immediately that such melodies
made no appeal to the Chinese ear.

The general also found Manning another Chinese servant,
ostensibly to do the humbler tasks which the Munshi naturally disdained. He was the Sid who had brought Manning
dishes of stewed lights on the journey. Sid, a Chinese Moslem,
had attached himself to the general in Lhasa, following him
to Phari, and now wished to return to the capital. Manning,
bound in that direction, appeared to the general the ideal
employer, and found himself pressed into accepting a servant
whom he did not want and whom he could hardly afford,
since he was awaiting funds from Rangpur which had not
arrived. Fear of offending the general, on whom he depended
for his pass to Lhasa, made him accept Sid and even, on the
general's insistence, pay him four dollars a month, twice as
much as he had originally offered. It turned out a bad
bargain. Sid had boasted of being an excellent cook, and
while Manning was in Gyantse the Chinese meals he was
served were excellent, but when he left it soon became
evident that this had not been due to any culinary talents
on Sid's part, but to 'a good body of a Tibetan woman . . .
accustomed to Chinese cookery' who had worked with him
in the kitchen at Gyantse. Nevertheless, Sid had his uses,
including 'a full share of impudence' which led him to claim

things on the way for his master 'which a more modest man would have let go by', while he was 'expert in little domestic offices: folding up clothes, pasting up a hole in the paper, making up parcels, driving a nail where it is wanted, tacking and stitching'.

If we are to believe Manning's accounts, he was indeed unfortunate in his servants, but this appears to have been due at least in part to his own inability to play the master or to protect himself in any effective way from being imposed upon. With the Munshi, in particular, he seems to have lived in a state of perpetual apprehension, not daring to protest when this employee appropriated his only waterproof chest, and only after a long period of extraordinary passivity keying himself up to the point at which, in Gyantse, he at last rebelled against the Munshi's uncontrolled displays of temper.

He was angry with me but once during our stay at Giansu, when upon some trifling occasion he broke out with such bitterness and fury as was scarcely endurable. I begged of him not to eat me up, as I wished to proceed farther on my journey; and then for the first time opened my mind to him on the unfortunate state of his temper, and lamented my ill luck in having a person with me to whom I was so afraid of putting a question, that I was perpetually deterred; it being necessary for me first to go round about, and with civil speech and preface bring him into the humour to listen to it and answer it. That this necessity was a grievous burden to me; that I never used the same precautions with any English gentleman, whatever his rank. He answered these remarks without much asperity; only observing that he wondered why I brought him with me from Rangpur; that I should have done better for myself to have left him behind. When these fits were over his behaviour returned to its usual cross level, and I to my usual serenity; never on any occasion taunting him with what had passed, or making any allusion to it whatever.

At last the awaited letter arrived from one of the ambans in Lhasa. Manning—under whatever unrevealed false name he had chosen to travel—was to be allowed to make his way to Lhasa. What the Tibetans had refused to Bogle and Turner as representatives of the Company, the Chinese had granted to Manning as an individual traveller whose pose of being an Asian can have deceived no one.

Manning received the news with some trepidation, since at the same time he learnt that the other amban was a Tartar chieftain of particularly suspicious nature who had been sent into a bureaucratic exile in Lhasa because of his tactless handling of the British in Canton; if this official recognized him, Manning's position might become very difficult. But the desire to continue his journey was too strong for this vague threat to deter him, and he made his plans for departure, ordering an appropriate dress for his entry into the capital. It was made for him by the general's soldier tailors.

> It was an ample coarsish red woollen-cloth robe with fur cuffs; it was lined with cotton cloth, and upon the cotton cloth was stitched a dressed sheepskin with all the wool on. I had also bought stockings of the same kind of sheepskin, under which, if I pleased, I could put one or two pairs of common worsted or cotton stockings, and over all draw my Chinese boots, so that I was able to keep my feet cosy whatever weather might ensue. I had a sort of fur tippet, and a quilted cap to defend my face and ears. . . .

The general entered eagerly into Manning's plans for departure, since his own interests were involved. He did not wish it to be known in Lhasa that he had exceeded his duty in assisting a stranger, and so he not only enjoined Manning never to mention that he had accompanied him to Gyantse, but arranged the date of his departure so as to make it appear that he had waited in Phari for the news from Lhasa. Manning's journal does not tell when he actually left Gyantse. There are no dates in his narrative between the 5th November, when he left Phari in the general's company, and the 17th December, when he was already established in the capital, but we can certainly assume that he did not go from Gyantse until early December.

The day of departure came; Manning paid a courtesy call on the general, who in turn came down to see that his guests had everything needed for the journey; they made a jesting farewell to him and his soldiers, and rode out of the town. They had been provided with good horses, and the prospect for their journey as they took the road towards Lhasa, which no European had yet travelled, looked excellent. Unfortunately the local magistrate, piqued by the Munshi's insolence, had neglected to give them 'a passport of the best sort', which the general had promised them and which would have assured them good mounts for the rest of the journey. Instead he had merely extended the passport on which they had travelled from Phari, and they found, when they had got barely three miles out of Gyantse, that their good horses and pack yaks were taken away and replaced by 'sorry jades, lean kine, and half-starved, tottering asses'. One of the horses did not even have a bridle; it was unnecessary, Manning was assured, because the beast was so gentle. Manning's own nag had a saddle 'so small and narrow from head to stern, besides being imperfect and having a great brass bump in the middle, as to cramp me and render my ride uncomfortable'. Because of the poor mounts, they rode slowly in the scorching daytime heat of the valley eastward from Gyantse, and by the end of the day Manning found one side of his face completely blistered from the strength of the high-altitude sunlight reflected from the hard, sandy soil. The one fortunate aspect of this stage of the journey was the fact that on the road from Lhasa to Shigatse the Chinese had recently built post-houses similar to those that existed on the main trunk roads of China, and since a Chinese soldier—usually with a Tibetan wife—lived in each of these to forward the despatches, the accommodation was relatively clean. Describing it, Manning could not refrain from giving free rein to his anti-Tibetan prejudices.

> The Chinese are really civilized, and do not live like cattle; and it is a comfort, after having lodged in smoke and dirt with the native animals of Tibet, to take shelter in a Chinaman's house where you are sure of urbanity and cleanliness at least.

After two days riding up the valley, their guide led them into a range of snowy mountains and over the great Karo La pass, which—though Manning had no instruments to record the altitude—rose to approximately 17,000 feet, crossing the great central range of the Himalayas. They had to ride precariously over frozen stream beds and small icefields, and for some distance the road led along the base of a glacier. Riding slowly with the guide before the yak drivers, and letting the Munshi and Sid gallop ahead, Manning found his new sheepskin-lined gown excellent protection from the bitter cold. Eventually they came down into 'a large stony plain, at the end of which stood a considerable town on the margin of an extensive lake, or little sea, as it is called'. The lake was the great Yamdrok Tso, the Turquoise Lake; whose beautiful colouring was thus described nearly a century later by Perceval Landon: 'near inshore the innumerable ripples are indeed blown in over the white-sanded floor as colourlessly as wavelets on a South Pacific strand of white coral, but twenty yards out the bottom drops suddenly, and the lake glows deeply with the colour from which it takes its name'. Meadows of deep green grass bordered the lake, where many yaks grazed; a peninsula deceptively like an island, with its own diminutive mountain range, jutted into the lake, and on the far side, in its grove of willow trees, stood the monastery of the successor to Hamilton's friend, Dorje Phagmo, the Thunderbolt Sow.

The town, which they reached towards the end of the day, was Nagartse, an overgrown village with a grim white-washed fort built on a spur above it. Here Manning ran into some passing difficulties. Their guide had gone up to the castle to report to the Tibetan governors, and Manning and the Munshi began to search for a lodging. Unfortunately Sid, the only member of the party who knew the town, had quarrelled with the local Chinese postmaster, and did not wish to approach him, while the Tibetans saw no reason to accommodate strangers who appeared to lack any official approval.

> We rode up one way, and down another, and loitered about, until at last we were shown into a wretched place, where the apartment had walls only on three sides, the fourth being open like a coachhouse, without doors.

Here they were told that they could be given nothing to eat. Manning decided that this was no cause for despair, as they had food in their wallet, including 'a piece of excellent pickled pork that the General had, among other things, given us for prog on the road'. So he left the Munshi and Sid to quarrel noisily with their hosts, while he went up and sat on the roof of the house to enjoy the sun setting over the purple hills around the Yamdrok Tso.

He was soon disturbed from his contemplation by the return of the guide, who told them that his mission was at an end and he was now returning to Gyantse. This came as a surprise to both Manning and the Munshi, who had expected him to accompany them all the way to Lhasa. Manning tipped him, and he went off, but immediately the travellers regretted that they had not waited until he had found them another guide, for they discovered that, now they were on their own, nobody would provide them with horses and yaks. There was nothing for it but to apply to the postmaster to whom Sid had refused to take them, and when the Munshi did this, the Chinaman came round to investigate their difficulties.

> He sat down in one of our chairs, and affecting all the decisive gravity and authority of a magistrate, determined what horses we wanted, and provided us a conductor, to whose care we entrusted all our goods and chattels.

Not wishing to offend a man who acted with such show of dignity by offering him money, and having no more appropriate present, Manning wrapped some silver coins in a paper and sent the Munshi to present them to their benefactor's wife, a proceeding which was accepted as tactful and sufficient.

The next day they went by slow stages around the shores of Yamdrok Tso, and at their first stopping place Manning eventually met 'the first Tibet people I had seen that I at all wished to be acquainted with'. They were an old farmer and his family who went to the trouble not only to feed the travellers, but even to take a pan of charcoal into the room where they ate so that they could warm their 'fingers and noses'. 'Though I could not speak,' Manning concluded, 'I tried to express by my manners and countenance that their kindness was not thrown away upon me; and as in these cases there is undoubtedly a great sympathy, I trust they partly understood my sentiments.'

Travelling farther along the lakeshore, Manning came to villages so afflicted with bad harvests and late frosts that they were too poor to offer anything but tea and tsampa (barley meal). The road became a narrow, stony path winding between the lakeshore and the mountains, and in the afternoon, after hours of travel, Manning realized that they were opposite Nagartse, and no great distance away. 'Turning my head back towards the west [he noted], I had a noble view on a set of snowy mountains collected into a focus, as it were; their summits empurpled with the evening sun, and their majestic, graceful forms ever varying as I advanced into new positions. Though I kept a long, long lingering eye upon them, yet I heartily wished that I might never see them again. My lips almost spontaneously pronounced this wish repeatedly, as I apostrophized them in my mind.' And, later, he was to add, 'Fruitless wish!' For all his desires to travel on into China were to be frustrated, and he was to come this way again.

That night he stayed in another small town on the shore of Yamdrok Tso, in the shadow of a castle that belonged to Dorje Phagmo, of whom the local people complained that she was 'capricious and tyrannical'. Manning, who was not given to writing extensively on natural curiosities, was so fascinated by the ravens which he saw swooping and gliding about the castle and over the lake that on this occasion he broke his rule to describe them.

I did not know that they were so social, so frolicsome, and so joyous. They wantoned about in a thousand different manners and postures, sometimes pursuing each other, and making a mock fight; sometimes separately; sometimes rising; sometimes falling with closed wings; sometimes floating awhile in the air on their backs, sometimes lying edgewise; sometimes whirling round the building with vast rapidity; and all with an eagerness and joyousness of motions and cries and screams that showed the overflowing of happy sensations too plainly to be mistaken.

That night there was no food at all to be spared in the
place where they stayed, and they fried some bacon from the
stores which the general had so thoughtfully provided. The
next day a long journey lay before them, since they had to
travel six miles along the lakeshore and then cross the
Khamba La pass, more than 15,000 feet above sea level,
before they would reach a place to lodge. The morning
started badly, with slow mounts, and Sid's horse fell and
smashed their china cups. At the last village on the lake there
were no remounts ready, and they had to wait more than an
hour. The actual ascent to the top of the Khamba La from
the level of the lake was not very great, but the descent
into the Tsangpo Valley was long and, though Manning
does not go into details, 'in many places troublesome'. It
was 'dark and silent night' when they reached the village
that was their destination, and their guide was still far back
up the mountain with the slow baggage yaks. They rode
from house to house vainly seeking a place to stay the night,
until the noise they made aroused the Chinese postmaster,
who showed them to a house where they were given a kind
of open gallery to sleep on; the night was cold and frosty,
but Manning preferred it to the smoky house, and, sending
for straw and pulling his red woollen nightcap down over his
ears, lay down in his warm padded clothes to sleep.

Looking out next morning, Manning found himself in a
region more congenial than any he had yet seen on his
journey. Though he was not wholly unappreciative of wilder
landscapes, it was wide valleys that really attracted him,
with the mountains visible but distant, with clear rippling
streams and white villages scattered over the landscape, with
trees and cultivated fields, and all these he found that
morning, 'and an air of gaiety was spread over the whole,
and, I thought, on the faces of the people'. Even the place

where they changed their horses was a clean paved yard with a shelter where cushions were set out for them, buttered tea was served and they were given a joint of roast mutton to eat on their journey.

About midday they came to the ferry over the Tsangpo, and crossed, men and horses, yaks and baggage, in a single large boat which aroused such undefined 'reminiscences' in Manning as to bring on 'a fit of European activity'; in other words, a display of chronic eccentricity.

> I could not sit still, but must climb about, seat myself in various postures on the parapet, and lean over. The master of the boat was alarmed, and sent a steady man to hold me tight. I pointed to the ornamented prow of the boat, and assured them that I could sit there with perfect safety, and to prove to them how commodiously I was seated, bent my head and body down the outside of the boat to the water's edge; but finding, by their renewed instances to me to resist, that I made them uneasy, I went back to my place and seated myself quietly. As the boat drew near shore I meditated jumping out, but was pulled back by the immense weight of my clothes and clumsiness of my boots. I was afraid of jumping short and having the laugh against me.

Across the ferry they rode beside the tributary Gya Chu in the direction of Lhasa, Manning cantering ahead with the guide to the night's destination, a house full of Tibetan soldiers, armed with bows and long muskets, on their way to military exercises in Lhasa. The following day the Munshi appeared in a state of great agitation over what would happen on the morrow; it would be an unforgivable fault if they did not arrive in Lhasa in time to present themselves to the ambans before noon. By now Manning's Sinophilia was beginning to wear thin, and he mocked the Munshi's anxieties, but to no effect; the headstrong Chinaman insisted on galloping ahead, with Sid in attendance, to make arrangements for the following day at the night halt of Litong. Manning followed at a leisurely pace with the guide, finding time at one stage to tend to a child in convulsions, at another to watch a peasant ('scratching his head as naturally as countrymen do in like situations in England') pleading his case before a Tibetan magistrate, and at a third drinking tea and eating tsampa at a kind of oratory in the charge of a nun, 'a great masculine woman' who came every now and again to stare at him from the doorway. In this house there were many 'whirligigs', as Manning irreverently termed the Tibetan prayer wheels, and, with a strange perversity for one who would prostrate himself before image or man at the tip of a hat, he refused to follow the guide's example by giving them a pious twirl, 'for though I am a great conformist in certain ways,' as he explained with great complacency, 'take me in another line and I am a most obstinate non-conformist, and would sooner die than swerve a little'.

They rode on over the stony plain beside the river, splashing through shallow streams, to the tinkling of the bell that hung from the neck of the guide's horse, until they came to a rough and rocky hill that blocked the way. The guide dismounted, but Manning refused. His heels had been too much galled by tight boots. In the end, however, he had to get down, to descend on the opposite side a path so steep as to be 'an absolute staircase'. They arrived in Litong to find the Munshi in a state of 'dole and wrath'; his hurrying had been wasted, for the postmaster was 'so drunk that he could neither stand nor go'. It was late the next morning before he had sobered enough to set them on their way, and Manning was delighted to see the Munshi so frustrated. To reach Lhasa before noon was now impossible, and he rejoiced at the thought that he would not have to appear 'before the mandarins, sweltering and heated, my boots hurting me every step I set'.

They had not gone far that morning before 'a respectable person on horseback' appeared from the direction of the capital; he was the representative of the Tibetan authorities of the city who, after the amban had given Manning permission to enter Lhasa, had assumed that civic duty of hospitality which was necessary in a land with no hotels and few inns. Not far beyond the town where they changed their horses towards midday, the great edifice of the Potala came into view, so immense that in the clear upland light it appeared close at hand, though it was at least five miles away. They approached it over a stretch of marshy land which reminded Manning of what he had read of the Pontine Marshes, and rode under a great archway 'whose gilded ornaments at top were so ill fixed that some leaned one way and some another, and reduced the whole to the rock [sic] appearance of castles and turrets in pastry work'. Beyond the archway they rode out on to a level and 'royally broad' road, swarming with monks and infested with beggars 'lounging and basking in the sun'. Manning was curiously inexplicit about his reactions to the Potala; he admitted that it had exceeded his expectations, and was 'perfect enough', but though his eye 'was perpetually fixed on the palace, and roving over its parts, the disposition of which being irregular, eluded my attempts at analysis'. But it was then virtually the same as the Potala known to twentieth-century travellers, the mountain of masonry built upon a mountain of living rock which the Fifth Dalai Lama started in the seventeenth century and which grew into a vast cascade of stone topped with gilded roofs and turrets that to this day fascinates architects in its felicitous harmonization of the human construc-

tion with the natural rock that is both setting and foundation.

'If one approached within a league of Lhasa, saw the
glittering domes of the Potala, and turned back without
entering the precincts,' said one of the British correspondents
in 1903, 'one might still imagine it an enchanted city.' He
went on—as other travellers have done—to give a description of its unregenerate squalidness which was no more
evocative than the brief but telling passage in which Manning recounts how, if the Potala had exceeded his expectations, 'the town as far fell short of them'.

> The habitations are begrimed with smut and dirt. The
> avenues are full of dogs, some growling and gnawing bits
> of hide which lie about in profusion, and emit a charnel-
> house smell; others limping and looking livid; others
> ulcerated; others starved and dying, and pecked at by the
> ravens; some dead and preyed upon. In short, everything
> seems mean and gloomy, and excites the idea of something
> unreal. Even the mirth and laughter of the inhabitants I
> thought dreamy and ghostly. The dreaminess no doubt
> was in my mind, but I never could get rid of the idea; it
> strengthened upon me afterwards.

It was only in the last point that other travellers have ever
disagreed with Manning. To all but him the cheerfulness of
the Tibetans in Lhasa, despite all the filth and want, seemed
real, the projection of an extraordinary national personality.

# XIII

## *Manning in Lhasa*

When they entered Lhasa, the Tibetan who had met Manning and his party led them into a narrow by-lane, and thence into a courtyard where they dismounted; they walked through into an inner court and climbed by a ladder into a gallery where a room had been provided for them: the **kind** of room whose primitive discomfort might be regarded as an oblique assessment of a traveller's importance. It was large indeed, but that was its only advantage. The small windows to the north and the west were placed so that no sunshine entered, but, since they were unpapered, there was a liberal flow of cold air, while 'in the middle of the roof was a very large aperture (four feet square or more) through which the freezing wind came eddying day and night'. The floor was rough and uneven; indeed, Manning insisted that it must be called 'ground' rather than floor, yet here, for many days, he was forced to spread out his bedding in utter discomfort.

But for the moment there was no time to consider such matters. The Munshi insisted that homage must be paid at once to the Chinese authorities (he had little regard for the Tibetan grandees), and the first necessity was for Manning and him to acquire suitable hats. Off they went to the hatter, who measured their heads and lent them hats so that they could pay their visits. By this time they had found that the ambans were holding a review of Chinese troops, and would not be back to Lhasa until the evening, so that the Munshi's conscience was stilled, and in due course they set out and walked, Manning inwardly complaining of his galled heel, to the building where the Chinese officials held audience. Manning went in trepidation, for now he would come face to face with the Tartar mandarin who might have seen him in Canton 'or remember having heard of an Englishman of my description, strangely residing at Canton, and suspected of wanting to get into the country'. Even if the mandarin did not recognize him, there were servants in his entourage who had come from Canton and 'are still more likely to have seen and heard of me'. To give himself a little added disguise, Manning put on a pair of 'China spectacles', and to dispel any thought that he might be an Englishman (that race having a well-known objection to bowing the head) he promptly performed a most humble kowtow, falling to his knees and touching the floor with his brow. He need not have been apprehensive, for the Tartar mandarin was so shortsighted that at a moderate distance he could recognize no one, and the interview went off with a few harmless questions and some polite enquiries about health that filled Manning with a quite unjustified sense of the security of his position. His visit to the local generals the next day should have put him on his guard, for though one of them was related to the general in Gyantse, which assured Manning a polite reception, another of these high officers stared at him for a long time and then asked him whether he had been in Canton. Manning was momentarily at a loss for words, but the Munshi quickly answered on his behalf that he had never seen the city. Manning at this moment felt a perverse and perilous rush of Anglo-Saxon pride:

I was inclined to speak the whole truth from the first, and

declare myself an Englishman, for I had been guilty of no offence; but Munshi earnestly dissuaded me from it.

Having satisfied the Munshi's feeling of the innate superiority of the Han race by visiting all the Chinese officials, they began to make the rounds of the Tibetans, beginning with two of the Khalons, or ministers, members of the four-man cabinet of Tibet. It was a matter of sitting on cushions and drinking buttered tea and talking about lodgings in a roundabout way, since the Munshi insisted that Manning should speak no Chinese publicly in Lhasa, owing to his poor Peking pronunciation and his inability to converse in the Szechuan dialect spoken by most of the Chinese who lived in Lhasa. English also was out of the question except in private, and the procedure actually followed when Manning and the Munshi appeared among Tibetans was a singularly cumbrous one. Manning would address the Munshi in Latin which the latter had learnt from the priests in Macao. The Munshi would translate this into Szechuan Chinese for the benefit of the Tibetan interpreter, who in turn would translate it into Tibetan. In this way even politenesses occupied a great deal of time, and the only serious business discussed at Manning's visit to the Khalons was to plan his visit to the Dalai Lama, which they advised him to postpone until he had recuperated his strength after the long journey. Manning welcomed the advice, since it gave time for the sun blisters that disfigured his face to heal.

By the time of Manning's visit, the Dalai Lama, who had been a child when Bogle came to Tibet and had come of age just after Turner's visit, had already lived his reign through, an obscure and holy man who emerged only briefly into the sun of temporal power, and then, in his early thirties, allowed a powerful regent, Tatsa Rimpoche, to take the substance of authority out of his hands. His successor, Lungtok Gyatso, the Ninth Dalai Lama, had been discovered in 1806, and was now a bright and vigorous child whose early and mysterious death on the verge of adolescence nobody yet anticipated. The real power still lay in the hands of Tatsa Rimpoche, whom Manning called 'the Ti-mu-fu'.

In preparation for the audience, Manning assembled the presents he had brought for the Tibetan hierarchs. They were sadly reduced from what he had originally intended, and spread out before him they seemed scanty indeed. He had brought from Calcutta a good quantity of fine broadcloth, but only a third of it had escaped the depredations of the Bhutanese. He had succeeded in getting a pair of 'china ewers' into Tibet, and these he had thought of filling with decorative arrangements of artificial flowers, but his servants had contrived to leave these in Gyantse. To compensate for his losses he found in his baggage a pair of fine brass candlesticks belonging to the East India Company which his Chinese servant in Canton had mistakenly packed into a parcel sent on to him in Calcutta, and these he polished and fitted with wax candles to make a show. He also had thirty mint silver dollars and, having been told that foreign coins were considered acceptable presents in Tibet, he wrapped twenty of them up into a silk scarf. By the time he had filled 'two large handsome phials' with Genuine Smith's Lavender Water and added some Nankin tea, which was a rarity in Tibet, he felt he had after all prepared a present worthy of any hierarch. For the Regent he put together a much humbler gift of six silver dollars, one phial of lavender water and some Nankin tea.

On the 17th December he set out with the Munshi, with his Chinese servant and a newly engaged Tibetan Moslem boy carrying the presents behind them. They went on horseback to the Potala, and rode only a short way up the

mountainside, since the ramp for the use of riders ended at a
platform, from which they had to climb four hundred steps,
some of them stone stairs cut in the mountainside and others
consisting of ladders that went from story to story within
the vast winter palace that was also the centre of Tibetan
government, until at last they reached the great flat roof on
which stood the audience hall. Here, as is still customary
when one visits a Dalai Lama, even in exile, visitors were
expected to wait as a tribute to the greatness of the spiritual
being who would be receiving them. Manning and the
Munshi spent the time arranging the presents, and confer-
ring with the Dalai Lama's interpreter, a lapsed monk,
with a family and a reputed liking for women, who had
already visited Manning and impressed him with his oral
knowledge of many Asian languages, none of which he could
read or write. 'He was a strange, melancholy man, severe
in his manner, and extraordinarily sparing in his words, except when he made a narration or continued speech, and
then he was equally profuse.'

At last they were ushered into the hall. As he was entering
Manning realized that beside the youthful Dalai Lama,
seated on his lion throne, was the Regent, a middle-aged
monk in maroon and yellow dress, who occupied a lower
seat. This confused the visitor, who had not been tutored in
the protocol necessary for such an occasion, and did not
know how much ceremonial he should go through with the
Regent in the Dalai Lama's presence. However, with an
alacrity Bogle or Turner would have found astonishing, he
immediately flung himself down in front of the Dalai Lama
and performed three kowtows; he repeated the performance
once for the Regent, and this procedure seemed to meet
with approval. He then presented his gifts, putting the
coins in their silk scarfs with his own hands into the hands

of the Dalai Lama and the Regent. While he was doing this, one of his servants managed clumsily to break the bottle of Genuine Smith's Lavender Water intended for the Regent, and though Manning was embarrassed to smell 'the odoriferous stream', he judged it best to ignore the incident which, with Tibetan courtesy, everyone else did. The presents given and accepted, Manning took off his new hat, and presented his head, freshly shaven for the occasion, for the Dalai Lama to bless. The holy hands were laid directly on his head; he was accepted as a member of the higher order of mankind, though one doubts whether Manning had the same kind of fine eye as Bogle for the symbolic acts that marked the subtler social distinctions in Tibet. He and the Munshi were invited to sit on cushions which placed them well below the level of the Dalai Lama's throne, and there they received none of the ample gifts which, on his first audience with the Panchen Lama, had been placed before Bogle. At first they were merely given some buttered tea, and, while this was 'most excellent', Manning was astonished to see the cup whipped away from him before he had even been able to empty it. Only at the end was a small gift of dried fruits set before Manning; he did not rate a dried sheep's carcass. It was obvious that the Tibetans were in no mood to confer special favours upon Manning, and their reception of him was almost certainly linked to the fact that he appeared to have entered Lhasa under Chinese auspices.

But in the visitor's mind the lack of gifts was amply overborne by the charm which the Dalai Lama exerted, and Manning was perhaps even more deeply affected by meeting this young hierarch than Turner had been in his meeting with the infant Panchen Lama. He was so fascinated by the 'Lama's beautiful and interesting face and manner' that he was almost unaware of the rest of his surroundings. 'I could have wept through strangeness of sensation,' he related. 'I was absorbed in reflections when I got home.' And no sooner did he reach his frigid room than he hurriedly noted down: 'This day I saluted the Grand Lama. Beautiful youth. Face poetically affecting; could have wept. Very happy to have seen him and his blessed smile. Hope often to see him again.' Having written this, he was still so stirred by his experience that he sat down and tried to draw the Dalai Lama's portrait, 'and though very inexpert with the pencil, I produced a beautiful face, but it did not satisfy me. I drew another which I could not make handsome, yet there was in some respects a likeness in it which the other wanted.'

Behind his erudition and scholarship, behind all the sophisticated chatter that filled his letters, there was an innocent being with an overbearing desire for love existing within the bizarre persona Manning presented to the world. Lamb, I think, recognized it, and this was why he rated Manning so highly; he had a touch of the same absurd innocence himself. As for the Dalai Lama, whether he perceived this quality in his visitor, or merely saw him as a figure of outlandish comedy (for which he could hardly have been blamed), it is hard to tell. Manning's account can be interpreted in either way.

> Sometimes, particularly when he looked at me, his smile almost approached to a gentle laugh. No doubt my grim beard and spectacles somewhat excited his risibility, though I have afterwards, at the New Year's festival, seen him smile and unbend freely while sitting myself unobserved in a corner, and watching his reception of various persons, and the notice he took of the strange variety of surrounding objects.

The audience took its formal course. The Dalai Lama asked questions about health, about the journey, never about

Manning's plans, and the visitors would pop up from their cushions each time to give the appropriate reply; Manning especially prided himself on one answer. The Dalai Lama had asked whether he had not met with 'molestations and difficulties on the road'.

> I said I had had troubles, but now that I had the happiness of being in his presence, they were amply compensated. I thought of them no more. I could see that this answer pleased both the Lama and his household people. They thus found that I was not a mere rustic, but had some tincture of civility in me.

Beaming with self-satisfaction, Manning made his way backward out of the presence, to be stopped by the interpreter who asked if he had any request to make of the Dalai Lama. Manning replied that he would like the opportunity to study the religion and the ancient history of Tibet, and asked the Dalai Lama to appoint a monk who knew Chinese to instruct him, and to give him some books that would inform him. The message that came back was ambiguous. The Dalai Lama had no copy of the books he would like to give his visitor, but would have one made. All Manning received afterwards was what the Dalai Lama described as 'the most essential part of their prayers and meditations'; as he could not read Tibetan and the Dalai Lama never answered his request for a teacher, these were of little use.

Nevertheless, during the four months that he remained in Lhasa, Manning had fairly free access to both the Dalai Lama and the Regent, and their reception of him became increasingly friendly, perhaps because the Tibetans recognized his harmlessness, perhaps because they felt a sympathy with him in his growing difficulties with the Chinese.

Those difficulties threw a steadily darker shadow, of frustration and often of fear, over his days in Lhasa. Not very long after he reached the capital he became aware of the particular attention that was being paid to him. One day a group of Chinese officials arrived, and a mandarin among them began to question Manning, and asked him to write 'a sentence in my character', which Manning did, presumably to keep up pretences, in Latin. 'He was vastly civil, vastly inquisitive.' But to the Munshi, who was Chinese, and who, it turned out, had committed what might be regarded as a crime in leaving his country to take up service with a foreigner, the mandarin was much more pressing. He made him go over the whole story of their journey, which the Munshi contrived to do without revealing that Manning had come from Canton. Night after night they returned to question the Munshi. He and Manning had moved to a new apartment with several rooms, and Manning would sit quietly in his own chamber, waiting. 'They would stay a most unreasonable time, and at coming and going, as if by mistake, open my door, and take a survey, to see if I conspired with any one of nights.'

Eventually one of the officials admitted that they had been sent by the Tartar mandarin from Canton, who had a peculiar detestation of Europeans, and suspected Manning of being either a missionary or a spy. He even asserted that the stranger's coming was associated with a comet that for some months had been visible in the heavens. And while Manning passed, as he tells us at this point, for a 'Calcutta man', presumably meaning some kind of fair Indian, 'we could not conceal that Calcutta (in Bengal) was under the British'.

The fact that Manning became aware of what was going on almost entirely indirectly, through the Munshi's partial reports of the interrogations to which he had been subjected, made the situation seem even more disturbing than it might otherwise have done, and both the Munshi and Manning were thoroughly alarmed when they learned that a report on them had been sent to the Emperor in Peking; its contents which they could not learn exactly were meanwhile exaggerated by the rumours that spread in the little Chinese colony.

Manning was swayed by alternating bouts of hope and depression. When the mandarins told the Munshi that he would not be allowed to return to Calcutta, but would have to go through China back to Canton, they would sometimes hint that Manning might be allowed to accompany him on the same route, which of course would provide the very opportunity for studying Chinese life he had been seeking when he made his way to Lhasa. At the thought of such a possibility he would be—for a brief time—elated and optimistic.

Yet he could not ignore the report which the Munshi found most disturbing with regard to his own situation— that he had been denounced to the Emperor 'as a runaway, associating himself with foreigners', in which case 'a decree might come ordering, or at least authorizing his execution'. If this happened, Manning wondered, would he not be threatened? He heard the story of a righteous mandarin, who had refused to share in the corruption of his fellows in Lhasa, and had been executed as a result of false charges laid against him by the Tartar mandarin. And, if the Tartar mandarin hated the English, what guarantee was there that Manning himself, even though he was a foreigner who had come to Lhasa with the permission of the Chinese authorities, was not in danger? 'If he had the power put into his hands, who could say that he would not use it; and what resource could I have? All this was very true, and very unpleasant.'

247

For most of his time in Lhasa, until the Emperor's reply arrived, by swift courier, about the beginning of April, Manning remained a victim of these fears, and he noted with great vividness the course his thoughts followed. Reading this passage, which I quote at length, one remembers that Manning was the contemporary and acquaintance of William Godwin, whose famous novel, *Caleb Williams*, was the first great thriller, the first story of a man pursued by hostile forces whose power lies in the fear even more than in the fact of the atrocities they may wreak on their victim. Manning, in this passage, seems a Caleb Williams caught in real life.

I never could, even in idea, make up my mind to submit to an execution with firmness and manliness. The sight of the despotic pomp of mandarins at Canton, where I was perfectly secure, has almost turned me sick. What I read of their absolute power, not only in China, but in various Asiatic countries, had always appalled me. I put myself in imagination into the situation of the prisoner accused; I suppose myself innocent; I look round; I have no resource, no refuge; instruments of torture, instruments of execution are brought by florid, high-cheeked, busy, grinning, dull-hearted men; no plea avails; no kind judge to take my part, as in England, but, on the contrary, because I am accused (and perhaps by my judge) I am presumed guilty. They harshly and inequitably examine, not to discover whether I be guilty or not but in order to force out the conclusion that I am guilty. I am before evil-minded men, void of conscience, who proceed according to the forms, and violate the spirit of justice—no honest jury, who will incline to mercy when the man's character is good, and when the imputed crime is not heinous in its own nature, but only by the accidental regulations of society. If one is before a generous-minded man, who is wantonly exercising his power, one may appeal to what is noble in his nature, and excite a flame that will dissipate his malice and dark suspicions; but these evil-minded men, who outwardly are perfect politeness, and inwardly are perfect selfishness, have no touchwood in their heart; nothing for the spark to catch hold of; one may as well strike fire against the barren sand as appeal to their hearts. This friendlessness, this nothingness of the prisoner is what sickens me to think of. I had rather be eaten up by a tiger than fall into such a situation and be condemned. I own I push this dread too far. Death is death; the form ought not to make so great an impression; but this superstition, to which, perhaps, my mind is by its natural texture prone, has grown upon me by reading and meditation. I have often striven to rectify my sensations, often, often, at Lhasa; but the associations are too strong to be thoroughly disengaged, though I hope and believe I can so far master them as to be able to submit to any fate without acting like a coward.

These thoughts and fears darkened Manning's private thoughts throughout his period in Lhasa without materializing into any of the horrors that he feared. Indeed, except that he was not allowed to leave the city in the direction of China, no attempt appears to have been made to limit his freedom of movement or his intercourse with the people of Lhasa except in so far as he or the Munshi thought that necessary in self-protection. And, as Manning's repute as a medical 'Lama' spread through the city among Tibetans as well as Chinese, he became involved on a professional and sometimes on a personal level with many people of both races.

Certainly his fears seem to have coloured his attitude towards the people he met, for the striking feature of his recollections of Lhasa is that the image of the Chinese as civilized and polished people, which is evident when he is writing of those he encounters in his wanderings between Phari and Lhasa, is replaced by a much harder and more grotesque image, while it is the Tibetans who begin to take on the amiable qualities which the Chinese general from Gyantse had earlier personified.

Shortly after his arrival in Lhasa, Manning and the Munshi had moved into a new apartment with separate rooms for each of them as well as a kitchen; they were in a house that belonged to the Chinese officials in Lhasa, and paid a modest rent of 2s. 8d. a month. Again, Manning's was a gloomy room, for the walls were so thick that, though in the winter months when the sun was low it shone through the window, as the spring came on it rose too high to give any direct illumination. The Munshi and Sid papered up the holes and rents in the walls of the room, and Manning did not trouble to decorate it any further, though he noted that the Munshi 'embellished his in various ways, until it reminded me of a little milliner's back parlour'. Manning still slept uncomfortably for several weeks on the floor, 'as my bedstead, though boarded in the middle, was now built up with mud, which dried very slowly, and I was afraid to lie in it while any dampness remained'. In fact, he had suffered greatly from rheumatism every evening since he came to Lhasa, the pain coming on and lasting until towards morning, though in the daytime he felt perfectly well. He was, thus, his own first patient, and used his medicines liberally upon himself, prescribing pills of opium and camphor, Dover's Powders, and doses of antimony. Attacked by such rigorous methods—or perhaps merely retreating before the onset of spring—his sickness gradually waned and disappeared.

The room where he lived and slept and furtively kept his journal was also the consulting-room where he received the less important of his patients. For minor sicknesses he charged nothing, but there were certain complaints— probably those of venereal origin—for which he demanded twenty pieces of silver for a course of treatment, telling his patients that the medicines were costly. He found that the Chinese, while happy to be treated gratis, were reluctant to pay the full price, and with one such patient he quarrelled so dramatically that the ordinary Chinese in Lhasa treated him afterwards with a respectful caution. The man paid nothing for his early treatments, and when Manning threatened they would cease if he did not pay, he brought three coins wrapped in a piece of paper. Manning refused them, but the man argued that he should be expected to pay only in so far as the cure appeared to be progressing satisfactorily. Manning demanded twenty pieces for his services, cure or no cure, and refused to guarantee success. The argument mounted in fury, until the Chinese violently pushed a table and upset Manning's pills.

> I could bear it no longer. I snatched up his dirty paper of money, flung it out of the door, and bid him go after it. He turned pale with anger; he advanced towards me in a menacing manner. I was on my legs in a moment and fronted him firmly. I told him if he came near me with his insolence, by heaven! I would knock him down. I believe I spoke English or Latin in my anger; but he pretty well understood me; he faltered, and was glad, I believe, to have the other Chinamen interfere. One laid hold of him, another fetched him the money. The most respectable among then came to me, begged me to be pacified and to sit down, which I did. The man poured out a torrent of abuse against me and my Munshi, very little of which I understood. They soon had him out of the room.

Manning afterwards found that his conduct had been thought very bold: 'To fling a Chinaman's money out of the door: I not being a Chinaman.' But the story spread, and from that time on—outside his difficulties with the authorities

—Manning had no trouble in Lhasa 'with any man, Chinese or not'.

There were alarming moments when his patients died on him, like the dropsical Chinese who, having achieved a partial cure under Manning's prescription, proceeded to gorge himself immoderately and expired of the surfeit. But no one blamed him in this case, or for the death of the mad mandarin who for a time was receiving treatment at his hands. This mandarin was one of those involved in the bringing of false accusations against the official who had been executed at the instigation of the Tartar mandarin; he had since become a bitter enemy of the Tartar, and it was said that the whole affair had turned his head, though this seems unlikely, since he had a long record of corrupt dealings and had, indeed, been sent to Lhasa as a kind of punishment at the hands of the Emperor.

In Lhasa he was regarded as a man of influence who—if he recovered—would eventually return to a prominent position in Peking, and Manning's willingness to treat him was not entirely disinterested.

If I could make a cure of him, my Munshi said, it would be nothing to ask him to get me admitted to Peking: he was of a great and rich family. His servants also said, if I could cure him I might have whatever I asked for, and a grand Chinese title bestowed upon me. . . .

The prospect of finding an easy way to Peking turned Manning into an amateur alienist over night, willing to attempt the cure of the mind as well as the body. For fear of the Tartar mandarin, everything was done in secret, the mandarin's servants sending after dark a guide to fetch Manning on horseback to their master's house.

Manning found the mandarin 'uncombed, unwashed, beslimed with his own spittle and dirt, storming and scolding, and almost intractable'. The madman took a liking to Manning, and used to tell him long rambling tales about the Tartar, who he believed intended to kill him. In the end, after trying a few drugs in vain, Manning decided that it was no longer worth the risk of discovery by the Tartar mandarin, since the chances of his patient becoming sane enough to help him reach China were remote indeed.

As a physician in Lhasa, Manning faced two difficulties, one of which he admitted, and the other he did not; indeed, he may not even have been fully aware of it. The difficulty he did experience was that his patients, to whom his remedies were unfamiliar, would rarely follow his prescriptions to the letter. 'A few who had the sense to submit themselves entirely to my directions were completely cured, and acknowledged it with gratitude and thanks.' The unacknowledged difficulty lay in the rivalry of both Tibetan and Chinese physicians, whose methods differed from those of western medicine, being in some respects—such as their reliance on sympathetic magic—inferior, but in other ways—and particularly in the wide knowledge of the properties of herbs —superior. Patients whom Manning did not cure quickly were likely to return to their native doctors.

An advantage of his practice was that it brought him into closer contact with the Tibetans. Indeed, he found his intercourse with them less inhibited than with the Chinese, since the Munshi did not insist on the same caution in dealing with them, and was so contemptuous of Tibetans that he would not deign to accompany Manning unless he were visiting a person of some consequence. Instead, Manning would usually take Sid, who was able to speak with great facility a kind of atrocious pidgin Tibetan, or the Tibetan servant boy, who in turn spoke a vile Chinese.

One of his more interesting visits was to the mother of

one of the Khalons, and on this occasion it was a matter of
two curiosities meeting, for the lady was anxious to see the
fantastic stranger of whom everyone talked, and Manning
was glad of the chance to meet a high Tibetan noblewoman.
There was no artificial ceremony in the way the Khalon's
mother, who was still 'young, plump and rather handsome',
received Manning and the Munshi. Manning—having
seen so many dirty Tibetan faces—was impressed that hers
was washed and clean; he was even more impressed by the
splendid headdress she wore, with its profusion of pearls,
which the Munshi declared were real, but which Manning
thought, because there were so many of them, must at least
be partly artificial. The lady was suffering from an affliction
of the eyes, and Manning carefully inspected them, somewhat
distracted by the maids who 'stood tittering and giggling
about, turning away their pretty faces when I looked at them
with a smile, and again looking on giggling when I closely
inspected the dame's eyes'. She attributed her affliction to
praying too long in the temple with the cold wind blowing
upon her. Like many Tibetans, she was extremely devout,
and intended to retire to her chamber the next day for a
month of devotions and self-mortifications. Manning promised to send her a lotion to use on her eyes, but she believed
to do this while in retreat would be a breach of her religious
rules. Manning could not budge her from the opinion.
After drinking buttered tea, and receiving some baskets of
dried fruits, he took his leave; he sent the medicine, but
learnt that she never used it.

The freedom from constraint among Tibetan women
brought Manning other female patients, and he showed
himself susceptible to the particular rose-petal and ivory
beauty that characterizes the girls of Lhasa. He was especially delighted one day when 'two handsome, well-dressed,

clean-washed lasses' found their way to his room in the company of their mother. 'It was so long since I had seen female charms of this order that feeling their pulses rather disordered my own.' Manning could find nothing wrong with these laughing, high-spirited girls, but he gave them some innocent medicine, and within a few days they were again on his doorstep, bringing a present of fresh mutton. 'They were welcome to come as often as they liked, without bringing mutton or anything but their own pretty faces. I understood they were the family of a rich Tibet merchant.'

Manning was well on the way to becoming as susceptible to the charms of the Tibetan character as Bogle had been before him. Yet here again his odd perversity came into play, for, though he had expressed to the Dalai Lama an interest in the Tibetan religion and had asked him for a tutor, he behaved with far less respect than his predecessor towards the outward manifestations of Buddhist belief. The reason for his disrespect undoubtedly lay in the urgings of the Munshi, who told him that both the Chinese mandarins and the Tibetan Khalons had asked whether he had yet paid his respects to the 'great saint', whose name is illegible in his journal; probably Tsong Khapa, founder of the Gelugpa sect. The Munshi told Manning that if he were to pay homage to the image of this notable guru it would remove the suspicion that he was a Catholic, and, since Catholics were the only missionaries Tibetans had known, it would also remove the suspicion that he was a missionary intent on commencing once again the evil work for which the Capuchins had been expelled fifty years before.

This statement provoked Manning's contrariness. He had bowed before images in Calcutta, but he had done it voluntarily. If it were expected that he should do the same in Tibet, and if there were ceremonies to go through before

the image, then he would refuse to go. He believed the
religion of the Tibetans to be sincere, but he would go beyond
that only if he were assured that other unbelievers, like the
mandarins themselves, did it as a matter of course and
regarded themselves as in no way bound by the act of homage.

On being assured that this was the case, he decided to
set out. The Munshi refused to accompany him, since he
had no respect for the Lamaist religion, so Manning walked
to the Jo-khong, the great temple of Lhasa, in the company
of his Tibetan servant, who, as one of the despised local
Moslems, knew nothing of Buddhist religion. As they left
the house, the Munshi thrust a bundle of joss sticks into the
servant's hand, and asked Manning if he had a white scarf.
Manning scoffed at the idea. At the temple the servant
proved so ignorant of even the elements of Lamaist religion
that he could not answer a single question. Manning stoutly
berated him, and a crowd of worshippers gathered round.
To placate them, he prostrated once before the principal
image, and afterwards, more angry than ever, strode out
of the temple, leaving the servant to put the incense where
he wished. On the way home, to show that he was impartial,
he stopped to enter a Chinese temple and perform a similar
prostration. Later he went into other Tibetan temples and
made no homage of any kind, merely to show that he considered himself free to bow or not to bow as he saw fit. But
when he failed to bow, he wanted it understood that it was
not Christianity that prevented him.

> All religions as they are established have a mixture in
> them of good and evil, and upon the whole they all perhaps
> tend to civilize and ameliorate mankind: as such I respect
> them. As for the common idea that the founders of all
> religions except our own are impostors, I consider it a
> vulgar error.

The season went its course, interspersed with ceremonials. There were parades of Chinese troops, and Chinese plays were acted before the temples; Manning was always present, sometimes taking dinner with the lesser mandarins, who were often more sympathetic to his predicament than their superiors. But he also kept up with the Tibetan ceremonial calendar, visiting the Dalai Lama before he went into a month of retreat, to receive from him some sacred pages wrapped in yellow silk, and going again on the day the young hierarch came out of his retirement, distressed to find him 'pale and worse in health, I thought, for his seclusion'. He also became friendly with the Regent, whom he judged 'a very good-natured kind-hearted man', though somewhat vulgar in his behaviour; the Regent was curious about the outer world, and asked many questions. When New Year came on the 12th February, Manning took his place in the procession of people carrying gifts to the Dalai Lama, and presented him with a telescope for which he had found little use, since he was scared to make any kind of observations while in Lhasa lest he appear to confirm the Tartar mandarin's suspicions that he was a spy.

By this time Manning's money was beginning to run low. He had continued to expect funds from Rangpur, but it is likely that they were intercepted on the way, probably by the thievishly inclined Bhutanese, and he found it necessary to turn merchant—an occupation by no means despised in a trading country like Tibet—and to sell as many of his possessions as he could spare.

> I sold some silk and crepe I had brought with me, and which had escaped the hands of the Bhutanese. I sold some sheets, a piece of cotton cloth, gauze gowns, a belt with stone clasp, a large tea box, handkerchiefs, which I at first meant to have kept; a few empty bottles; two or

three bottles of cherry brandy, which I had offered to the mandarins on my arrival and again on their birthdays, but which had not been accepted; a handsome opera-glass; a fan; in short, everything I could muster up, except the clothes I should probably want to use, and a few keepsake trinkets that I was unwilling to part with.

Even the trinkets he had to give away as New Year's presents; he had reduced his possessions to a very small compass, but had gained a fair amount of money, and, by showing that he was in straitened circumstances, had found an excuse to get rid of his useless servant Sid. He gave him a little money to set up as a butcher, a trade regularly followed by Moslems in Tibet, but Sid failed in this and also as a sweetmeat-seller; eventually, having spent his credit in Lhasa, he set off on the way home to Szechuan.

Manning wrote up his Lhasa journal at length until shortly before the Tibetan New Year in February. After that he kept only the most laconic of notes, but from these the building up of events during his last month in the capital is obvious. His financial condition became more and more precarious; the comparative reactions of the Chinese and Tibetans he must have found mortifying, for while the former ceased to invite him to dinner, the latter helped him in various ways. The Regent made him presents of rice, and there is—probably written towards the end of March—a brief reference to 'the Dalai Lama's kindness'.

Because of Manning's haphazard way of mingling European dates and Tibetan lunar dates, it is not easy to establish exactly the sequence of events that led up to his departure from Lhasa, but it appears that matters began to assume a critical turn at the end of March. By that time it was clear that the Munshi would be sent back to China. Manning still hoped that he would be allowed to travel with him to Canton, and actually went to the mandarins to ask their leave to do this, presumably in the hope that the Munshi would not be treated as a criminal. All hope vanished when the decree from the Emperor arrived, and the Munshi, having gone to the mandarins to see what could be arranged, was brought back to the house in chains, presumably to frighten Manning. 'I anxious,' he noted, comprehensibly.

Then comes a curious note. 'Glad when Munshi goes. Why? Because he writes to me. He comes again to see me.' One must assume that, in desperation, the Munshi was making appeals for help which Manning had no means of giving, feeling himself endangered. Clearly, he must have felt, if the Munshi went—as he had to—his own position might become less perilous.

There was reason for anxiety. For the first time the mandarins openly took an official interest in him, sending for him, and showing him opened letters, presumably intercepted on the way from Calcutta, which they asked him to identify. They were civil, promised good news and even urged him to stay a while longer. But Manning lived now in perpetual fear, dreading the arrival of a second decree that would implicate him, dreading the intrigues of the Jesuit missionaries at Peking, dreading 'something coming to light: that I have been at Canton'. He heard rumours: the Khalons were said to have remarked that he would have to go in a few days. He snatched at hopes: a Chinese magistrate felt his eyes had benefited from Manning's treatment, and might be of help.

About the 1st April he went again to the mandarins to find what his situation might be. 'Strangely put off,' he notes. He sold his empty bottles, a sign of the desperate nature of his finances, and began to get his things together preparatory to leaving. By this time anything that happened to him seemed strange and threatening. He contracted a fever and cough, and imagined he was poisoned. An Armenian visited him and wanted to accompany him from Lhasa, and he suspected the man's motives. Even suggestions by people who had seemed his friends appeared to have sinister possibilities. The Regent advised him early in April to wait until the new mandarin came to replace the Tartar, who had at last been totally discredited. 'Why? Uneasy,' he noted. Then, about the middle of April, he visits the Regent again who tells him to expect 'good news' in a few days, meaning presumably that he will be allowed to leave, but obviously not for China. He meets the Khalons, and they make him presents of silk and tea, a sign that they consider his departure imminent. Then the Munshi goes, and with his going is connected another enigmatic entry: 'Munshi bribes the treasurer.' There is no explanation why the Munshi did this, or whether he gained anything by it, but with this note he disappears entirely from the story, and no one knows what happened to this proud, irascible man whose involvement in Manning's enterprise had led him into such peril.

On the 16th Manning went, 'with a sorrowful heart', to take his leave of the Dalai Lama. 'I said I would tell my king (Governor of Bengal) that I was well treated. His heart rejoices. I thank the Grand Lama, and promise that if afterwards a Lhasa man comes to Bengal it shall not be forgotten.' He was just as sad to bid farewell to the Regent. In their turn, the Tibetans, and even some of the Chinese, appear to have treated Manning in a kindly way as he took his leave, perhaps regretting the difficulties he had experienced through the suspicions of the Tartar mandarin. He departed on the 19th April, loaded with presents, and made his way quickly down to Phari, which he reached on the 1st May. On the 3rd of May he crossed the border into Bhutan. At Paro he was held up again for three weeks, obviously under the impression that he was an agent of the East India Company, for there appears in his diary the angry note, 'Do they think I am a tradesman? How should I know the prices of things in Calcutta, or whether *this* cloth be prime or second?' At last, on the 24th May, he left Paro. There follows a list of dates and the names of the stages where he stopped the night, until on the 31st May he reached Tazijong, and on the 1st June celebrated his descent from the high mountains with the note, 'Village. Palm trees.' He reached Cantalbary on the 3rd June, and there he was held up again; it was not until the 6th June, when he picked up his bundle and threatened to walk out of Bhutan, that they gave him a horse and let him go on his way. He reached Cooch Behar on the 10th June.

As he travelled south from Lhasa along the now familiar trails of Tibet and Bhutan, Manning's thoughts must have turned to dejection. He had failed yet again in an attempt to enter China. The man he had induced to accompany him —whatever his faults a faithful companion—was now enduring some unknown but certainly uncomfortable fate. He himself had been forced to leave Lhasa just at the time when he was beginning to acquire a real appreciation of the Tibetan way of life as something more complex and interesting than the barbarian culture it had seemed to him when he first crossed the frontier from Bhutan. And always at the back of his mind there must have been the question why the Chinese had allowed—indeed had seemed to encourage— him to visit Lhasa, only to treat him with the utmost suspicion as soon as he got there. Was it mere bungling? Or was it an elaborate trap to catch the spy they imagined him to be, only to find themselves with a bizarre innocent on their hands? The Chinese records that might throw some light on this incident are unlikely to be revealed even if they exist.

But just as puzzling to Manning as the attitude of the Chinese officials in Lhasa must have been that of the British officials in Calcutta. They had refused to give him official status when he departed from Calcutta, doubtless because they thought no man so eccentric and so practically inept would get far upon his journey. And when he returned, having performed a geographical feat of considerable importance, having done what Bogle and Hamilton and Turner, their own men, had failed to do, they neglected to give him the glory that was his due. Doubtless they would have liked to profit from his experiences, but concern with the Himalayan kingdoms was low in 1812, and their interest was too lukewarm to melt Manning's obstinate resentfulness, to assuage his injured pride. Still refusing to satisfy the curiosity of Calcutta, he returned to Canton as soon as he could find a berth. Yet, ironically, it is probable that the very lack of the official status and support which he craved was precisely the advantage that allowed Manning to do what he did, and to become, inexperienced, ill equipped and eccentric traveller though he was, the first Englishman to reach Lhasa.

# XIV

## *Epilogue*

When Thomas Manning returned from Lhasa, it marked the end of a phase of British relationships with Tibet. The agents of Hastings had gone there primarily as the representatives of a great trading corporation, seeking commercial relations with Tibet itself, but, even more, a way of improving their mercantile position on the China coast. Manning had gone as a lonely scholar, following his own search for knowledge and for a personal fulfilment he had not found in the West. When British attention turned again to Tibet, its aims had changed radically. Trade had become far less important than politics.

It is symptomatic of changes in the British, Chinese and Tibetan attitudes that Manning was the last Englishman to go as an individual traveller to Lhasa. By the end of the nineteenth century the British saw Central Asia from the viewpoint of an imperial power contending there with another great power—Russia. The Chinese, becoming more nationalistic in a modern sense, began to think of Tibet, with other outlying dependencies, as integral parts of China rather than as border states over which Peking exercised suzerainty. And the Tibetans themselves, protecting their traditions within the ramparts of their mountains, became steadily more intolerant of outside interference until, when a great leader at last arose in the Thirteenth Dalai Lama, it was Tibetan rather than Chinese obstinacy that provoked the British to embark on the Younghusband Expedition, and it was Tibetan separatism that led to the expulsion of the Chinese in 1912 and the cautious acceptance of the British as advisers in the decades that followed.

Even after the acceptance and establishment of intercourse between Tibet and Britain during the present century, individual travellers were still discouraged from entering the country; the British who did so and produced the best accounts of Tibet and the Tibetans during the first half of the present century were all men who had gone to Lhasa as political officers, such as Sir Charles Bell, Sir Basil Gould and Hugh Richardson. The traveller whose exploits most closely resembled those of Manning was, of course, the French occultist, Madame David-Neel, since she also reached Lhasa in disguise, but though she too went native—to an even greater extent than Manning—her aims were strikingly different. If the official visitor to Tibet in the twentieth century tended to be politically oriented, rather than commercially as he had been in the eighteenth century, the rare individual visitor has been inclined to seek personal spiritual fulfilment as much as the kind of humanist knowledge which Manning pursued, and so, in writers like Madame David-Neel and Marco Pallis and even Giovanni Tucci, the great Italian expert on Tibetan iconography, one finds a directly sympathetic involvement of a kind Manning certainly did not share, and which even Bogle did not fully admit.

Perhaps this is merely a statement of the obvious—that travellers like all men are greatly the creatures of their own time—and that in ages when men are conscious of the collapse of their religious preconceptions, as many men in the West are today, they will seek in other cultures the grounds for faith which they have lost in their own. The absence of such a motivation is far from diminishing the importance of

264

the pioneer journeys which Bogle and Turner made to Tashilunpo and Manning to Lhasa. Indeed, once British interest in Tibet re-emerged in the 1860's, their contribution to the knowledge of that region was to be invaluable. Later, indeed, it was often regretted that with the departure of Hastings the policy of the Company changed to such an extent that Manning's achievement seemed irrelevant to British aims as they were conceived in the final years of the Napoleonic wars. Ironically, indeed, it was Francis Young-husband, leader of the mission that in 1903 fought its way to Lhasa with bayonets and artillery, who pointed out that 'all this need never have been if we had followed Warren Hastings' example and continued to send agents into Tibet to keep the Tibetans in touch with us and accustomed to look on us as friends'.

It remains to complete briefly the stories of the travellers whom we have accompanied on their pioneer journeys into Tibet. The deaths of Bogle and Hamilton have already been noted. The eventual fate of the energetic Purangir Gosain is not known. But Samuel Turner went on to a spectacular career in the Company's service, fought with distinction in the siege of Seringapatam in 1792, was envoy to Tippu Sultan of Mysore, and retired to England with a nawab's fortune, buying himself a country estate and reaping the credit for his Tibetan travels when his *Account of an Embassy to the Court of the Teshoo Lama* was published in 1800 and he was elected to the Royal Society. In 1802 he died of a stroke in a London street.

Manning survived the longest, and eventually fulfilled the ambition that had led him to Lhasa, though he seems to have been little satisfied with the manner of its fulfilment. Having gone back to Canton, he originally intended to return to England in 1815, but delayed his homecoming because of an opportunity to carry out at last his great desire to enter the mainland of China. It had been decided to send a British embassy to Peking in an attempt to improve the Company's trading position at Canton, and Lord Amherst had been chosen as its leader. It was necessary for the Company to provide the staff of interpreters and Chinese secretaries from among men who had lived long enough in Canton to have acquired at least some knowledge of the Chinese language and of Chinese customs. Sir George Staunton, President of the Company's Select Committee in Canton, became Second Member of the Commission, and picked the Chinese secretaries whom he wished to accompany him. Robert Morrison, the great Chinese lexicographer, was one of them; another was John Davis, son of the Samuel Davis who had accompanied Turner as far as Tassisudon in 1783; a third was Manning.

From the beginning there appears to have been little mutual respect between Manning, on the one hand, and Lord Amherst and Henry Ellis, Third Member of the Commission, on the other. To Amherst the eccentric Manning, whose beard by now had grown nearly to his waist, and who dressed habitually in Chinese clothes, seemed the very reverse of a British diplomat, and at first he refused to accept him in the mission. Sir George Staunton stood up for Manning, and eventually a compromise was reached by which the latter abandoned his Chinese garb for the duration of the mission, but retained his beard. His subsequent behaviour can hardly have endeared him to Amherst or the sycophantic Ellis, for John Davis—later a great Sinologist—told Clements Markham that Manning continued to do everything 'in his own odd and eccentric way'.

Being one day roused by a strange shouting, I went out and discovered it was Manning, who, wishing to cross the water, and finding nobody who would attend to him, commenced a series of howls like a dog, supplemented by execrations derived from the Chinese vernacular. This led our attendant mandarins very naturally to infer that he was mad, and they lost no time in conveying him over the river to the other side, which was all he wanted.

Undoubtedly it was the antipathy Amherst and Ellis conceived for Manning which led to the curious fact that, after being mentioned as joining the Embassy at Hong Kong in 1816, his name does not occur on a single occasion in Ellis's long and detailed account of the proceedings of the Embassy. Either his contribution was deliberately ignored, or he was quite as deliberately prevented from making any contribution. The latter is possible, for the major part of the Chinese translation appears to have been entrusted to Robert Morrison, who had arrived in Canton after Manning and almost certainly knew no more Chinese than he, while Davis was usually chosen as an intermediary with the mandarins.

In other respects, the journey provided less than Manning expected. There was a running dispute with the Chinese mandarins who accompanied the Embassy from the coast to Peking as to whether the Ambassador should kowtow to the Emperor. (It is possible that here again Manning's views about the expediency of prostrating oneself when it can serve any purpose may have increased his unpopularity in the mission.) When the Embassy did reach Peking, early one morning after a night's journey, the mandarins tried to force its members into the Emperor's presence immediately, unwashed and without court dress or credentials; when Amherst protested, he was accorded no audience at all, and the Embassy was hurried back, by devious waterways through the heart of China, to rejoin its ships at Canton. Thus, though Manning did in fact see Peking, the prize of his journeying was snatched away from him as the cup of tea had been snatched away in the Dalai Lama's presence five years before, and he saw the rest of China as a member of a closely escorted party which was never allowed to linger long enough to make any close contact with the real life of the country and its people. Afterwards the *Alceste*, on which Manning was sailing, was shipwrecked in the Indonesian archipelago, and the passengers taken to Batavia; Manning returned thence to Canton, but almost immediately left for England, on a ship that put in at St. Helena on the way, where at last he was able to meet Napoleon.

Manning's bitterness over his treatment by the representatives of authority in India and in China affected his actions for the rest of his life. He never wrote of his experiences, which would have made an extraordinarily interesting book, and, apart from his Chinese jokes, all he published was a paper on the consumption of tea in Tibet, Bhutan and Tartary. For a decade after his return to London in 1817 he was a figure in literary London, seen at Lamb's parties and other gathering places of the intelligentsia, listening with ironic silence to Coleridge holding forth, and sometimes himself talking a little on Oriental religions. Only Lamb really seems to have taken him seriously; other writers wondered what Elia saw in this man of vast but apparently wasted experience and knowledge. In 1827 Manning went to Italy and lived there for two years; he returned to England and went to live in the country, almost a hermit, spending his time—as his great beard turned white—in an enormous unfurnished room, surrounded by his collection of Chinese books which, presented to the Royal Asiatic Society and now in the possession of the University of Leeds, forms the only memorial to his great knowledge of Chinese, which some of his contemporaries regarded as unequalled in Europe.

In 1838 he experienced a paralytic stroke, and moved to Bath, where he could receive better medical attention. It is here that we catch the last glimpse of him, in March, 1840, as Henry Crabb Robinson calls on him in the company of Walter Savage Landor, and Landor is 'charmed with Manning's personal beauty and especially with his beard'.

Within six weeks of that meeting, Manning was dead. The child Dalai Lama, who had looked upon him with so much laughter and so long ago, had been dead already for twenty-five years, and his successor for three years, victims of the lust for power among the Regents which in the nineteenth century made every Lhasa hierarch die young, while Tibet closed its frontiers to the world and embraced the illusion of a divinely protected land where change could not enter.

# Bibliographical Notes

The only account of any of the early British journeys to Tibet that appeared in the lifetime of the traveller himself was Samuel Turner's *An Account of an Embassy to the Court of the Teshoo Lama*, published in 1800 and reprinted in 1806. Sir Clements Markham's *Narratives of the Mission of George Bogle to Tibet and of the Journey of Thomas Manning to Lhasa*, published in 1876, is an invaluable compendium, since it contains not only all the essential surviving material about their journeys, but also useful notes on other travellers to Tibet up to the 1870's, as well as some of the actual accounts of the Jesuit and Capuchin missionaries. There are quantities of unpublished material relating to Bogle's journey in the British Museum, the Public Record Office, the India Office Library and the Mitchell Library in Glasgow, but surprisingly little that adds significantly to the material Markham collected. A useful article on Bogle's mission, with some interesting appended papers gleaned from the archives in India, is 'Bogle's Embassy to Tibet' by D. B. Dishalkar in the *Indian Historical Quarterly*, June, 1933.

On Manning, thanks to his friendship with Lamb, there is other published material of some value to be found, particularly in *The Letters of Thomas Manning to Charles Lamb*, edited by G. A. Anderson, 1925, *The Letters of Charles Lamb*, edited by E. V. Lucas, 1935 and *Charles Lamb and the Lloyds*, by E. V. Lucas, 1898. Glancing references to the Manning of later years occur in several of the memoirs of the period, including those of Crabb Robinson, Procter and Allsop. As background to Manning's final success in reaching Peking there is Henry Ellis's *Journal of the Proceedings of the Late Embassy to China*, 1817, remarkable for the skill with which the author conveys the impression that Manning was present only as a name.

Two excellent works giving the general picture of British penetration into the Himalayas, and bringing the Manning, Bogle and Turner expeditions into true perspective, are *Trade through the Himalayas: The Early British Attempts to Open Tibet* by Schuyler Cammann, 1951 and *Britain and Chinese Central Asia: The Road to Lhasa 1767 to 1905* by Alastair Lamb, 1960. A small but useful guide to the minor realms of the region is *The Himalayan Kingdoms: Bhutan, Sikkim and Nepal*, by Pradyumna P. Karan and William E. Jenkins, 1963. As for Tibet itself, a good general account, perhaps too heavily weighted towards the twentieth century, is H. E. Richardson's *Tibet and its History*, 1962, but nothing on Tibetan life has yet replaced the three great works by that extraordinary man (who has long needed a biographer) Sir Charles Bell: *Tibet: Past and Present*, 1924, *The People of Tibet*, 1928 and *The Religion of Tibet*, 1931. Those who are interested in earlier travellers will find valuable information in *Early Jesuit Travellers in Central Asia* by C. J. Wessels, 1924 and *An Account of Tibet* by I. Desideri, published in an English translation in 1937. E. Huc's *Travels in Tartary, Thibet and China*, which appeared in English translation in 1879, gives a vivid picture of Lhasa, thirty years after Manning's visit, as it was seen by the only other Europeans to reach the 'forbidden city' in the nineteenth century, and Peter Fleming's *Bayonets to Lhasa* is probably the best account of the first British journey to Lhasa (that of a miniature army) since Manning's departure more than ninety years before; Fleming's account lists all the contemporary accounts of the Younghusband Expedition which, since they belong to the century after the events of which this book tells, have only a distant bearing on it.

# Index

*Account of an Embassy to the Court of the Teshoo Lama* (Turner), 15, 184, 205, 265, 270
*Account of Tibet* (Desideri), 26–7
Amherst, Lord, 198, 266–7
Amitabha, 106
Andes, 56
Andrada, Father, 24
Assam, 32, 35, 37, 49, 61
Avalokiteshvara, 106

Bell, Sir Charles, 20, 26, 264, 271
Benares, 113, 121
Bengal, 13–14, 31–2, 35–6, 40, 42–3, 46, 48–52 54, 57, 59, 61, 64, 67–8, 81, 83, 88, 96, 99, 113–17, 144, 150, 152–3, 158, 161, 165–6, 171, 173–6, 192, 260
Bhatgoan, 32–3
Bhutan, 14, 18, 32, 35–8, 42, 49, 51–2, 54–5, 57–91, 93, 98–9, 111, 113, 115, 124, 151–2, 154–155, 161, 164–6, 171–2, 175, 180, 182, 184–5, 193, 206, 210–41, 260–1, 269–70
Blavatsky, Madame, 21
Bodh Gaya, 113, 176
Bogle, Anne, 44, 46–7, 73–5, 180
Bogle, George, 13–15, 18–22, 27, 42–181, 183–6, 188–9, 191–2, 194, 197, 207, 210, 217, 222, 242–3, 255, 262, 264, 270
Bogle, Robert, 47, 173, 180
Bon, 134
Brahmaputra, River, 54, 59, 97, 102

Buddhism, 21, 26, 32, 38, 61, 63, 66, 71, 78–9, 87, 94, 110–11, 114, 117, 129, 132–5, 144–5, 158, 163–4, 176–7, 179, 213, 255–6

Cabral, Father, 24
Cacella, Father, 24
Calcutta, 15, 39, 46, 48, 50–1, 57, 70–1, 75–6, 92, 149–50, 155–6, 160–1, 166, 172–4, 176, 179–80, 182, 184, 193–4, 205–11, 213, 217, 223, 241, 246–7, 255, 262
*Caleb Williams*, 248
Canton, 24, 32, 34, 159, 177, 201–2, 205, 208, 211, 223, 227, 239, 246–7, 258–9, 265–6, 267–8
Capuchins, 22, 25–7, 116, 255, 270
Cathcart, Colonel, 193
Catherine the Great, 188
Chandler, Edward, 91–2
Changay Lama, 150, 177
Chanzo Cusho, 119, 122, 136, 181–2, 185–9, 192–3
Chapman, Spencer, 91–2
Cheyt Singh, 121–2
China and Chinese, 15, 19, 20, 23–5, 28, 32, 34–5, 39, 41, 54–5, 70, 100, 106–8, 110, 115, 117–119, 131, 148, 150, 157, 159–60, 171, 175, 179, 181–2, 187–8, 190, 192–4, 197–205, 207, 210, 215–17, 221–5, 229–34, 238–40, 245–53, 256, 258–62, 264, 266–268

China, Emperor of, 159–60, 174, 177–9, 189, 247–8, 252, 258, 267
Chinchu, River, 61, 64–6, 84–5
Chomolhari, Mount, 92, 96–7, 102, 217
Chuka, 67–9
Chum Cusho, 137–9, 158, 169
Chumbi Valley, 18
Chungpa Tulku, *see* Chanzo Cusho
Clive, Robert, 32
Coleridge, Samuel Taylor, 197–8, 268
Cooch Behar, 32, 36–8, 40, 42, 57, 59, 70, 85, 166, 177, 206, 210, 261
Cornwallis, Lord, 193–4, 208
Curzon, Lord, 19, 131, 188

Dalai Lama, Fifth, 107, 236
Dalai Lama, Seventh, 107
Dalai Lama, Eighth, 38, 41, 52, 55, 77, 82, 93, 107, 121, 126, 135–7, 148, 150–2, 154, 159, 179, 181, 186, 188, 193, 240
Dalai Lama, Ninth, 21, 240–5, 255, 260, 268–9
Dalai Lama, Thirteenth, 20, 107, 263–4
Dalai Lama, Fourteenth, 22, 94, 100, 116
D'Anville, Jean Baptiste, 27–8, 59
Darjeeling, 18
David-Neel, Alexandra, 21, 264
Davis, John, 266–7
Davis, Samuel, 184–6, 266
De la Condamine, Charles Marie, 56
Deb Judhur, 36–41, 82, 85, 89, 94, 111
Deb Raja, 36, 38–9, 60, 62, 69–86, 88–90, 92, 94, 100, 164–6, 171, 175, 185, 192
Debo Dinji, 131

Desheripgay, 105, 108–9, 112–13, 115, 121, 129–30, 137, 150, 164, 170
Desideri, Ippolito, 25–8
Dharma Raja, 35–6, 39, 71–2, 76–7, 88, 164
Dinajpur, 57, 166, 210
Dorje Phagmo, 137–9, 158, 169, 230, 232
D'Orville, Father, 24, 25
Du Halde, Father, 27

East India Company, 13, 31–7, 47, 49–53, 55, 59, 77, 84, 107, 110, 114–16, 123, 137–8, 150, 152, 155, 157, 176, 178, 181, 183, 192–4, 201–2, 206–7, 209, 215, 227, 241, 261
Elliott, Alexander, 50, 173
Ellis, Henry, 266–7, 270

Fitch, Ralph, 31
Fort William, 34, 39, 44, 47, 49, 51, 53, 209
Francis, Philip, 173–4

Gabet, Father, 15
Ganges, 150, 192
Gelugpa Sect, 78, 110, 163–4, 188, 190, 193, 255
Godwin, William, 198, 248
Gould, Sir Basil, 264
Grueber, Father, 24–5
Gurkhas, 33–4, 37, 108, 113, 153, 162, 194, 208
Gyantse, 98, 100–2, 104, 164, 187, 216, 221–8, 230, 239, 241, 250
Gyurmé Namgyal, 25, 131

Hamilton, Alexander, 51, 57, 62, 67, 69, 76–7, 82–4, 86, 93, 97–8, 101–2, 104, 110–12, 121–2, 128–130, 133, 138, 141–7, 151, 158,

161, 164, 169, 174–5, 181, 183–
184, 186, 193, 230, 262
Hastings, Warren, 27, 35–7, 39–
41, 43–4, 50–5, 59–60, 69, 71,
75, 80–1, 83–4, 97, 111–12, 115,
135, 142, 148–50, 155–6, 159,
165–6, 170, 171–8, 180–4, 188–
194, 207, 263, 265
Hazlitt, William, 198, 201
Hilton, James, 22
Hong Kong, 267
Huc, Father E., 15, 271

India, 13, 18–19, 24–5, 31, 33, 35,
41, 43, 48, 50, 119–20, 140, 150,
160, 172, 176, 180, 183, 192–3,
201, 207, 209–10, 212, 217, 223,
268
Indo-China, 15, 203–4

Jehol, 178, 194
Jesuits in Tibet, 22, 24–7, 270
Johnson, Samuel, 172
Jones, Captain John, 37, 60–1, 63,
81, 85
Julian the Apostate, 134

Kalimpong, 18
Kalmucks, 115, 132, 137
Kashmir and Kashmiris, 25, 54–5,
57, 84, 115, 125, 131, 161, 188
Kathalbari, 210
Katmandu, 20, 23, 32–4
*Kim*, 19
Kinloch, Captain, 33–5, 37
Kipling, Rudyard, 19
Kokonor, Lake, 23, 178
Kumbum, 178

Ladakh, 25, 111
Lamb, Charles, 197–202, 204–6,
208, 244, 168–70
Lamb, Mary, 201, 206
Landon, Perceval, 229–30

Landor, Walter Savage, 269
Lang Dharma, 134
Lhasa, 14–15, 18–20, 23–7, 38–9,
41, 52–4, 56–7, 81–2, 91, 94,
100–1, 104, 106, 108, 114–16,
137, 148–50, 152–3, 155–9, 165,
175, 181, 187–8, 190, 192, 194,
197–8, 203, 216, 221, 224–5,
227–8, 230, 234–65, 270–1
Litong, 235
Logan, James, 34
*Lost Horizon*, 22

Lumbulong, 69, 71, 86
Macao, 203, 210, 240
Macartney, Lord, 194
Macaulay, Colman, 19
Manning, Thomas, 14–15, 18–22,
28, 45, 92, 194, 197–270
Markham, Clements, 18–19, 167,
207, 266, 270
Marques, Father, 24
Minto, Lord, 50, 205, 207–8
Mirza Settar, 57, 59, 84, 120–1,
161
Moghuls, 31
Mongols, 24–5, 107–8, 119, 129,
132, 141, 178, 188
Morrison, Robert, 203, 266–7
Müller, Max, 21
Muri-Jong, 65–6
Murshidabad, 57

Nagartse, 230, 232
Namling, 70, 76, 102, 104, 105,
113, 162
Napoleon I, 200, 208, 268
*Narratives of the Mission of George
Bogle to Tibet and of the Journey of
Thomas Manning to Lhasa*, 18, 270
Nepal, 18, 24, 27, 32–4, 37, 49, 81,
93, 113, 140, 155–6
Newaris, 23, 32, 33, 37, 49

Odoric of Pordenone, Friar, 24

Pachu, River, 84, 87, 89, 212–13
Padma, 39, 41, 52, 84, 94–7, 102, 114, 147, 161–2, 166, 217
Painam, River, 97, 162, 186–7, 221
Pallis, Marco, 264
Panchen Lama, Third, 13–14, 21, 34, 38–43, 51–2, 69–71, 75–7, 82, 84, 93–5, 98, 101, 104–29, 132–9, 142, 148–56, 158–62, 166–81, 183, 185–6, 189–92
Panchen Lama, Fourth, 21, 182, 186–7, 189–93, 243
Paro, 88–90, 164, 175, 212–13, 260–1
Patan, 27, 32–3
Patna, 192
Peking, 21, 23, 107–8, 150, 159–60, 177–9, 182, 190, 194, 198–9, 203, 205, 240, 247, 252, 259, 263, 266–7, 270
Phari, 90–5, 101, 152, 214–16, 225, 228, 249, 260
Potala, 236–7, 241–5
Prinsep, H. T., 208
Prithvi Narayan, 33, 37–8, 113
Punakha, 164, 175, 185, 192
Purangir Gosain, 39, 42, 51–2, 57, 69–70, 75–6, 82, 101, 103, 111, 161, 166, 174, 176–8, 181–2, 186, 192–4, 265

Quito, 56

Rangpur, 35–6, 42, 57, 59, 81, 84, 120, 165, 174, 180, 185, 192, 210, 225–6, 257
Richardson, H. E., 167–8, 264, 271
Rinjaitzay, 142, 144–6, 158
Robinson, Henry Crabb, 197, 269–70

Russia, 19, 41, 131, 160, 187–8, 201, 209, 263

Sakya Lama, 22, 137
Sarnath, 176
Saunders, Dr. Robert, 184, 186, 191–2
Shigatse, 24, 38, 79, 93, 125–6, 161–2, 229
Siberia, 54, 115, 119, 129, 132, 138, 161
Sikkim, 18–19, 32–3, 124, 153, 162, 270
Simtoka, 82–3, 85
Sinkiang, 41
Solpon Chenpo, 111–12, 119, 121–122, 178, 181, 186, 189
Staunton, Sir George, 266
Szechuan, 240, 258

Taranatha Lama, 188
Tashilunpo, 14, 24, 38, 51–2, 70, 76, 93, 99, 100, 102, 106–8, 114, 121, 126–7, 129, 131, 134–5, 137–8, 141, 143–4, 147–8, 150, 152, 156, 158, 161–2, 164–6, 169–70, 174–9, 181–2, 185–90, 192–4, 207, 209–10, 265
Tassisudon, 38–9, 61, 64–5, 69, 71–3, 76–7, 79, 81–4, 88, 94, 164–6, 170, 175, 185, 213, 266
Tatsa Rimpoche, Regent, 240–5, 260
Terpaling, 187, 189, 190
Tibet, 13–15, 18–28, 31–5, 38–44, 49, 51–2, 54–5, 57, 59, 62–3, 65–6, 80–1, 83–179, 181–94, 197–9, 205, 207, 214–65, 268–71
Tibet and its History (Richardson), 167, 271
Tsangpo, River, 97, 102–4, 123, 125, 147, 162, 233–4
Tsaparang, 24

Tsomoling Nomenkhan, Regent, 181, 193
Tsong Khapa, 255
Tucci, Giovanni, 264
Turner, Samuel, 14–15, 18, 20–2, 27, 45, 183–92, 205, 207, 222, 242, 262, 265, 270

Urga, 188

Van de Putte, Samuel, 23–4
Verelst, Henry, 24
Victoria, Queen, 188

Wordsworth, William, 197–8

Yamdrok Tso Lake, 137, 229–32
Younghusband Expedition, 19–20, 81, 91, 264–5, 271